W9-ABF-698

WITHDRAWN

WALTER BENJAMIN

Kritik: German Literary Theory and Cultural Studies
Liliane Weissberg, *Editor*

Books in this series

Walter Benjamin: An Intellectual Biography,
by Bernd Witte,
trans. by James Rolleston, 1991

WALTER BENJAMIN,

AN INTELLECTUAL BIOGRAPHY

BERND WITTE

TRANSLATED BY JAMES ROLLESTON

 Wayne State University Press   Detroit

Originally published as *Walter Benjamin: rowohlts monographien,* copyright © 1985 by Rowohlt Taschenbuch Verlag GmbH. Revised and enlarged English translation copyright © 1991 by Wayne State University Press, Detroit, Michigan 48202. All rights reserved.
No part of this book may be reproduced without formal permission.
Manufactured in the United States of America.
95 94 93 92 91   5 4 3 2 1

Library of Congress Cataloging-in-Publication Data

Witte, Bernd.
   [Walter Benjamin. English]
   Walter Benjamin : an intellectual biography / Bernd Witte ;
translated by James Rolleston.
     p.   cm. – (Kritik)
   Translation of: Walter Benjamin.
   Included bibliographical references and index.
   ISBN 0–8143–2017–1
   1. Benjamin, Walter, 1892–1940. 2. Authors, German–20th century-
-Biography. I. Title. II. Series.
PT2603.E455Z95413   1991
838′.91209–dc20
[B]   91–7666

Grateful acknowledgment is made to Inter Nationes for its financial assistance in the translation of this work.

Designer: Mary Krzewinski

Contents

Translator's Preface

> While all individual elements of foreign languages—words, sentences, structure—are mutually exclusive, these languages supplement one another in their intentions.
>
> —Benjamin,
> "The Task of the Translator" (1923)

To translate a study of Walter Benjamin is to enter a force field dominated by his own intensely linguistic consciousness. Benjamin became convinced early on that language systems define ideas, feelings, political possibilities, the simplest perceptions of the world. And the systemic power of languages is, for him, complemented by a dimension of longing ("intention" in the essay cited above). Verbal languages are only one kind, the highest yet achieved, but still impelled to self-transcendence, towards the imaginable but seemingly unattainable language in which the entirety of history would become coherently legible.

Benjamin's life demands to be interpreted in this context: his shifting relations with ideas, literary works, historical data, personal commitments, and political action must be seen as a process of reading. Benjamin struggles to read himself and his times as a single, often nightmarish text—a text whose transformative "intention" might thus become discernible; a conventional biography, in which private desires drive ideas and public values, could not do justice to this linguistic dynamic. Bernd Witte, however, keeps faith with his subject by establishing three intertwined yet distinct modes of reading (and thereby producing) the text defined as Walter Benjamin's life. First, a life is what this book very clearly is, beginning with birth and ending with death: chronology is respected and there is no excess speculation on Benjamin's posthumous "significance." Second, the dominance of ideas and literary texts in Benjamin's experience of the world is kept in steady focus; although no important event in Benjamin's personal life is omitted, Witte makes clear that such events were inseparable from his continuous reading and mapping of European culture, in its immediacy as well as in its historical constellations. And third, Witte maintains an understated yet legible perspective from our own time, a time for which Benjamin's life, both expressed and consumed in the extreme atmosphere of the Weimar Republic and Nazi-dominated Europe, has become at once exemplary and remote. Particularly when recounting Benjamin's often-conflicted relations with Gershom Scholem and with the directors of the Institute of Social Research in New York, Witte obviously feels that, while ax grinding would be pointless, an ethical stance is both incumbent on a biographer and attuned to Benjamin's own ruthless self-awareness.

Benjamin's importance for contemporary German-language culture is not in doubt. The present translation of Witte's book is a contribution to a relatively new and unpredictable process, the confluence of Benjamin's apocalyptic perspectives with the pragmatic American tradition. I am grateful to Dr. Witte for his suggestions in response to the first draft of the translation and to Norma Dockery, my assistant at Duke University, for her unfailing patience and thoroughness in preparing the manuscript.

I

Childhood and Youth in Berlin

1892–1902

alter Benjamin is the heir and in some way the epitome of that enormously productive German-Jewish cultural tradition that had flourished in Berlin since the days of the friendship between Moses Mendelssohn and Gotthold Ephraim Lessing. He was born into a family of well-to-do business people, established for centuries in Germany: "an upper middle class child," as Walter Benjamin accurately characterized himself in the autobiographical sketches of the *Berlin Chronicle*.[1] His father, Emil Benjamin, born in 1866, descended from a merchant family long settled in the Rhineland and spent his youth in Paris. The ancestors of Walter's mother Pauline, born Schönflies, "at one time lived as dealers in grain and livestock in Brandenburg and Mecklenburg."[2] After 1871 the two families of Benjamin's grandparents moved to Berlin, the burgeoning capital of the newly founded empire, where during Walter's childhood they lived on the same street of the old western district. After their marriage in 1891, Benjamin's parents also settled in this area southwest of the zoological gardens. There, on July 15, 1892, their eldest son was born, his name registered as Walter Benedix Schönflies Benjamin. Three years later his younger brother Georg was born, and in 1901 his sister Dora.[3]

Emil Benjamin acquired "his sometimes considerable wealth" as auctioneer and partner in Lepke's art dealership on Koch Street. After he retired from active involvement in this enterprise, he invested his money "speculatively" in a series of smaller companies, among them a "retailer of medical supplies," a "building society" and a "wine distributor." From 1910

9

The Benjamin family: Émile and Pauline (née Schönflies) Benjamin with their children Walter and Georg.

onward he belonged to the consortium that operated the "ice palace," a Berlin music hall.[4] Even though these paternal business dealings remained hidden from the son, the signs of the family's prosperity were unmistakable. In *Berlin Chronicle*, Benjamin recalls in detail the high-bourgeois atmosphere of the apartment at 24 Nettelbeck Street: deliverers of groceries and French nannies, summer residences in Potsdam and Neubabelsberg, and years of private tutoring in a small circle of children "from the better classes." All this must have given the child an idea of his family's high rank–as did the numerous social evenings at home, when the luxurious deployment of porcelain and silver so impressed him that, thirty years later, he evoked it with the amazement, blended from awe and disgust, of the passionate collector and materialist historian.[5]

In the remembered images of his *Berlin Childhood around 1990*, which Benjamin began to note down in his fortieth year, he sought to locate the seeds of the destruction that was to bring the world of the nineteenth century to an end in war and inflation, in the sheltered atmosphere of his upper-middle-class childhood. The short prose texts that, mosaic-like, make up the book are not so much historical documents as prophecies projected backwards, installing the perspective of the materialist historian of 1932 already in the unconscious sensations of childhood. The total embeddedness of these sensations in the nineteenth century is seen to be precisely what imperils them. The furniture of the 1870s (*Gründerzeit*), which filled his family's large apartments, becomes for the child a second, confining natural order, preventing him from realizing his own identity. More and more he comes to resemble his surroundings, a world dominated by the commodities of the fully industrialized late-nineteenth-century society; but from his "own image" he becomes ever more estranged.

As an archetypal evocation of this self-alienation, Benjamin describes two photographs, one of which resembles the one reported as being taken in the "Diary for Wengen" (1902). It shows him as a ten year old with his brother Georg in an artificial "vacation world" with a painted backdrop of mountains.

> Wherever I looked, I saw myself surrounded by screens, cushions, pedestals which lusted for my blood like the shades of Hades for the blood of the sacrificial animal. Finally I was placed before a coarsely painted Alpine view and my right hand, which had to hold up a goatee hat, cast its shadow upon the vista of clouds and glacier-snow. Yet the worried smile around the mouth of the young mountaineer is less depressing than the gaze penetrating me from the childish face in the shadow of the household palm tree. This tree belongs to one of those studios that, with their stools and tripods, vases and easels, partake of

11

Walter Benjamin and his brother Georg as
"mountaineers," ca. 1902.

both the boudoir and the torture chamber. I'm standing bareheaded, holding in my left hand a mighty sombrero, which I allow to dip down with studied grace; the right hand is occupied with a staff whose lowered handle is visible in the foreground, while its end is hidden in the bundle of ostrich plumes, which flow forward off a garden table. Quite to one side, next to the door curtain, my mother stood rigid, in a tight bodice. Like a mannequin she gazes at my velvet suit, which for its part, overloaded with trimmings, seems cut from a fashion magazine. But I am disfigured by my similarity to everything around me here. I dwelt in the 19th century as a mollusk dwells in its shell, and the century now lies hollow before me like an empty shell.[6]

This text, designated by Benjamin as a photographic self-portrait, suggests the perspective in which the author himself perceived his childhood. Intensely opposed to the idealistic as well as to the psychological concepts of the individual, he derives the formation of the child's identity from the

12

Franz Kafka at the age of five.

socially marked space of his everyday life. The streets, courtyards, and schools of the imperial capital, the furniture and architecture of the Bismarck Era are deployed again and again as symbols of this false second nature in *Berlin Childhood*. In the artificiality of the accessories with which the human subject is programmed for the camera—so that it falls into a deathly rigidity even before being captured on the photographic plate—Benjamin found the metaphor in which he is able to articulate the relationship between the unconscious self-alienation of the Wilhelminian Age and the child growing up within it. The image also crystallizes the fear and melancholy that this state of being imposes on both individual and collectivity. It is thus entirely characteristic of the methodology of Benjamin's autobiography, being the exact opposite of the traditional developmental novel, that the second photograph he describes is not at all a portrait of himself. Two years before the

13

drafting of the autobiographical text, he had already used almost identical sentences in a reflection on a picture of the five-year-old Franz Kafka.[7] The unlabelled self-quotation simultaneously conceals and reveals Benjamin's identification with the Prague author who, also born into a Jewish merchant family, found in writing the strength to break out of his original milieu. The involved reader of Benjamin grasps that the text of *Berlin Childhood* is concerned not so much with the private self of the author, as with the social construction of an individual growing up among the Jewish upper bourgeoisie before the turn of the century.

The ambiguity surrounding the distorted images of this childhood is dissipated only in the rare moments when the child achieves self-identity by transcending his class limitations. It is thus that his habit of loitering is interpreted, his "custom of always remaining a half step behind. It was as if I wanted no kind of united front, not even with my own mother." This form of protest against his own social origins is brought, in the text "Beggars and Whores," into a productive relationship with his first independent attempt at writing: "The poor: for rich children of my age they existed only as beggars. And it was a great step forward in my understanding when, for the first time, I glimpsed the presence of poverty in the shame of poorly paid labor. That was in a little text, perhaps the first I composed all by myself. It concerned a man who hands out leaflets, and the humiliations he endures from a public with no interest in the leaflets."[8] This linkage of social revolt, the discovery of appropriate expressivity, and identity formation is projected by Benjamin into even earlier layers of experience, when he describes the infant's games of hide-and-seek:

> The child standing behind the door curtain feels himself to have become something diffused and white, a ghost. The dining table, under which he has crouched, converts him into the temple's wooden idol, with the carved legs as the four pillars. And behind a door he has become himself a door, has put it on like a heavy mask and, as a shaman, will bewitch all who unknowingly enter. Above all, he must not be found. . . . Thus, with a loud cry, I expelled the demon who was transforming me, whenever the person looking for me laid hands on me. Indeed I didn't wait for that to happen, but anticipated it with a cry of self-liberation.[9]

The magical perspective in which the child is absorbed, with no mental separation, into his animistically experienced surroundings is shattered for the first time by the self-affirmation of the cry. This very early, still inarticulate expression of the self appears in memory as an allegorical promise of self-liberation from passive absorption into a bad world, a liberation that later he will achieve through writing. Thus, in a "dialectical image," the

The Benjamin brothers with their sister Dora.

child is constructed as a writer, and the writer authenticates the origin of his own activity in his childhood.

Benjamin always maintained extreme discretion in relation to the circumstances of his personal life. The author who regarded it as a merit "never to use the word *I*" in his writings, also reveals in them nothing about his family, his parents, or younger siblings.[10] It is only in his memories of childhood that a striking exception is made. There the image of the father's "power and stature" appears in connection with the telephone, introduced

15

in Berlin in 1892, through which he was accustomed to conclude his stock exchange transactions: "Differences of opinion with the bureaucracy were the rule, to say nothing of the threats and insults which my father directed at the complaints department. Yet his real orgies involved the phone-crank, to which he devoted himself for minutes on end, to the point of self-forgetfulness. And his hand was like the dervish who surrenders to sheer voluptuousness. But my heart was beating fast, I was sure that in such cases the operator was threatened by a stroke, as punishment for her dilatoriness."[11] The angry tyrant has allied himself with the most modern technology, enlists it in the service of his affairs, while at the same time exploiting and castigating those in a weaker social position. In this constellation the mythical structures of the patriarchal social order become visible. Powerless suffering, registered by Benjamin as a reaction to the excesses of paternal domination, appears in his private life as the origin of his subsequent extremely tense relationship with his father, and in the public realm as the source of his uncompromising rejection of bourgeois life-styles.

The maternal image is different. Her consoling and healing power counterbalances the father's punishing authority when she comes to the bedside of the frequently ailing child to tell him stories: "Pain was a dam that resisted the narrative only at the outset; later, as the story grew stronger, the dam was undermined, then dissolved into the abyss of forgetting. Stroking prepared the bed for this river. I loved it, for in my mother's hand I sensed the rippling flow of stories, which were soon to pour abundantly from her mouth."[12] The tenderness with which the son looks back on the childhood bond with his mother is intensified by his endowing her with the storyteller's archaic powers—the capacity to transmit experiences and heal sicknesses. In his 1936 essay "The Storyteller," he mourns this as long departed from the modern world. Thus his mother becomes the guarantor of that harmony between body and text, which appears to the adult as the no-longer-accessible source of happiness in his childhood.

In his autobiographical fragments Benjamin does not merely reproduce the role distribution of the patriarchally governed nuclear family. Nor does he draw from these fragments psychological conclusions about the socializing processes of his early childhood. Rather they acquire an allegorical meaning, wherein the social experience of the child reveals itself as identical with that of the adult recording it in memory. Nowhere is this clearer than in the text with the significant title "Society." In this reinterpretation of the opening motif of Marcel Proust's *Remembrance of Things Past*, whereby the subjective childhood memory is transformed into a materialist-historical image, the mundane ritual of soirees at his parents' villa brings the fragility of family relationships into the open. The "monster," as society is labeled

16

by the child's anxious shrewdness, drags the afternoon preparations, which seemed to anticipate a gathering of peace—as suggested by the cornflower motif of the place settings—into the dirt and installs itself in the heart of the family. The child in his remote room is powerless against the demonic force of the consumer society, which simply takes over the table decorated for other purposes. Yet he glimpses, what as an adult he sees with certainty, the truth about whence the monster derives its destructive power: "And since the abyss that had produced it was the abyss of my own class, I first made acquaintance with its power on these evenings."[13] His father confronts it with weapons drawn from its own arsenal. His "formal shirt, blank like a mirror," appears to the child as "armor," the father himself as a "warrior" marching into battle against the monster.

Here too the mother's peaceful image is contrasted with that of the man who must take up the struggle for existence. From the outset she is illuminated by the colors emanating from the stones in her brooch. For the reader, who has encountered these stones in another text in *Berlin Childhood*, as an allegory of art in the sense that Goethe calls it "life's colorful reflection," the figure of the mother appears in the same harmonious light as surrounds her in the text in which she appears as a storyteller. Thus at the end even her departure is not, as in Proust, experienced as withdrawal of love, but as a promise of future happiness. "And without knowing it I experienced in my bed, just before falling asleep, the truth of an enigmatic little proverb 'The later the evening, the lovelier the guests.'"[14] This final sentence of the text identifies the mother, who late in the night comes once more to the child's bed, as the late guest and makes her the forerunner of those even-later guests whom the remembering writer anticipates at his table of peace.

The ambivalent relation of the child to his family is replayed in his attitude toward Berlin, the city of his childhood. On the one hand Benjamin sees himself in his childhood as captive of the old and new western districts of Berlin: "My clan occupied these two districts at that time with an attitude that blended obstinacy with self-confidence and made them into a ghetto perceived as a fiefdom. I was enclosed in this territory of property owners without knowing of any other."[15] In retrospect this place, whose architecture, produced by "Schinkel's very last students," retained, in Franz Hessel's words, "remnants of Graeco-Prussian culture,"[16] also appears to Benjamin as the refuge of a bourgeois-humanist way of life. To this way of life the child owed his sheltered happiness, and the adult, having experienced its destruction, transforms it, through the image of the garden where the golden apples of the Hesperides are ripening, into a distant utopia.

What in childhood can only be reconstructed from later self-analyses

The Kaiser Friedrich Gymnasium on Savigny Square, ca. 1900.

has become tangible, during Benjamin's schooldays, in the form of the earliest preserved texts and attested modes of behavior. At Easter 1902 Benjamin entered the academic track of the Kaiser Friedrich Gymnasium on Savigny Square. Previously he had received exclusively private instruction, initially in a small group of children with rich parents. The *Berlin Chronicle* gives, as a mark of the elite rank of this group, the names of two fellow pupils of noble and upper-middle-class origins, Louise von Landau and Ilse Ullstein from the weathly publishing house family. After that he was prepared for entry to the higher school through individual instruction from a preparatory school teacher. Evidently, however, the often-sickly boy with the sheltered upbringing did not adapt well to the public school system. For after only three years he was removed from the high school by his parents and sent to Haubinda, a country boarding school in Thüringen,

18

where he remained almost two years and, so it appears, repeated one year of study. Not until 1907 did he return to the Kaiser Friedrich Gymnasium, where he graduated at Easter 1912 at the age of twenty. In the same year his family moved to a villa in the suburb of Grunewald. At number 23, Delbrück Street, "Emil Benjamin had purchased a castle-like villa. . . . The family lived now in a spacious flat with a greenhouse and had a pretty garden next to the house."[17]

The high school of the Wilhelminian Era, where in the lower grades "beating, place changing, or detention" were the customary punishments, filled Benjamin the student with confusion and anguish. In his memories written down thirty years later, "the turreted molding above the classrooms" still appears as an "emblem of confinement," to which the thoughts of the worried child retreated during long hours of instruction.[18] In his melancholy brooding the molding became a symbol of "inwardness shielded by power," to use Thomas Mann's stringent characterization of the Wilhelminian Era, and opened his eyes to the structure of school and society at the turn of the century.

Still more upsetting than the pedagogically primitive disciplinary measures was the feeling of being hemmed in by the mass of his fellow students: "These stairs were always hateful to me; I hated them whenever I had to climb them in the herd, with a forest of feet and calves in front of me, helplessly exposed to the bad exhalations from all the bodies shoving so closely against mine."[19] In these lines there speaks the fundamentally physical revulsion of the loner against being drafted into a collectivity. Sickness, tardiness, unobtrusiveness are the impotent attempts of the child to evade this compulsion. Once he has learned to express himself, there grows from this instinctive rejection of class affiliation a marked awareness of the value of his own individuality. Thus the study of Pindar prescribed in the curriculum of the "humanistic" high school provoked Benjamin to his "first philosophical essay," whose title, "Thoughts on Aristocracy," may be an indication of its author's elitist ambitions.

The two-year stay in Haubinda gave a decisive impetus to the further development of Benjamin's mind and character. This country boarding school, founded in 1901 by Hermann Lietz for students of junior high school age, had been directed since 1904 by Paulus Geheeb and Gustav Wyneken, who sought to implement the program for educational reform conceived by Wyneken. Here Benjamin felt for the first time that his idealism was taken seriously, that students and teachers encountered each other as free and equal partners dedicated to the same spiritual goals. Life in this idealistic educational community shaped his ideas into the war years and made him an enthusiastic proponent of school reform.

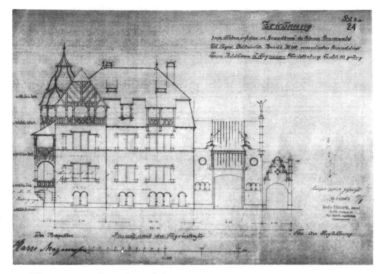

The construction plan of the Benjamin house at 23 Delbrück Street.
The house was destroyed during World War II.

In the student journal *Der Anfang* (The Beginning), devoted to Gustav Wyneken's ideas and edited beginning in 1908 by Georges Barbizon (George Gretor), initially in hectograph format, Benjamin published in the summer of 1910 his first creative efforts. While still derivative in form and content, they suggest an awareness of his future social role as intellectual outsider. Thus one may read his earliest published text, a poem sketching the figure of the poet in traditional metaphors, as the outline of a model for self-identity:

> Look, at the edge of the monstrous abyss
> You see a lonely man carelessly standing
> Between black night and colorful life.
>
> He stands in changeless serenity
> Alone, apart from the road of life.[20]

At the age of sixteen Benjamin, together with Herbert Belmore and other fellow students, founded a reading and discussion circle, at whose weekly meetings plays from world literature were read and discussed. Here too educational reform ideas were central, as shown by the essay "The Sleeping Beauty," which Benjamin published, as he did his earlier texts, under a pseudonym—Ardor—appropriate to his sense of commitment, in the second number of *Der Anfang*. In this piece classical and modern figures from dramatic literature, Tasso and Faust, Karl Moor and Max Piccolomini, Hamlet and Gregers Werle, are interpreted as forerunners of the Age of Youth, which Benjamin sees as imminent. "Youth is the beauty who sleeps and has no inkling of the prince approaching to liberate her. And that youth should awaken, should take part in the struggle being waged for its soul—to this end our journal is contributing its maximum effort."[21]

Benjamin's intellectual and organizational activities in the next few years were devoted almost exclusively to the endeavor sketched here. In the last article written in his school years, the programmatic text, "The Free School Community," published in May 1911, he tries, with long quotations from Wyneken's *Yearbooks of the Free School Community*, to summarize the tasks of the new generation. In the process he takes over from his teacher the mixture of Hegelian metaphysics and enthusiastic faith in technological progress that typified the times. In his attempt to characterize the "signature" of the age, one can already glimpse the positive evaluation of technology's impact on cultural processes, which was to become normative for the author of the essay "The Work of Art in the Age of Mechanical Reproduction": "In socialism the spirit confronts the degenerations of the struggle for existence, in evolutionism it acknowledges the logical development of the world, in technology spirit takes up the fight with the powers of nature. The world has been penetrated by the human spirit, which was earlier oppressed by 'the domination of the material.'" From this scarcely original analysis of the situation Benjamin derives the "task of the individual in the present day": "It is to place oneself in the service of this objective spirit and to fulfill one's duty in work on behalf of the highest good. There is a religious impulse in the conscious evolution of this thought from metaphysics."[22] These pathos-ridden sentences by the high school senior, however imprecise, can stand as a motto for Benjamin's efforts, during his first years of study, at influencing the youth movement in Wyneken's spirit. In his unconditional engagement with this goal, the idealistic outsider believed he had found the meaning of his actions in society and at the same time realized the dream of integration into a community.

II

Youth Movement, Judaism, Philosophy of Language

1912–1917

nlike many persons of letters who find their own voice only gradually, Walter Benjamin is, in his writings, immediately and fully himself. Thus there is no question of viewing his earliest texts, from the time of his membership in the youth movement, as in any sense external to the body of his work as a whole. To this intellectual identity formed already in youth he owes the self-confidence and authority with which he interacts with friends and contemporaries and which permits him, already in his first literary utterances, to speak highly apodictically and didactically.

In the years immediately preceding the First World War, when he began his studies, the protest against the bourgeois way of life and the anticipation of coming catastrophes were captured in the literary works of the Expressionists. Benjamin kept his distance from them, although he knew many of them personally, since they generally belonged to the same generation and came from the same social background. To their generalized pathos of humanity, the twenty-year-old Benjamin already consciously maintained a religiously grounded counter-pathos of truth; a few years later he was to develop, with the concept of the "expressionless" as the metaphysical center of his theory of art, an intellectual model in opposition to the "expressionism" (*Ausdruckskunst*) of his contemporaries.

To achieve backing for the view he expounded, Benjamin joined the radical wing of the youth movement. In the summer semester of 1912 he went to Freiburg to study philosophy with the neo-Kantian Heinrich Rickert.

22

There he devoted a large part of his time to the organization of student groups who were to propagate, on the basis of Gustav Wyneken's writings, the idea of an independent youth culture among students. He freely acknowledges that as a result, he neglected his own studies almost totally. In June 1912, in a letter to his school friend Herbert Belmore, who had stayed in Berlin, he portrays himself ironically as a "hero of school reform" ready to "sacrifice learning."[1] The "group for school reform," which Benjamin joined in Freiburg, had been founded in the winter semester 1911–12, as a consequence of a public appeal of Gustav Wyneken, within the framework of the Free Student Movement. The Free Students, in contrast to the conformist cultivation of tradition within the fraternities, stood for a conception of learning oriented toward Humboldt's ideal of freedom and self-determination, and they demanded a political voice for students in university affairs. Within this loosely organized movement Wyneken's supporters represented the most radical wing. They turned their backs on the debates about the university's political organization, which they deemed futile, and expressed their absolute opposition to Wilhelminian society in the demand for "serving pure spirit," which, in their view, could only be accomplished by the still uncorrupted youth.[2]

Benjamin had committed himself to this extremely idealistic concept of social change through cultural revolution ever since his "decisive spiritual experience," which was how he perceived his stay in Haubinda and the personal encounter with Wyneken.[3] In the summer semester of 1912, the unit for school reform in Freiburg, under the direction of its founder Christian Papmeyer, organized a series of lectures on issues of the youth culture, which were collectively published in the pamphlet *Student and School Reform* and distributed, in a printing of ten thousand copies, to the Free Student groups at all German universities. Even though Benjamin had only just arrived in Freiburg, he contributed an essay with the programmatic title "School reform, a cultural movement." In it he summons youth to productive activity in freedom, since only thus could "a revision of values" and a consequent advance in culture be possible.[4]

After Benjamin returned to Berlin in the winter semester 1912–13, he founded the *Sprechsaal* (speaker's corner), a free association of his friends, at whose evening meetings aesthetic and moral questions were debated. The group, which included young women, rented an apartment, "the home," in the Old Western quarter near the Landwehr canal, as a meeting place to which every member had unquestioned access.[5] Clearly the main goal was to realize a free way of life for youth unsupervised by parents or other authorities of the bourgeois world. In his second Freiburg semester in the summer of 1913, Benjamin reorganized the unit for school reform, at Wyne-

23

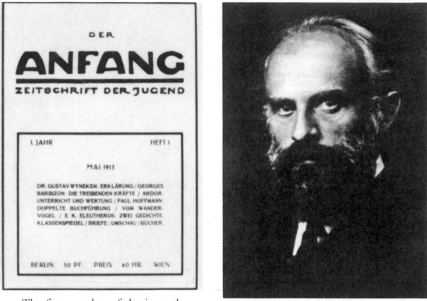

The first number of the journal
Der Anfang.

Gustav Wyneken, ca. 1916.

ken's express wish, in an effort to mobilize the Free Student group as a whole for its goals.[6] At the same time he sent regular contributions to the "journal for youth," *Der Anfang* (The Beginning), edited by Georges Barbizon and Siegfried Bernfeld in Berlin. In each of the first six issues of 1913 he is represented by an article in which he propounds the usual positions of the radical youth movement. His protest is directed against repression in school and home, against the "scepticism and world-weariness" of the philistines, and against the hypocrisy of bourgeois morality. His positive demands testify to his characteristically elitist sense of mission. Thus in the essay "Teaching and Valuing," invoking Nietzsche, he outlines the image of an anti-reformist high school, where Greek culture would be "not a fabulous realm of 'harmonies' and 'ideals'," but "that misogynist and homoerotic Greek culture of Pericles, aristocratic, based on slavery and the dark myths of Aeschylus." To educators he poses the question "whether they are capable of creating this school, which would have to be hostile to the present, undemocratic, joyous."[7] In the light of such theories, it is hardly surprising that the publication of *Der Anfang* provoked, as Siegfried Bernfeld put it

24

Walter Benjamin, ca. 1912.

later, "an outcry of anger in the world of principals and rectors and among political parties even at the liberal end of the bourgeois spectrum."[8]

Drawing on his feeling of intellectual self-worth, Benjamin peremptorily rejected the academic profession as he came to know it in Freiburg: "Cohn's seminar on the *Critique of Judgment* and Schiller's *Aesthetics* is chemically purified of all ideas. . . . I sit in Rickert's seminar and chew on my own thoughts." Instead he felt able to satisfy his intellectual ambitions in personal conversations with friends and communal reading of Spitteler, George, Rilke, and Kierkegaard. In the discussions within the small, like-minded group he formed around himself, he endeavored to "restore people to their

25

youthfulness."[9] These personal conversion efforts on Wyneken's behalf achieved some success. At the end of the 1913 summer semester Benjamin could announce to his Berlin friends: "The meetings on school reform (with an attendance of eight to ten) are always on a high level. The essential thing is that evening after evening Wyneken is discussed, that we don't hold back with our committed discipleship—everything else follows from this."[10]

Benjamin's emphasis on following his teacher and his various attempts to gather a group of students around himself could claim authority in Gustav Wyneken's theory of youth culture. The latter's Hegelianism, appropriately trimmed down for the Wilhelminian Era, presented world history as the progressive penetration of nature and humanity by Spirit, whereby the beginning of the twentieth century was distinguished as the moment in this "self-recognition process of nature" when for the first time youth as such intervened. This idealistic ideology was addressed to older high school and university students, who at that time came almost exclusively from the middle and upper bourgeoisie. For them it provided the justification for a hierarchical social structure, which was reproduced in the educational model to which Wyneken aspired. According to the model only the culturally productive, the geniuses, were the bearers of Spirit; hence they were preselected as leaders of the "self-educating communities." For the majority of young people, however, service to the Spirit could consist only in "free commitment to the self-chosen leader."[11]

Although Benjamin's social action appears at first to be wholly marked by this elitist spirit metaphysics, his publications and letters from the years immediately before the war reveal that he committed himself to it only because it enabled him to stave off concrete political involvement and to maintain an individual viewpoint. Alienated from the cultural and religious traditions of Judaism by his upbringing in a liberal home, he experienced for the first time in August 1912, during a vacation in Stolpmünde with Zionist schoolfriends Kurt Tuchler and Franz Sachs, "Zionism and Zionist activity as a possibility, hence perhaps a duty."[12] The following winter, in a correspondence that he himself labeled "programmatic" with Ludwig Strauss, a poet his own age, he worked out an independent attitude to the question of Judaism. This was to become for him the source of the articulation and renewal of spiritual life. Strauss, as a "Zionist activist" and translator of Eastern Jewish literature, was among the most outspoken proponents of Jewish self-determination. In contrast Benjamin distanced himself from Zionism as a political and social movement; its "nationalism," he felt, was diametrically opposed to the mission of Judaism to become an international "radical cultural will." His critical comments on the advocates of a political Zionism were relentlessly harsh: "Their personality was inwardly by no means defined by Jewishness; they preach Palestine but drink like Germans."[13]

Benjamin committed himself instead to a "cultural Zionism which sees Jewish values everywhere and works for them."[14] In this sense his Jewishness meant for him a duty toward the development of European culture. "My life experience led me to this insight: the Jews represent an elite in the ranks of the spiritually active. . . . For Judaism is to me in no sense an end in itself, but the most distinguished bearer and representative of the spiritual."[15] Essentially Benjamin held to this position throughout his life. It immunized him against the repeated and urgent attempts by his friend Gershom Scholem to persuade him to move to Palestine, and he continued to defend it even when historical reality, in the shape of Nazi rule, had turned his dreams of a European cultural mission for Judaism into an illusion. His despairing efforts during his Paris exile to reconstruct the nineteenth century testify to the fact that even the physical threat to his very existence could not derail his utopian projection of a fulfillment of European culture through the spirit of Judaism. That threat did demonstrate however the truth of the prophetic sentence with which, in the correspondence with Strauss, Benjamin justified his involvement in this matter: "For me it is idle to ask which is more important, Jewish work for Palestine or Jewish work for Europe. I am tied here. And it would be bad indeed for Europe if the cultural energies of the Jews were to be withdrawn from it."[16]

Benjamin's attitude toward Judaism can in no way be equated with the traditional assimilationist tendencies of the newly successful Jewish bourgeoisie. Underlying it is an intense awareness of his own special position in society and the shaping of that position by his Jewish origins. In his "Dialogue on Religious Feeling Today," which he circulated in typescript among his friends in 1913, he established for himself, following on his debate with Ludwig Strauss, a highly personal intellectual model, which also presupposed a confrontation with the bourgeois ideology of progress through individual cultivation. Opposing the classical, "pantheist" tradition that marked this outlook, Benjamin insists on the fundamental dualism of Nature and Spirit—and thereby expressly contradicts Wyneken's optimistic assumption of a progressive spiritualization of nature. Historically Benjamin bases his point of view, which he regards as being the only one of actual value, on the distinction between sense perception and reason, which Kant had rendered fundamental to modern thought, and on Romanticism's discovery of the "dark side of nature."

The decisive elements in the religious point of view Benjamin outlines in his "Dialogue" are, however, his secret affinity for Jewish monotheism, in which nature as mythical force is profoundly suspect, and his personal

27

life experience in metropolitan Berlin. Thus to him the real carriers of the longing for a new religion are the outsiders, the coffeehouse denizens, since they are the furthest removed from all "natural" living.

> Religion will once again emanate from the enslaved—but the class which today endures this historically necessary enslavement is the writing class. Writers want to be honest, they want to express their enthusiasm for art, their 'love of the distant,' in Nietzsche's phrase, but society rejects them: they are themselves driven to eliminate, in a process of pathological self-destruction, everything that is all-too-human yet necessary for life. So it is with those who would transmute values into life, into life's conventions: and our untruthfulness condemns them to life as outsiders, and to an excessive emotionalism which renders them sterile.[17]

Thus speaks one who has become aware early on of his limits as an author, who knows he lacks "the unity of the moment, of ecstasy, of the great visionaries,"[18] but who also, by conceiving the writer as the extreme embodiment of his own Jewish outsider status, projects him as the marginal figure from whom future salvation is to be expected.

In spite of his revolt against the bourgeois milieu of his origins, Benjamin always refused to define his own practice as purely social or political. "I am thinking (not in a socialist but in some other sense) of the mass of the excluded, and of the Spirit which is in league with the sleepers," he writes in November 1913 to Carla Seligson, who like himself took an active part in the meetings of the Berlin Sprechsaal.[19] This sentence is to be understood as a position taken in a dispute that developed in the winter of 1913–14 and led ultimately to the breakup of the Wyneken group in Berlin. Under the influence of Siegfried Bernfeld, founder and director of the Viennese Academic Committee for School Reform, a group around the editor of *Der Anfang*, Georges Barbizon, sought to politicize the Berlin Sprechsaal. "There were thoughts of winning over political parties; or of strikes, or of an emigration of the youth from town and university." Fritz Heinle and Simon Guttmann, supported by Benjamin, opposed such efforts. The policy struggle in which, as always in the debates of the youth movement, personal rivalries and leadership claims were also involved, was fought through with the aid of written polemics. Benjamin finally addressed Wyneken directly, in a ten-page "open letter" wherein he stressed that in all his actions he had been concerned only to maintain the pure community of youth and finally dissociated himself formally from "what had hitherto been the youth movement."[20] In consequence he ceased his collaboration on *Der Anfang* and withdrew from the Berlin Sprechsaal.

His refusal to engage himself politically, either as a Zionist or as a socialist—a refusal he saw as keeping faith with the "spirit of youth"—signified above all a theoretical grounding of the individual's responsibility to act and think for himself. In September 1913 he wrote in a statement of belief to Carla Seligson:

> The central point is: we must not settle upon a given set of concepts, even the idea of the youth culture should be for us only the illumination which draws the most distant spiritual zones into the circle of intellect. But for many, Wyneken's ideas, even the Sprechsaal itself constitute a "movement"; they root themselves within it and cease to perceive the Spirit in its even freer, even more abstract manifestation. It is this unceasing, vibrant awareness of the abstractness of pure Spirit which I call youth.[21]

This fundamental holding open of one's own life, on which Benjamin insists here, is premised on a hope of fulfillment, which he himself calls messianic. Such fulfillment is conceived as coming not from practical involvement with the world, but from a community of the like-minded mediated by literature, ultimately from a turn toward the inner world. "Today I feel the immense truth of Christ's saying: Behold the Kingdom of God is neither here nor there but within us. I would like to read you Plato's dialogue on love, where that truth is more beautifully and deeply articulated than anywhere else."[22] In these enthusiastic words, with which the letter to Carla Seligson culminates, both the life context and the religious grounding of Benjamin's "metaphysics of youth" receive their most explicit formulation.

After his withdrawal from the Sprechsaal, Benjamin attempted one last time to implement his ideas about an independent youth culture in a practical way, by having himself elected president of the Berlin Free Student Group at the end of the winter semester 1913–14. In his speech at the opening meeting of the summer semester 1914, he directed his polemic primarily against the students' social engagement, which was for him "an extreme and objectionable manifestation of relativism," since "there exists no inner, authentic link . . . between the spiritual existence of a student and his charitable interest in workers' children."[23] Once again he demanded the "constitution or, better, the making possible of a community of youth based solely on inwardness and intensity, and no longer in any way on politics."[24] Benjamin's fellow students in Berlin refused to endorse this elitist program. One month later he repeated his speech at the annual meeting of all the Free Student Groups, the "Free Student Day" in June 1914 in Weimar. Here too he was disappointed. His plea to "found a new university based on itself, on Spirit as such" was ignored or rejected. Afterwards he travelled to Munich to visit his fiancée of the time, Grete Radt, and reported bitterly on the "uniform ill-will of this assembly" and the "brutal, daily negative votes."[25]

The double defeat caused Benjamin to retire completely from organizational work in the youth movement. Instead he published the speech he had given in Berlin and Weimar, amplified by a few important methodological sections in the introduction and conclusion, under the title "The Life of Students" in Efraim Frisch's journal *Der Neue Merkur* (The New Mercury) in 1915. In this context it reads like an anarchist manifesto, questioning the foundations of bourgeois society, namely family, profession, and sense of social responsibility, in order to open up for youth the free space of a "community of creative human beings."[26] In developing his speech Benjamin had worked with Fichte's "Theoretical Plan for an Institution of Higher Education to be Established in Berlin" and with Nietzsche's "On the Future of Our Educational Institutions." Thus he states at the beginning of his essay with regard to their methods: "The only way to approach the historical position of students and universities is through a philosophical system." He adds: "As long as various conditions of possibility are lacking for this project, there remains only the task of liberating, through understanding, the forms of the future from their distortions in the present. Critical thinking is devoted solely to this task."[27] Critical thinking, to become Benjamin's royal road toward understanding, appears here for the first time as a replacement for a philosophical system that has lost its validity and, still more decisively, as a substitute for his failure in social practice.

Benjamin grounds his critical procedure in an explicit historiographical framework that views the present not as an empty, neutral historical continuum, but as a moment tending toward the messianic future. "The elements of the end of history reveal themselves not as shapeless, progressive tendencies but as the most endangered, despised, and ridiculed thoughts and productions, which are embedded deeply in any present moment. To purify the immanent state of perfection into absolute presence, to render it visible and dominant within the present: that is our historical task."[28] In these sentences, which recapitulate his earlier statements about the writer on an objective level, Benjamin for the first time described history as the medium for the religious experience to which he aspired, and discovered historical-critical thinking to be the essential intellectual tool, with its mission to "liberate, through understanding, the forms of the future from their distortions in the present." The price he pays for this new form of understanding is the renunciation of all practical intervention upon history itself. It is only theoretically that the critical thinker can anticipate the historically decisive turns that he hopes will facilitate the arrival of the "messianic realm."

Among Benjamin's relations with people his own age, the link with

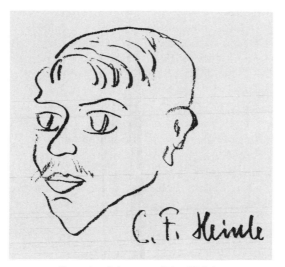

Portrait of the poet Fritz Heinle.

Fritz Heinle was of the utmost importance to him. Certainly they sometimes quarrelled, after the young poet had followed his friend from Freiburg to Berlin. But Benjamin saw in the tension prevailing between them a constellation that was decisive for his future life, in which the "necessity of the idea" became manifest. Thus he wrote to Carla Seligson about his reconciliation after an argument with Heinle: "He confronted me in the name of love and I opposed him with the symbol. You will understand the simplicity and fullness of meaning which both these concepts have for us . . . although each of us identifies with the other, he must necessarily remain truthful to his own spirit."29 There is much evidence that Benjamin saw in the interaction between the two of them the archetypal realization of a pure spiritual community, hence at the same time the desired symbiosis between Germans and Jews. Heinle was for him the productive one, the poet entitled to speak in the name of love, while he identified his own role as that of the writer whose project was to decode the spiritual meaning of all life's manifestations. "Fritz Heinle was a poet, the only one of all my friends whom I encountered not 'in life' but in his poetry": thus Benjamin described his friend even eighteen years after the latter's death.

At the outbreak of the First World War in early August 1914 Benjamin, "without a spark of war enthusiasm in his heart," volunteered for service in the cavalry barracks in Bellalliance Street in Berlin, in order not to be

31

separated from his friends during military service.[30] Then occurred "the event," after which for a long time everything else, even the bloody conflict between the European states, paled into insignificance for him. On 8 August Fritz Heinle and Rika Seligson, Carla's sister, in despair over the war, took their lives in a suicide pact in the "home" of the Sprechsaal. For Benjamin this death became a kind of primal experience. It marked for him the end of the youth movement and the hopes he had associated with it. This is how he himself interpreted it in one of his earliest literary essays, the analysis of Dostoyevsky's *Idiot*, in the summer of 1917. With the directness characteristic of his early essays, Benjamin locates the "metaphysical identity" of the novel in the fact that Prince Myshkin, the hero, is led by the episodic structure of the whole, and by the subordination to him of all the other characters, to appear to be immortal. Benjamin equates this result of his literary analysis directly with his personal experience: "But the pure word for life in the condition of immortality is: youth. That is Dostoyevsky's great lament in this book: The failure of the movement of youth. . . . The whole rhythm of the book is like a monstrous volcanic implosion. In the absence of both nature and childhood, humanity becomes conceivable only through a catastrophic self-destruction."[31] Benjamin's friends read these sentences correctly "as an esoteric comment about Fritz Heinle."[32]

Even more than the destruction of his hopes of forming a spiritual community, Heinle's death meant for Benjamin an experience of survival, of outliving another, which was to be decisive for his existence. As the survivor he testifies to the poet's productivity, which was both destroyed and metaphysically fulfilled in death. The point here is not so much that Benjamin throughout his life surrounded the figure of his friend with a "kind of cultish secrecy" and was active years later, even in his own testament, in pressing for the publication of Heinle's literary manuscripts. In a more general sense the meaning of his friends' death for Benjamin was that purity of spirit is found not in life but only in poetically shaped language, and that this purity is to be rendered visible and effective, not through social action but only through the language of sobriety, which for him meant the prose of critical theory.

In Benjamin's mind the figure of his dead poet-friend blends with the figure of the late Hölderlin, as rediscovered at the time by Norbert von Hellingrath, to form a new ideal image of human existence. In his "first larger work, a study of two Hölderlin poems," written in the months following Heinle's suicide and dedicated to him, Benjamin intensifies the meaning of Heinle's fate, through a comparative interpretation of Hölderlin's odes *Dichtermut* ("Poet's Courage") and *Blödigkeit* ("Foolishness"), into an apotheosis of the poet as savior of the world. The poet is deemed to be the unity-creating "principle of form," holding together a disintegrating world. By giving to people and gods their intelligible image, he also endows "himself with form." But such an achievement is only possible for a person "who gives himself over to the danger, so that in the event of his death he expands it into a universal danger–and simultaneously overcomes it."[33] Death is accordingly, as later in the study of German tragic drama, defined as the principle that gives to the poet himself a definite outline, to his text meaning, and to his work as a whole impact and credibility. This "existentialist" view of literature interprets the poet's fate as a tragic one. He must necessarily come to grief, so that he can fulfill his true task, the production of universal symbolic connections. This insight, which Benjamin finds in the transformation of Hölderlin's early poem into its later form, and which he views as archetypal for all poetry, dominates Benjamin's thinking from now on, its "sobriety" displacing his enthusiasm for "youth." Paraphrasing Hölderlin, he formulates this development: "With ever more focussed concentration as their goal, things strive for an existence as pure idea, thereby crystallizing the poet's destiny in the pure world of forms. The plasticity of achieved form is revealed as the spiritual. Thus has the 'thinking day' emerged from the 'day of joy.'"[34]

Looking back at this period of his life, Benjamin subsequently defined the historical location of the radical wing of the Berlin student movement, which he helped to found, in a reflection on the geographical location of the "home" of the Sprechsaal in the Old Western sector of Berlin:

> That spot, where by chance we opened our meeting place at that time, is today for me the precise and concrete expression of the historical position that this last genuine elite of bourgeois Berlin assumed. It stood as close to the abyss of the great War as its meeting place stood to the steep bank of the Landwehr canal; it was sharply cut off from the proletarian youth, just as the houses of this pensioners' district were set apart from those of Moabit; and the young elite was the last of its kind, just as the inhabitants of those large bourgeois houses were the last who could assuage the demanding shades of the dispossessed by acting out the rites of philanthropy. Nevertheless–or perhaps for that very reason–it is certain that at no later time did the city of Berlin penetrate my very existence as powerfully as it did then, when we thought we could leave the city itself untouched and simply focus on improving its schools, on eliminating the inhuman treatment of children by their parents, on making the words of Hölderlin or George resound in its cultural life. It was the ultimate heroic attempt to change the attitudes of people without challenging the structure of society itself.[35]

The crisis of 8 August 1914 signified for Benjamin the failure of this attempt. Its aftereffects on his life lasted well into the first two years of the war. His initial indifference toward the war was rapidly transformed into a sharp, theoretically argued oppositional attitude, which contrasted vividly with the widespread sense of release and expansion dominant among Germans in the fall of 1914. He avoided military service by presenting himself at the recruiting office "as someone afflicted with tremors, as previously rehearsed." Gerhard Scholem, who became close friends with Benjamin in the summer of 1915 as a result of a discussion on the "essence of the historical process," tells of "his utter revulsion against talking about the political events of the day and military actions."[36]

Benjamin broke his silence only once. When Gustav Wyneken published his manifesto *Youth and War* at the end of 1914, Benjamin responded in March 1915 with a letter of farewell, in which he reviewed once more all that Wyneken had meant to him as "bearer of an idea and principal guide toward the life of the spirit." Benjamin then charged Wyneken with betrayal of this very idea and broke with him definitively. Despite this explicit rupture with his own past, Benjamin clung to its theoretical viewpoints, as the pathos-ridden and self-conscious conclusion of the letter testifies: "Youth however belongs only to those who see clearly, who love it and love in it the idea above all. It has slipped away from your erring hands and embarked on a destiny of suffering. To live with it is the legacy I am wresting from you."[37]

At the end of October 1915, Benjamin moved to Munich, where his fiancée Grete Radt was studying, in order to take cover from the war and to continue his studies at a distance from the all-too-painful Berlin memories. Here too he gave the academic instruction an extraordinarily negative evaluation. He declared the lecture course by the renowned art historian Heinrich Wölfflin to be "very bad."[38] "His seminar has no viable relationship to the significance of his theme (early medieval miniatures), it is completely disoriented and he has no access at all to the outlook on life involved here." Only the colloquium given by the Americanist Walter Lehmann "on the culture and language of ancient Mexico," in which Rainer Maria Rilke among other figures of Munich society participated, was reckoned by Benjamin to be "of intellectual and social value."[39]

The significant degree of snobbism permeating such judgments is linked subjectively to Benjamin's constant self-analysis, whereby he strove to justify his own viewpoint from ever-changing external perspectives. In the same letter, in which he reports on his Munich studies, he endeavors characteristically to draw the new paths of his thinking and writing into a single analytical context:

34

It is theory that really constitutes the living fruitfulness of our intellectual production, its health in the highest sense. The relation of productivity to life (to the importance of which a disaster like Wölfflin's bears witness) is structured and sustained by theory. It is within the framework of theory that the creative person's life is filled with rhythmic production. Theory guarantees its purity by maintaining its distance from all intellectual violence (the real impurity of the creator), and it can do this by surrounding with a clear, constant fire the images of that primary, most simple idea on which all productivity must constantly draw in order to grow and become form. Theory's light, being light as such, is infinite no matter how limited the objects it illuminates.[40]

Philosophy of history, literary criticism, and theory are the paths on which Benjamin is striving experimentally toward his own method of cognition. All of them converge in the goal of situating life, the objects of this world, in a relationship with that pure reality he had previously called spirit, and for which now, writing in the Platonic mode, he uses the neo-Kantian term *ideas*.

In his philosophy of language Benjamin came closest to the successful mediation of these two poles, whose antithetical tensions still dominate the conceptual labor of the "Epistemological Preface" to his book on German tragic drama. His interest in language was, as he himself stated in a late curriculum vitae, awakened by studies with the Berlin teacher Ernst Lewy on Wilhelm von Humboldt and furthered by his work with Lehmann in Munich. The impetus to develop his thinking in written form was given by the intensive discussions with Scholem, who at this time was still studying mathematics but was already occupied with Jewish mysticism. Benjamin's pioneering essay, "Concerning Language in General and the Language of Man," completed toward the end of 1916 in Munich, originated in his desire to continue the discussions with Scholem on the essence of language in a written forum.

This text is thus extremely hermetic in its linguistic posture, being conceived as a medium for self-questioning and communication with a friend preoccupied by the same questions. Its author had no intention of publishing it. Benjamin gave access to the manuscript to only a few people who were close to him at the time: Ernst Schoen, Herbert Belmore, and Werner Kraft. He describes the essay's concern as being to "engage himself with the very essence of language . . . specifically as it pertains to an immanent understanding of Judaism and of the early chapters of Genesis."[41] The self-interpretation in this letter shows to what extent the original constellation of Benjamin's thinking remained the same through all the processes of transformation. He had, after all, understood his efforts on behalf of a spiritual

35

community in the youth movement as the purest realization of the meaning of his Jewishness; this is true to an even higher degree of his early philosophy of language.

Benjamin begins by defining language as "the principle whose mission is the communication of spiritual contents." As such it is universal: "There is no happening, no entity in either organic or inorganic nature that does not participate in some sense in language, for it is of the essence of all things to communicate their spiritual content." This general principle is then differentiated in the course of an intepretation of the first chapters of Genesis. Benjamin distinguishes initially three levels of language, to which corresponds a "structuring of all spiritual being into qualitative levels": the divine creative language, in which the Word creates things directly in unity with their names; the language of Adam, which constitutes pure cognition through the assigning of names; and the mute language of things.[42] In this system of pure language, which Benjamin finds developed in the language mystic Johann Georg Hamann, whom he cites, words are defined by "receptivity and spontaneity at once"[43]; that is, they are not mere linguistic signs, but the "spiritual being" of both the speaker and the named entity that is present in them.

From this ideal language system, the present-day language of human beings is separated by the Fall, which has ruptured it into the multiplicity of national languages and introduced into it the elements of judgment and abstraction. It is clear that only this fallen language is directly accessible to our minds. However Benjamin's linguistic-philosophical commentary on the early chapters of Genesis, wherein he establishes the cited hierarchy of languages, is not to be understood as exclusively theological. Rather, a double movement can be read into it. What appears in Benjamin's formulation as the interpretation of a sacred text reveals itself, through a dialectical reversal, as a grounding of linguistic hierarchies from the perspective of critical theory. In the study of language Benjamin puts into practice what he had described in "The Life of Students" as the historico-philosophical method. Here too it is his goal to liberate through cognition, from the fallen state of contemporary language, the utopian condition of its perfection.

Human language, in its defective state, is characterized by a fundamental duality. On the one hand it is referential language, designates concrete things that, Benjamin writes, are communicated *through* it. On the other hand language is the expression of a spiritual essence that transmits itself only *within* it. In the process of translating the mute language of things into words, human language at the same time expresses the spiritual essence of the speaker. Benjamin here employs the concept of translation not in the customary, as it were horizontal sense of transmission from one language into another, but in the vertical sense of transmission from an imperfect language, such as that of things, in its postlapsarian muteness, into a more perfect one, such as the human language. With this concept Benjamin thus ensures continuity within the hierarchy of linguistic levels.

In human language, according to Benjamin's speculation, there is similarly an extreme point at which the boundary to the linguistic level immediately above it can be crossed. This boundary point is the name. "Because man's spiritual essence is language itself, he cannot express himself by means of language but only within it, in its texture. The embodiment of this intensive totality of language as man's spiritual essence is the name."[44] Through the name, then, today's language participates in the primal Adamic one, which is defined as the pure language of naming. Based on this system of continuous transitions between hierarchically conceived linguistic levels, the task of linguistic critical theory should be understood as the translation of human language into the more perfect Adamic one, or as the activation of that which functions in language as symbol of the non-communicable. Through this theory of language, poetry, which encodes the symbolic supplementarity of language within the text, and literary criticism, which soberly names the inexpressible elements encoded into poetry, can move to the center of Benjamin's future critical work.

In the spirit of his mystical theory of naming, Benjamin also worked through his mourning at the loss of his friend Heinle. In place of the actual person of the dead man, his name, distilled into pure language, moves gradually to the center of Benjamin's remembering consciousness. Benjamin himself assigned this meaning to the act of writing whereby he freed himself from the extreme shock of his friend's death during the war years, in the first of his cycle of fifty sonnets addressed to Fritz Heinle and Rika Seligson.[45] In it he summons up the memory of the physical and spiritual figure of his friend, in images variously adapted from Rilke's and Georges's poetry, in order finally to assert that he can live "serenely" without his presence,

> If within me you but build your sacred name
> Imageless, like an infinite amen.

To these lines from the opening poem corresponds the conclusion of the fiftieth sonnet, hence of the whole cycle, wherein the goal, the manifestation of pure language, is proclaimed in images drawn from the prophetic and Kabbalistic tradition:

A liberated gaze stepped into the tropic
Of high mourning where from out of pale

Winters arose the new shoot
In whose calyxes slumbered the seeds
Of coming children from the promised name.[46]

The early essay on language is close to the limit of the sayable and the comprehensible. In a letter to Martin Buber, whom Benjamin saw as outside his circle, he himself sought to convey the extremism of his position (Buber had in July 1916 asked him whether he would contribute to his journal *Der Jude*, an offer Benjamin declined):

> In however many guises language may show its effectiveness, it achieves that effect not through the transmission of contents, but through the purest expression of its dignity and its essence. . . . My conception of style and of objective and as such highly political writing is: to lead the reader toward that which escapes the word; only when this non-verbal realm is opened up in its pure, inexpressible power, can the magic spark fly between word and motivating deed to the point of unity between these two equal realities. Only the intensive compression of words toward their center of inner silence attains to a genuine impact.[47]

The motive behind such struggles on the edge of silence is the rescue of experiences that are inaccessible to rational classification. The unity of Benjamin's various sketches for an autonomous theory, following the failure of the youth movement, can be seen to reside in a synthesis of philosophy of history, literary criticism, and theory of language; in this unity "language is presupposed as an ultimate, inexplicable, and mystical reality, only observable in its effects."[48] The "critical theory" into which these elements are woven constitutes the center and origin of Benjamin's thought. From this theory he expected that truth would be revealed in it as a world-changing, messianic force with immediate impact.

III

Art Criticism in the Spirit of Romanticism

1 9 1 7 – 1 9 2 3

verything, except for those few elements through which I gave my own life a new direction, everything to which I had drawn closer in the last two years had ended in downfall; here I find myself rescued in many senses, although I have not attained ease, security or mature living. But I have escaped those demonic, ghostly forces which, wherever we turn, dominate the world, and I have escaped the sheer anarchy, the senselessness of the suffering."[1] In these sentences, from a letter written at the end of July 1917 in St. Moritz to Ernst Schoen, Benjamin expressed his sense of relief that, by his move to Switzerland, he finally knew himself to be safe from the personal and historical catastrophes, which the great European War had meant for him. In the restless preceding months he had become closely acquainted with Dora Pollack, daughter of the Viennese Zionist and Shakespeare scholar Leon Kellner, who at that time had just separated from her first husband, journalist Max Pollack. It was she who helped Benjamin elude the threat of military service, when at the beginning of January 1917 another draft notice reached him. Attacks of sciatica, which he either simulated under her guidance or, as Scholem asserts, suffered under hypnosis, resulted in his being declared unsuitable for military service.[2] On 17 April 1917, Dora and Walter were married in Berlin. Shortly afterward he went to a sanatorium to be cured of his "illness." It was there that he received the medical "certificate . . . which made possible his emigration to Switzerland."[3] This first, still-voluntary exile signified, as it did for the few German intellectuals who took a comparable step, such as Her-

39

Dora Pollack (née Kellner), 1917.

mann Hesse, Hugo Ball, and Ernst Bloch, a conscious rejection of the bellicose atmosphere that dominated wartime Germany.

After summer sojourns in St. Moritz and Zurich, Dora and Walter Benjamin settled in Bern in the autumn of 1917, where their son Stefan was born the following April. In quest of a theme for his planned dissertation, Benjamin soon renewed his study of Kant's philosophy. It seemed clear to him, as he wrote to Scholem in October 1917, "that in the framework of philosophy and hence of the doctrinal field to which philosophy belongs,

Walter Benjamin, 1917.

indeed which it perhaps constitutes, there can absolutely never be a shattering, a collapse of the Kantian system, but only its ever more firm establishment and universal development. . . . Only in the spirit of Kant and Plato and, in my opinion, along the path of revising and expanding Kant, can philosophy become doctrine or at least be incorporated into doctrine."[4] By the word *doctrine*, in these very explicit sentences, is to be understood the representation of absolute truth in a philosophical system, such as Benjamin outlined soon afterward in his essay "On the Program of the Coming

41

The philosopher Hermann Cohen.

Philosophy." The self-conscious posture, with which he formulated his personal philosophical belief to his friend, should not however obscure the fact that the methodological principles he invokes are adapted from Hermann Cohen's study *Kant's Theory of Experience*, which he had just read. This book claimed that the basis of all progress in philosophy was the introduction of "Platonism into critical thought" or, more specifically, the reconception of the thing in itself as Idea.

In his essay "On the Program of the Coming Philosophy," which he wrote for self-clarification and as a basis for discussion with his friends, Benjamin is to be sure concerned above all to overcome the confinement of the concept of experience to the limits allowed by the mathematical natural sciences, which had been the program of the academic neo-Kantian philosophy of his time. Through an "annihilation" of the reduction of experience to "human empirical consciousness," such as Kant and his followers

42

had carried through, the "coming philosophy" will, as Benjamin views its task, project the "establishment of a higher concept of experience" in an objective medium.[5] As instrument of "pure cognition" Benjamin again designates language, since not only is the traditional subject-object anti-thesis overcome in language, but also language guarantees the continuity of experience, from the highest kind—still defined as the religious—to the lowest. At the conclusion of his essay he underpins this proposal histori-cally by a reference to the same authority that he invoked in his philosophy of language: "The great refiguration and corrective process, to which the one-sided, mathematically-mechanically oriented concept of cognition must be subjected, can only be achieved by a definition of cognition in relation to language, such as Hamann already attempted in Kant's lifetime."[6]

The programmatic sketch of 1918 has as its premise that a philosophical system can be articulated, whose hierarchy of ideas culminates in pure cogni-tion, "the sole embodiment of which, for philosophy, can and must be God."[7] In the place of mathematical-scientific experience, then, Benjamin proposes to install the religious kind, which has its origin in language. This restoration to philosophy of theological doctrine leads him, in the introduc-tion of his essay, to the speculation that "the chief problem of philosophy . . . must perhaps be recovered from the age of scholasticism."[8] This formula-tion suggests indeed that Benjamin's move back to theology is not to be understood as a private idiosyncrasy. Rather, a comparable theological turn is to be observed in the works of numerous intellectuals at this time. Martin Heidegger, for example, in his 1916 dissertation on Duns Scotus, took the path, which Benjamin considered but did not take, back to the language philosophy of the Middle Ages. Benjamin read this text in 1920, while searching for his own dissertation theme, and acknowledged its proximity to his own aspirations.[9]

Still closer are the links of Benjamin's thinking to Georg Lukács's *Theory of the Novel*, written in 1916, and to Ernst Bloch's first book, *Spirit of Utopia*, published in 1918. All of these works are grounded in the same historico-philosophical assumptions. These young intellectuals reacted more intui-tively than the general public to the shattering of the old social forms that was becoming apparent through the European war, which undermined the positivistic faith in progress of the Wilhelminian bourgeoisie. In retrospect Lukács defined the mental attitude that produced his work as a "mood of permanent despair at the condition of the world."[10] His moral condemna-tion of the war led him to depreciate modernity in comparison with Greek antiquity transfigured into the ideal, and to contrast the novel "as the form of the radically sinful age" with the immanence of meaning of the epic.

The case was similar with Ernst Bloch, with whom Benjamin became personally acquainted in 1918 and was on neighborly terms for a length of time in Bern. Bloch demonstrated, in the *Spirit of Utopia*, the unbridgeable gap between the world's utopian qualities, which he made the focal point of his speculation, and the events of the day. As he put it in the book's introductory sentences on the war: "What existed just now will probably soon be forgotten. Only an empty gruesome memory hangs in the air. . . . It's not worth talking about it any more." Thus the new life, which Bloch constructs as a synthesis of music and mysticism, metaphysics and socialism, is truly "conjured up out of the blue," as the author acknowledges in an accurate estimate of the romantic idealism of his undertaking.[11] In Lukács as in Bloch, the eschatological vision of a better world stands in unmediated juxtaposition with the actuality of the world's misery. This is equally true of Benjamin's projected renewal of theological doctrine; as youngest of the three he remains the most deeply involved with the language of traditional religiosity. For them all, who as declared opponents of the war stood in opposition to official German public opinion, the imagining of a meaningful cosmos constituted both escape and protest, protest against a condition of the social world that was unbearable to them, but to which, as socially and economically privileged people, they were not directly exposed.

Common to all three authors also is the historical basing of their theories on those of the Romantics. Just as the *Theory of the Novel* derives its conception of the philosophy of history from Friedrich Schlegel's early writings, so *The Spirit of Utopia* cites Schelling and Fichte as authorities. This re-energizing of Romantic thought becomes intelligible through the similar historical experience that links the two wartime generations. From the perspective of intellectuals not directly affected, the Romantics had reacted to the destruction of late feudal social structures in Germany with a swerve away from Kantian philosophy, which they criticized as formalistic, toward a new mythology. Lukács, Bloch, and Benjamin seek to transcend the collapse of the bourgeois worldview in the catastrophe of the First World War—a view variously manifest as vitalism, positivism, or neo-Kantianism— by charging the critical posture with metaphysical contents. Thus Bloch's chapter on Kant in *The Spirit of Utopia*, which in its tendency is completely at one with Benjamin's programmatic outline, criticizes the entrapment of Kant's philosophy in the inadequate metaphysics of his century. It tries to overcome its limits through "a greater phenomenological breadth of consciousness," which with blithe eclecticism is to embrace Japanese dance ceremonies, Chinese ancestor worship, and Christ's death as sacrificial rite.[12] This is to say: Romantic searching for God in response to a radical historical upheaval marks the year 1794 as well as 1918.

Benjamin recognized the actuality of Romanticism early on and let

Georg Lukács, ca. 1915.

himself be guided by it in his quest for a dissertation topic. After he had spent the spring of 1918 "introducing himself to the local seminars," primarily to that of his future supervisor Richard Herbertz, he turned during the summer to intensive reading of Romantic texts.[13] Already in November he was able to sketch the central thesis of his projected study in a letter to Ernst Schoen: "The work treats the Romantic concept of criticism (art criticism). The modern concept of criticism has derived from the Romantic one; but for the Romantics 'criticism' was a quite esoteric concept, with mystical premises in its relation to knowledge and, in aesthetic questions, synthesizing the best insights of contemporary and later writers into a new concept of art, which is in many respects our own."[14]

Benjamin devoted the winter of 1918–19 entirely to intensive work on his dissertation. The extent to which he sealed himself off from the news of the political changes in Germany can be gleaned from the letter already quoted, dated 9 November 1918: "Yesterday I received . . . the news of the

45

Ernst Bloch in a portrait by Willy Geiger, 1921.

proclamation of the Bavarian Republic. . . . In any case my commissions for the book auction will probably come to nothing, since it is hardly likely to take place." And after a review of his summer reading: "Since then, as I said, I am reading exclusively for my dissertation: to have to write it, precisely in times like these, involves a focussing of my mind which is both viable and beneficial."

The secluded life of the scholar, book-collector, and family man was also not without its farcical aspect. Thus he allowed himself to be installed by his disciple Gerhard Scholem, who spent the summer months with the Benjamins, as "rector mirabilis of Muri University," so named for the village near Bern to which he had moved in May 1918. In this role-playing Scholem's position was that of the janitor, which obviously was meant to express his dependence at that time on the older thinker. However the two took this

46

Gerhard Scholem, 1920.

schoolboy-style satire on the academic institution so seriously that they worked out the statutes and course announcements of the "university," and later had them printed by Scholem's father, who owned a printing press.[15]

Despite his outwardly reclusive existence, Benjamin developed in his intellectual work the most subtle sensitivity to the problems of the age. He himself was highly conscious of the contradiction between the conventional academic form of his dissertation and its far-reaching claims. In April 1919, after finishing the rough draft, he stated:

> It has become what it was destined to be: a signpost toward the true but hitherto completely unknown nature of Romanticism; a signpost is all it is because I could not approach the very center of Romanticism, its messianism—I only treated the art-criticism—or indeed any of the other aspects that are vitally actual to me, without cutting myself off from the possibility of the conventional and complicated, "academic" posture demanded by the dissertation format. The one thing I hope to have achieved in this work is that the reader can extract these dimensions from its essential core.[16]

Terror treibt manche Theorie
Durch feierliche Termini.
Jedes Problem: den Tod, die Zahl
Behandelt man transzendental.

A page from the publication "Muri University."

In these sentences Benjamin hints at the metaphysical background that the dissertation's academic form must veil. Through the privileged example of art and by invoking his Romantic predecessors, Benjamin establishes the primacy of critical thinking, as an epistemological method, over systematic thinking, which for him had been rendered obsolete by his historical experience since 1914. In this context critical thinking is defined as an absolutely "positive" procedure, releasing those elements in historical phenomena that can come together as an "idea." "Thus critical thinking, in total contrast to current definitions of it, is in its central intention not judgment but on the one hand completion, systematization of the work of art, and on the other hand the dissolving of it in the absolute."[17] As previously in his philosophy of language, indeed as a special case of that philosophy, individual works and forms of art are defined by Benjamin as a continuum, which in its entirety is coterminous with "the transcendental order of art." Understood thus, the critic's activity should achieve for the artwork "the revelation of its absolute dependence on the idea of art."[18] The metaphysical vocabulary of such definitions is evidence that here, as in the philosophy of language and the reconception of Kant's epistemology, an absolute is envisaged that cannot be named in a profane context, but to which Benjamin alludes at the end of his study, when he says of Friedrich Schlegel: "Critical procedure, as integration of the created work with the absolute, was for him the highest kind. It can be understood metaphorically as the creation of a blinding light in the work. This glare–the light of sobriety–dissolves the work's multiplicity. It is the idea."[19] This metaphor taken from the mystical tradition, which Benjamin uses in his–as he calls it–"esoteric postscript" to define Romantic critical thinking, permits a glance at the messianic constellation that conditions the overall conception of his study.

Having passed his doctoral examination, Benjamin remained in Switzerland until the fall of 1919, engaging in intense personal discussions with Ernst Bloch, whose *Spirit of Utopia* Benjamin characterized as "a truly contemporary and immediately relevant statement." It reinforced for him his "rejection of every current political tendency."[20] He spent the following winter in Austria, primarily with his wife's family in Vienna. By ostentatiously staying away from Berlin he was trying to keep a freedom of operation in relation to the plans of his father, who had suggested to the twenty-seven year old that, having concluded his studies, he might want to take up a "bourgeois" occupation. Benjamin on the other hand wanted to continue his life as an independent scholar with the goal of achieving his *Habilitation* (post-doctoral degree) as soon as possible; this plan presupposed continued financial support from his father. He spent the months in Breitenstein and Vienna in search of a working topic in "the large group of problems involving word and concept (language and logos)."[21] When in March 1920, the impact of inflation on his father's financial resources no longer permitted Benjamin to live away from the parental household, he was forced to move back with his family to the house in Delbrück Street in Berlin. The letters from these months tell of constant family arguments culminating in a "total falling out" with his parents; the quarrels did not end even when Benjamin moved to an apartment of his own in the fall.[22]

Benjamin saw a further danger to his plans for *Habilitation* in the involvement with Hebrew, which his friend Gerhard Scholem had urged on him. Here too he put up energetic resistance against the distortion of his own projects. "I cannot turn my attention to Jewish matters with full intensity, until I have extracted from my European apprentice years that which can at least provide some sort of chance of a more peaceful future, of support from my family and the like."[23] In this sentence from a December 1920 letter to Scholem, practical reasons are advanced to divert attention from the fact that "philosophy was occupying him exclusively." This way of arguing follows a model that was to become from then on the almost-instinctive basis for Benjamin's reactions to Scholem's advances throughout his life. Repeatedly he postponed the "entry into Hebrew" in favor of further engagement with the European tradition, until it was finally too late and his "European apprentice years" cost him his life.

In order to satisfy both his father's demands and his own intellectual needs, Benjamin conceived the plan of editing his own journal. The publisher Weissbach in Heidelberg, with whom Benjamin was negotiating about the printing of his translations of Baudelaire's *Tableaux Parisiens*, offered him in August 1920 the direction of a journal viewed as a replacement for the Expressionist organ *The Argonauts*, which Weissbach had published earlier. Benjamin conceived the *Angelus Novus*, the title of which was inspired by a picture by Paul Klee, which he had recently purchased in Munich. In his own formulation the journal was to be a strictly "private production."[24] On the model of the *Athenäum* of the Schlegel brothers and the *Blätter für die Kunst* (Pages dedicated to art) of the George circle, it was to "have a quite limited, closed circle of collaborators."[25] For the first volume, which Benjamin worked to assemble during the fall of 1921, he invited as contributors his friends Gerhard Scholem, Ernst Bloch, and the theologian and philosopher Florens Christian Rang, who much influenced Benjamin's political and religious thinking, particularly in the book on tragic drama. Beyond this inner group he planned the collaboration of Erich Unger, Ferdinand Cohrs, Ernst Lewy, and S. J. Agnon.

Even in this selection of contributors the tendency is apparent to make the journal into the mouthpiece of a small circle united by esoteric religiosity. Benjamin put it explicitly in his "Announcement of the journal: *Angelus Novus*": "For it the general validity of statements about the spiritual life must be linked to the question whether such statements have a legitimate claim to an intellectual place in the coming religious orders of things. Not that the shape of such orders can be predicted. What can be predicted is that what is struggling for life in these, the first days of a new age, will not be born without them."[26] Benjamin was conscious of the fact that, with this program, he was from the outset excluding a wider public. Essentially he was limiting the circle of readers to the contributors themselves when he demanded of his journal that it should "with relentless thinking, uncompromising speaking and, if necessary, complete disregard of the public, hold fast to what is taking shape as genuine actuality under the sterile surface of the latest cultural novelties, the exploitation of which it will leave to the newspapers."[27]

Although in November 1921 Benjamin was able to assemble an initial volume consisting of poems from Fritz Heinle's manuscripts, Rang's "Historical Psychology of the Carneval," Agnon's story "Synagogue," and his own essay "The Task of the Translator," the journal did not survive beyond the project stage.[28] Because of continuing inflation the publisher could not or would not provide the promised subsidy for the printing costs of the exclusive publication. But even without these material obstacles the journal was, as Benjamin acknowledged after some hesitation, destined to fail because of its internal contradictions. Through the talmudic legend of the "new angel," which he had placed at the end of his announcement of the journal, in justification of its name, he had indicated the epistemology for which it would stand. In the process he made the figure of the angel, as a synthesis of ancient religious tradition and artistic avant-garde, into a secret symbol for his own project as a critic. Both Benjamin and the angel, reading the chaotic fragments of recent history, decode its salvation, which they then bear before God. Behind the demand that the journal should "restore power to critical language," there lies an ultimate arrogant definition of the journal's function.[29] In the last resort the *Angelus Novus* was not destined for human readers. Its editor's intention was in fact that it should speak directly to God.

"This non-existent journal could not be more real and dear to me if it were really there."[30] When Benjamin consoled himself in October 1922 with this sentence about the failure of his project, the intentions he had pursued with it had already been incorporated into the sketches for his first larger essay, originally planned as "exemplary criticism" for one of the first issues of the *Angelus Novus*.[31] The study of Goethe's novel *The Elective Affinities* fulfills paradigmatically the demands Benjamin had imposed on criticism in his dissertation, by simultaneously redefining the actuality of the artwork and using it as a point of entry to truth in a fuller sense.

The author already establishes this goal in the introductory reflections on methodology, asserting that his concern is not so much with a commentary, a "descriptive analysis" of the novel, as with a critical engagement with it. He tries to characterize the implications of this distinction metaphorically, through a comparison: "If, for the sake of an allegorical image, one views the work in its growth as a flaming funeral pile, then the commentator confronts it as a chemist, whereas the critical thinker is like an alchemist. For the former the wood and the ashes are the exclusive objects of his analysis, for the latter only the flame itself remains a mystery, that of the living being. Thus the critical thinker asks about the truth, whose living flame burns above the massive logs of what once existed and the light ashes of what has been experienced."[32] Implicit in this image is a singular conception of the work of art, which is understood not as a static object

51

but as a self-consuming process within history. As historical distance increases, the importance of specific content for understanding the work decreases, permitting the work's truth content to emerge all the more clearly. This destruction of the "logs of the past" is the point of entry for the work of the critic, who is concerned solely with living truth. With the metaphor of the flame as the exclusive focus of critical study, Benjamin expresses his claim to understand the artwork as the medium of both existential and metaphysical, that is, religious truth. The disturbing fact remains that he compares his own project, not with the rational research methods of modern scholars, but with the magic practices of a pre-scientific age.

Critical thinking in the specific sense defined here is always oriented toward the autonomous work of art as its true subject-matter; the first example of it, Friedrich Schlegel's interpretation of Goethe's *Wilhelm Meister*, established the tone and the mission. Benjamin links himself to this model when he takes *The Elective Affinities* as the focus of his critical project. Because of its compositional purity and unity, this last symbolic novel by Goethe was reckoned already at the beginning of the nineteenth century to be the perfect example of a classical work of art. Hermann Cohen, in his *Aesthetic of Pure Feeling*, which Benjamin consulted, had called it an "ideal type of the genre" of the classical novel, because its central theme, the problematics of marriage, is shaped in an exemplary fashion.[33] Formal criteria, however, were probably still more decisive in dictating Benjamin's choice of topic. The striking "constructedness," the classicistic severity of the novel's form thrusts its nature as artwork into the foreground, hence makes it a perfect object for an interpetation based primarily on internal linkages.

The concentration of critical activity on the work itself entails a polemical turn against contemporary literary scholarship, which could only understand poetry as the "expression and portrayal of life."[34] Benjamin encounters this methodological premise of Wilhelm Dilthey's concept of humanistic disciplines again in Friedrich Gundolf's biography of Goethe, first published in 1916, against which he directs a theoretical polemic in order to achieve "clarity concerning the theoretical relationship between life and work."[35] He makes the justifiable criticism that Gundolf constructs Goethe's life by analogy to an artwork, so that his life appears ultimately as his greatest work, with the author himself as its hero. In contrast Benjamin insists on the priority of the written text over the biographical "text": "Works are as irreducible as deeds," he states apodictically and thus automatically rules out any "explanation" of a text by means of facts outside itself.[36]

These methodological distinctions are drawn so precisely by Benjamin because he seeks to gain, from the critical discussion of the classical work of art, a historico-philosophical perception of his own times that would be

Friedrich Gundolf.

of true actuality. Goethe, in his story of the four-way relationship between Eduard, Ottilie, the Captain, and Charlotte, had embodied the vulnerability of marriage to passionate love – and permitted the social order to triumph at the end. But at the same time he made the lovers, whose longing cannot be fulfilled in this life and who therefore escape into death, into the truly justified ones. Ottilie becomes a saint, at the site of whose undecayed corpse miracles occur. In the critical tradition, as in Gundolf's book, this fable was taken as evidence that Goethe had wanted to depict in his novel the moral purification, indeed sanctification, of the natural human being. Gundolf emphasizes that marriage is the literary symbol allowing Goethe to advance from the natural to the mystery of the sacred: "The self, nature, culture, fate – all participate equally in marriage and only in marriage. . . . Only in this human structure could the law of nature be transcended by a miracle, fate be dissolved in sainthood, without an awkward and artificial shift."[37] In the commentary preceding and preparing his critique Benjamin opposes this view emphatically. For him the polar oppositions in which previous interpreters sought to contain the novel's ideological content—love and marriage, passion and social norm, sensuality and morality—belong in their entirety to the sphere of myth.

The concept of myth, which remained central up to his late works, constitutes the key to Benjamin's cultural critique. In the essay "Fate and Character," written in 1919, he had sought for the first time, with the help of the Kantian distinction between nature and supranature, to define myth as natural history. The two concepts that constitute the essay's title had been previously used by Hofmannsthal and the young Lukács, in order to derive from them the generic distinctions between tragedy and novel. Benjamin's procedure is the reverse, in that he shows how the concepts acquire their definitional content from the historical genres traditionally assigned to them. Following his own reflections on the philosophy of language he seeks to establish the priority of the essential human event, as expressed in poetic form, over conceptual abstraction. Accordingly fate, which defines the hero's life in ancient tragedy and propels it irresistibly to a catastrophic end, is defined as "the context of guilt in which all life is situated."[38] Character, which dominates comedy, understood as a specifically modern form of expression, is said by Benjamin to embody "the vision of natural innocence." However historically questionable such a categorization may be, it reveals Benjamin's tendency to decode the entirety of history as the history of nature, in order thus to oppose to it the "time of salvation or of music or of truth."[39]

The cultural relevance of his historico-philosophical construction is more clearly expressed in the essay "Toward a Critique of Violence," written in 1921 just before the study of *The Elective Affinities*. Here Benjamin takes over the antithesis between mythical polytheism and the single truth of the monotheistic religion, which Hermann Cohen had proposed in his book *The Religion of Reason and Its Judaic Sources* (1919). On these lines Benjamin contrasts the mythical violence of Apollo, who takes bloody vengeance on Niobe's children, with the "sanctified manifestation" of pure violence, such as the biblical God carried out against Korah and his fellow-priests, according to the narration of the Fourth Book of Moses.[40] But unlike Cohen this juxtaposition is for Benjamin not a question of philosophical religious knowledge, but of current political linkages. Thus he terms the "political general strike," as he calls the revolution of 1918–19, an act of mythic violence, since it has only replaced one ruling elite by another. In contrast he demands from the "proletarian general strike," which is to be "as pure means to an end, violence-free," the elimination of the whole structure of domination, hence a "rupture" of the mythic eternal repetition of the same, which is called history.[41] This utopian vision of an anarchistic revolution destroying the myth itself is theologically grounded throughout Benjamin's work. In the early "Toward a Critique of Violence" as in his final text, the "Theses on the Philosophy of History," the event is imagined as a rupture of history by God in the shape of the Messiah.

The history and constitutional law of a society, which are commonly thought of as subject to an ongoing process of rationalization, are magisterially banished by Benjamin to the realm of "natural life." Thus myth becomes for him a figure for the total negation of the world as it is and a basis for the demand for its destruction: as such it is intimately related to Lukács's definition of modernity as the "age of radical sinfulness." In the essay on *The Elective Affinities*, Benjamin transfers to art his fundamental opposition to a world persisting within a historical "state of nature," by demonstrating that the world of the novel is a precise reproduction of the domination of guilt over all life. Since Goethe himself, in the central metaphor that gives the novel its title, compares the relationship of the lovers to a chemical process, Benjamin confines himself in his commentary to pointing out the many symbolic references to the predominance of nature in the text of the novel: the magical influences of the earth, manifest in the transforming of the cemetery and in Ottilie's special sensitivity to telluric phenomena, or the function of water as the chaotic, death-bringing element. Thus he views the love between Eduard and Ottilie as a mere "harmony at the deeper levels of nature" and thereby locates it a priori within the sphere of mythic determinism, an interpretation that seems especially justified by the muteness of the two lovers.[42]

But Benjamin also assigns marriage to the mythic realm, which for Gundolf and other interpreters had functioned precisely as the focal point of morality within the novel. He feels justified in this because marriage operates in the novel as a mere legal norm that has long lost sight of its original purpose, namely to be the "expression of the persistence of love" and which, in its decay, releases the violence of mythic law.[43] Finally Benjamin sees the "context of guilt in which all life is situated" as imposing its demands at precisely the point where, according to the poet's will, the work was to transcend the natural sphere, in the figure of Ottilie. By renouncing the fulfillment of her passion and pressing her virginal self-denial to the extreme limit of voluntary death, she seems to master her fate and, as the legends of miracles twining around her death suggest, to become a saint. Benjamin disagrees with this interpretation, which Goethe's text overtly supplies. The girl's renunciation cannot, in his view, be reckoned as liberating, since it is based exclusively on a creatural attraction toward death, hence is in thrall to mythic ambiguity. He sees her becoming mute as a sign of this and states categorically: "No moral resolution can enter the world without being expressed in language and without having become, in a strict sense, something communicable. Hence, in the perfect silence of Ottilie, the morality of the death wish that is driving her becomes questionable."[44]

The sequence of these two sentences can stand as characteristic of Benjamin's interpretive mode of argument. The initial statement decrees authoritatively a general principle, drawn from Benjamin's "doctrine," his philosophy of language, without grounding its application in the new context. And in the second sentence a fact taken from the literary text is subjected to an evaluative judgment based on this principle: Ottilie's renunciation is redefined negatively as death-addiction. At the same time the appearance of supporting evidence is adduced for the theoretical premise, through linkage to the literary text. Thus, the individual aesthetic signs are no longer interpreted in terms of their immediate context, but are correlated with a system existing independently of them, one whose philosophy of history derives from Benjamin's own historical experience and whose tenets he had earlier worked out in the essay "Toward a Critique of Violence." In this system lack of language implies subjection to nature, nature implies the binding context of guilt, and the aesthetic reproduction of nature defines myth. By decoding the symbolic novel as an archetypal portrayal of natural life, Benjamin's critical perspective delivers on the whole Goethean "art epoch" the devastating judgment that its works are marked by ambiguity; the related judgment on traditional interpretation, such as Gundolf's, is that it is nothing but a perpetuation of the poets' mythic discourse in another medium: "Existence coalesces without differentiation into the concept of nature, which grows into something monstrous."[45]

For Benjamin trust in the goodness and creative energy of nature amounts to "idolatry." The religious allusion in this term is not coincidental. He refers to the theological doctrine, from which the critic must draw his standards of judgment, when he unmasks the classical work of art as mythic. And in doing so he transcends the negativity of his overall critique in the direction of a utopian goal. For the inner logic of his system ensures that the critical concepts point always to their polar opposites: Muteness to language, myth to truth, fate to freedom, and nature to God.

Benjamin's critique gains in cogency because he is able to demonstrate the presence of these positive poles in Goethe's work. By taking the "correspondences" and oppositions between the novel and the novella *Remarkable Young Neighbors*, enclosed within it, to be the "key" to his interpretation, Benjamin succeeds in locating within the work itself the place where the spell cast by the "law" of natural causation can be broken.[46] The sober tale concerns a youth who, on the day before the marriage of his childhood friend to another, rescues her from death by a courageous leap into the water, thereby winning back her initial love; this becomes for Benjamin an allegory for the "power of true love."[47] Whereas the lovers in the novel have a natural longing for each other, without acknowledging their own feelings by word or deed, here they take action at the decisive moment, hence are both rescued. The one story ends with shadowy dissolution and death, the other with marriage and happy life.

On the basis of these oppositions the critic argues that in the single extraordinary event of the novella "the day of decision . . . casts its light into the shadowy Hades of the novel."[48] The ultimate indication for this eruption of truth into the text is for Benjamin the fact that the youth in the novella undresses his beloved after he has pulled her out of the water. In Goethe's story this act is pragmatically motivated as a revival attempt. Under the allegorist's gaze it is transformed into a figure for the metaphysical ground of the text: "Man appears to us as a corpse and his life as loving, when they are in God's presence. Thus death, like love, has the power to make us naked. Only nature is indecipherable, for it retains a secret for as long as God permits it to exist. Truth is revealed in the essence of language. The human body is made naked, a sign that the person as such is entering God's presence."[49] These sentences, highlighted by their rhapsodic rhythm, move the argument openly into the theological dimension. They signify that the novella is to be read as a utopia, as an ideal image of married love that is possible only by escaping the realm of nature and appearing before the face of God. At the same time they stress that language is the originary structure enabling such theological certainty to exist.

The novel bears within its symbolic organization a specific level of meaning, which the critic elaborates and evaluates negatively as the "context of guilt in which all life is situated." In contrast the noticeably sober narrative form of the novella, refraining from psychological and moral judgments, is neutral in its signification. Its texture can therefore be filled out by the critic with the metaphysical purposes he brings to his reading. Allegorical substitution is the method he deploys to this end. His interpretation thus gains the function that allegorical reading has always had since its invention in antiquity: it rescues the artwork that has become obsolete by endowing it with a new metaphysical truth.

While the historical experience underlying Benjamin's critical stance can be unambiguously identified in the references to philosophy of language and the doctrine derived from it, the core of subjective experience, which gives it its existential seriousness, is much harder to describe. Benjamin alludes to it obliquely when he says of the ideal love he thinks he has discoverd in *Remarkable Young Neighbors*: "Its origin is the presentiment of an

57

Jula Cohn.

eternal life of happiness."[50] In this utopia, clearly indebted to his personal longings, one can discern, in a precise mirror image, the antithesis of Benjamin's own life circumstances at the beginning of the 1920s.

The essay on *The Elective Affinities* is dedicated to Jula Cohn. A sculptress and the sister of Benjamin's friend and classmate Alfred Cohn, she belonged to the outer circle of the school of writers and artists formed by Stefan George and was a friend of Friedrich Gundolf.[51] Benjamin had met her for the first time in 1912. After living in Heidelberg, she had returned to Berlin in April 1921 and lived for a while with Benjamin and his wife. Benjamin reports in *Berlin Chronicle* that she had, already before the war, embodied the "fateful center" of his circle of friends.[52] Only after his marriage in 1917 did he break off his relationship with her, because "despite

58

all the efforts we (Jula, my wife, and I) made to forge a harmonious and soundly based relationship with one another," living together had proved impossible.[53] Four years later the renewed attraction to Jula Cohn plunged Benjamin's marriage, as Scholem puts it, into a "destructive crisis with momentous consequences for his life."[54] He separated from his wife on a temporary basis and finally in 1930, "after seven years of hesitation," was divorced from her.[55]

The doctor and psychologist Charlotte Wolff, whose acquaintance Benjamin had made in 1922, reports in her memoirs that, on the occasion of reading his essay on *The Elective Affinities*, Benjamin had discussed with her the question "how great literary works develop through the stimulus of personal problems."[56] That seems to indicate that he recognized his personal life circumstances in the novel. This existential background finds its expression in the text of the essay itself, for example in the following characterization of the loving girl: "despite the complete passivity, which defines Ottilie in the erotic as in every other sphere, her wholly natural behavior makes her unapproachable to the point of being removed from the scene."[57] This description has a postscript in the sentences in *Berlin Chronicle*, where it is said of Jula Cohn: "Really she was never the center of human beings but rather, strictly speaking, the center of human fates, as if her plant-like passivity and lethargy had assigned her to these dimensions, which more than any other human things appear subject to vegetable laws."[58] As this parallel shows, the insight derived from *The Elective Affinities* and the experiences of his personal life become so close as to be indistinguishable. In his interpetation of Goethe's novel he endows, as a critic, the literary figure of Ottilie with the features of Jula Cohn. On the other hand, as a lover, he sees the relationship to his beloved as governed by "fate," thus situating it in the critical perspective that he applies to it in his essay on *The Elective Affinities*.

Benjamin turns the beloved woman closest to him into the one farthest away, by stylizing her as Ottilie, the loving woman who removes herself into the remotest possible distance, namely death. What drives him to such an act of distancing? Looking at comparable behavior of his toward other women, Asja Lacis for example, one is inclined to think that he sought to protect himself by fending off a permanent tie, because the prospect of love's death in the rhythm of daily life was intolerable to him. But questions of individual psychology are not of primary importance here. The issue is, rather, how does the actuality of love appear possible to a great lover? Only at a distance, through renunciation of fulfillment. In this it is Dante, whose distant glimpse of the beloved Beatrice on a bridge becomes the impetus for a life's work, who appears as the model for Benjamin the critic. Like the author of *The Divine Comedy*, he transforms the beloved woman into his text and the text into what is truly beloved. Only perpetual study is capable of bringing closer this transformed object of love. At the same time such study holds the beloved one at a reverent distance, without shattering her in banality. The writing and reading of a text thus becomes the sole indestructible act of love. For only thus can the ideal of a distance, no matter how close the actuality, be realized in relationship to a beloved human being.

The metamorphosis of passion through the reading and production of literary texts does not however imply for Benjamin the final renunciation of the beloved woman. In the autobiographical sketch "Agesilaus Santander," written in 1933, he linked the infinite patience with which he was resolved to wait for the beloved to the figure of the Angelus Novus.

> Taking advantage of the circumstance that I entered the world under the sign of Saturn—the planet that turns around most slowly, the planet of detours and delays—he sent his female form in pursuit of his male one via the longest, most fateful detour; although both had at one time been the most intimate neighbors, they did not know each other. Perhaps he did not know that the strength of the man he wanted to hurt revealed itself most fully in this process: namely through waiting. Where this man happened upon a woman who mesmerized him, he made the decision, without knowing it, to lie in wait for her along her life's path and to wait until, sick, aged and in torn garments, she fell into his hands."[59]

Scholem correctly linked these sentences to Benjamin's relationship with Jula Cohn, by whom he was indeed "mesmerized," as the identification of her with Ottilie revealed.[60] But what Scholem failed to see is the fact that a disguised self-interpretation of the essay on *The Elective Affinities* is in play here. The "longest, most fateful detour," along which the angel's female form pursues the male one, is the critical text itself. Only thus is to be understood the enigmatic statement that they had once been neigbors without knowing each other. They were "neighbors" in Benjamin's plan to write the disguised text about Jula Cohn for the journal *Angelus Novus*. The definition of happiness, furthermore, which the autobiographer of 1933 wills for the loved one, is derived from the earlier interpretation of the *Remarkable Young Neighbors*. "He longs for happiness: that conflicted state, in which the ecstasy of the unique, new, not yet experienced coexists with that bliss of renewal, repetition, the already lived."[61] Such happiness was experienced by the two children in Goethe's novella, who loved each other in childhood and rediscovered this love in marriage, transformed, after passing through mortal danger. Benjamin assigns this happiness to himself and his beloved,

Walter Benjamin, sculpted by Jula Cohn, 1926.

since he is certain that to them also, after they have passed through the alien-ation of the text, the longed-for reunion will be granted.

Guided by this "blissful presentiment" the critic finds in the text of the novel itself a sign of redemption: "The sentence that, in Hölderlin's phrase, contains the caesura of the work, in which everything pauses as the lovers seal their doom in an embrace, reads as follows: 'Hope sped like a star falling from heaven over their heads and away.'"[62] Benjamin quotes Goethe's words as a secure indication that, for the novel's characters as well as for the people of his own circle whom he recognizes in them, an act of liberation from the spell of the "natural context of guilt" could succeed. To place such

61

eschatological weight on this sentence is only possible because Benjamin extracts it from its context in the novel and juxtaposes it with Christian images of life after death. "Elpis remains the last of Goethe's primal words: the certainty of blessedness, which the lovers of the novella take home with them, corresponds to the hope of redemption which we nourish for all the dead."[63] That is Benjamin's interpretation. In the context of the novel Goethe's sentence must be read completely differently. In the image of the "falling star" he is evoking the deceptiveness of hope. In the expectation of a life together in the near future the lovers give free expression of their love for the first time. But it is precisely their embrace, impelled by hope, that leads to the accident on the lake, rendering their union forever impossible. By isolating the single sentence, as a quotation, from the context established by the poet, Benjamin turns it into a neutral sign, void of meaning, into which he can read his own truth just as he reads it into the "sober" narration of the novella. So strong is the absorptive power of his theological interpretive machine that in the end the critic destroys the original context of the work and arrives at a perspective contradictory to the author's intentions.

Benjamin's "redemptive" criticism, this example suggests, dissolves the symbolic network of the classical novel by extracting individual sentences from their original context and assigning them a new situational value within Benjamin's own metaphysical system. It thus proceeds formally in the same way as Medieval and Baroque allegory, which extracts elements from "natural" contexts, in order to construct from them moral and theological statements that are known in advance. To be sure this criticism pursues different goals: Whereas the emblematic poet is concerned above all to clarify generally known and accepted truths, the allegorical critic aims to certify the meaning of his subjective experience by the authority of the text, in which he installs that experience through the process of interpretation. This intention is served also by the strangely inverted dialectic that dominates the essay's construction. In the first part, conceived as thesis, the symbolic worldview is presented negatively, shown to be a reproduction of the "natural" dominance of guilt in human affairs. As contrasting antithesis redemption is then articulated as a positive goal. This inversion has as its effect that in the moment of synthesis, hope appears as not so much a "heightening" (*Aufhebung*), that is, a transforming preservation of the thesis, but rather as its anticipated destruction. Thus in the medium of aesthetic criticism one can trace for the first time the outlines of what was later to move, as "negative dialectics," to the very center of the philosophy of the Frankfurt School.

Benjamin was completely conscious of the methodological singularity of his interpretation. He reflects upon it by installing it as a further level

62

of meaning within the novel itself. To this end he interprets the figure of Ottilie as allegorical. She is not only the innocent-guilty loving woman, driven by fate to death, hence a specific configuration of the appearance of beauty (*des schönen Scheins*). Rather, she embodies the very appearance of beauty itself. Thus the story of her life can be read by the critic as an allegory of the structure of the beautiful presented diachronically, as an image for the transformations to which the appearance of beauty is subjected in the work of art. According to this interpretation, the annihilation of appearance is already announced in Ottilie's renunciation of the fulfillment of her passion and its metamorphosis into a quiet fondness; for the tearful emotion that unites the lovers in the novel's final chapters dislodges genuine harmony in favor of the "appearance of reconciliation."[64] But that too must disappear. With the death of the figure embodying the appearance of beauty, with the death of Ottilie, all appearance dissolves and truth intervenes. Read thus as a metastory of the metaphysics of art, the novel at the end takes on the work of criticism itself. By destroying the appearance of beauty within itself, the novel tells the truth that only through the destruction of appearance can truth become manifest in art.

> It is the expressionless in which the sublime power of truth manifests itself, just as it shapes the language of the real world according to the laws of the moral world. It is truth that shatters what still survives in all appearance of beauty as the legacy of chaos: false, deceptive totality–totality that would be absolute. It is truth that completes the work, by shattering it into shards, into a fragment of the true world, into the torso of a symbol.[65]

Instead of defining a positive goal these central poetological tenets of the essay attempt a negative formulation of the conditions of possibility for the cognition of truth in the work of art. The place of truth is defined as a deficiency, as absence of expression. That is, only where the sign-systems of language and art–which always already refer to objects from natural life– are neutralized, where the referential urge imparted to these systems by subjectivity is withdrawn from them, only at such a point can truth appear. Criticism makes this possible by keeping faith with the sober, "expressionless" novella, or by isolating individual sentences of the novel as quotations, or finally by dismantling the entire "natural" expressivity of the novel through allegorical reading. Accordingly, the condition of truth's possibility is the destruction of all deceptive totality. Into this category the critic places nature itself, as it appears in the symbolic artwork, shaped by aesthetic illusion into wholeness and, in this perfect form, justifying all particulars. But the symbolic artwork itself is also a deceptive totality, with the immanence of its totalized being functionally present in each one of its parts. This aesthetic wholeness appears illusory in the light of religious experience, which alone, through rupture, can mediate concrete totality. Benjamin had argued this point in his "Program of the Coming Philosophy," and it forms the background, in the essay on *The Elective Affinities*, for the negative evaluation of natural life.

The sentences quoted are of decisive importance for the aesthetic discussion of the first half of the century, because in them for the first time the symbolic work of art is put in question, on a systematic theoretical basis derived from the actual historical experience of the disintegration of the bourgeois world. They are thus Janus-faced. For it is only now that the Romantic expectations for criticism are fulfilled, given life by this last Romantic critic—and are thereby at the same time transcended. Given life: for the critical text absorbs into its being the transmuted life of the critic himself, and thus becomes itself an autonomous work of art, as Friedrich Schlegel had demanded of it, and as already could be seen happening before 1914 in the essays of Oscar Wilde and Rudolf Kassner and in Georg Lukács's collection of essays *Soul and Form*. Such breaching of limits by criticism is possible however only because it puts its real point of origin, the classical work of art, radically in question. The historical threshold on which Benjamin's critical procedure stands is most precisely expressed by the phrase "torso of a symbol," with which he designates the work of art as "completed" by criticism. To be sure, this metaphor has not yet dissolved its links to idealist terminology; still, in its imagery it evokes vividly the destruction of harmonious wholeness characteristic of the methods of allegorical criticism. The phrase suggests that the fragmentary state to which criticism reassigns the work in its act of "completion" gives a more accurate picture of existence than the deceptively harmonious world of the symbol. Moreover the formulation makes very clear the profound ambiguity of Benjamin's interpretation. The symbolic understanding of the world is negated only in order to rescue with all the more certainty the absolute truth-claim of art.

The fascination that emanates from the essay on *The Elective Affinities*, with its multiple levels of meaning and its enigmatic depth fueled by the author's existential involvement and concealed under the rich, indeed dazzling, surface, already mesmerized its first readers, Florens Christian Rang and Hugo von Hofmannsthal. Rang had written to Hofmannsthal in April 1923 about the failure of Benjamin's journal project, offering himself and Benjamin as contributors to Hofmannsthal's journal *Neue Deutsche Beiträge* (New German Review).[66] In November of the same year he sent him the manuscript of the essay on *The Elective Affinities*. Hofmannsthal's spon-

Hugo von Hofmannsthal.

taneous and enthusiastic response, as the first and for a long time the only document of the essay's reception, deserves to be quoted at length: "I can only say that it has marked an epochal change in my inner life and that, insofar as my own work does not claim my full attention, my thinking has hardly been able to let go of it. What I find extraordinary—to speak of apparent externals—is the exalted beauty of presentation in the context of such penetration into secret depths; this beauty emanates from a wholly secure and pure mode of thinking, to which I know few parallels."[67]

Hofmannsthal's unconditional endorsement reflects his insight that Benjamin's essay fulfills the demands that he himself had posed to criticism in his program for the *Neue Deutsche Beiträge*: "There is to be no criticism, unless, as in the rarest cases, it should become itself a work of art (Solger's

65

study of *The Elective Affinities*, which gave such pleasure to Goethe . . .)."[68] What Hofmannsthal thought he could find only in the classical past, he now saw before him in the manuscript of the unknown young writer. And so he published Benjamin's essay on *The Elective Affinities* as the central prose contribution of the first and second volume of the second series of *Neue Deutsche Beiträge*.

But for Benjamin too the place of publication could not have been more appropriate to his own intentions. Like his own *Angelus Novus*, Hofmannsthal's journal was conceived as extremely exclusive. Through its bibliophile format and private circulation, Hofmannsthal had ensured that it was read only by conservative journalists, politicians, and dilettantes with exquisite taste, whom he habitually described as the "larger circle of men associated with me spiritually." Conceived as a focal point for creative individuals who, though isolated from each other in time and space, could unite around the "spiritual possession of the nation," the journal was also close to Benjamin's ideas in its theoretical program: "Language, yes, language is all; but there is something beyond and behind it: Truth and Mystery."[69] This program of a unifying movement based on an esoteric philosophy of language was Hofmannsthal's response to what he experienced, after the collapse of the Habsburg Monarchy, as the crisis of loss of tradition and dissolution of the established literary public. Benjamin could identify unreservedly with Hofmannsthal's views and therefore expressed his enthusiasm at the opportunity for publication now opening to him: "From a creative point of view this mode of publication, in by far the most exclusive of the local journals, is altogether valuable for me. From an academic point of view a different one might have been more favorable but not comparably accessible. But as to journalistic impact, this place is absolutely ideal for my attack on the ideology of the school of Stefan George. Perhaps it is the provenance from this one place that will make it difficult for them to ignore my invective."[70]

In this prediction Benjamin turned out to be wrong. Not only did Gundolf majestically ignore the polemic directed at him, but there was also no wider public response at all. Thus the essay on *The Elective Affinities* became generally known to the literary public only after its republication in the middle of the 1950s. Nevertheless, the collaboration with Hofmannsthal certainly did a great deal to advance Benjamin's early career as journalist and critic. In Benjamin's letters Hofmannsthal was quickly named his "new patron," whose prestige and influence he deliberately invoked in his dealings with publishers.[71] In 1924, Benjamin used Hofmannsthal's laudatory comments on his work as a basis for obtaining from his parents "a modest annual income," which was to enable the thirty-two-year-old Benjamin to prepare himself, free from economic constraints, for his university career.[72] Finally we learn from a letter that his relations with the publisher Rowohlt-Verlag and its weekly journal, *Die literarische Welt* (The Literary World), founded in 1925, were given significant impetus by a letter of recommendation from Hofmannsthal.[73] These relations were to be central to his future journalistic activity.

IV

History as Catastrophe: Anti-Classical Aesthetics

1 9 2 3 – 1 9 2 5

Immediately upon completion of the essay on *The Elective Affinities*, Benjamin renewed his quest for a theme for his work toward the *Habilitation* or post-doctoral thesis, which would qualify him for a full professorship. While he had at first planned a study in the philosophy of language, he began in October 1922 to consider for the first time a "*Habilitation* in modern German studies."[1] This change of theme would facilitate the search for a philosophical faculty prepared to accept his work. Benjamin began by sounding out the University of Heidelberg, but realized while staying there, in December 1922, that his prospects for successfully carrying through his project were slight, among other reasons because of anti-Semitic sentiment. In early 1923 he stayed in Frankfurt, where the sociologist Gottfried Salomon introduced him to the Germanist Franz Schultz. After Salomon had delivered Benjamin's dissertation and his study of *The Elective Affinities*, and Benjamin himself had visited Frankfurt for a second time in March 1923, his plans crystallized to the point where he assumed permanent residence in Frankfurt in the summer semester of 1923.[2]

Benjamin sought the *Habilitation*, not because he wanted to initiate a university career, but as confirmation of his social status as independent scholar. Moreover, in relation to his parents he saw the degree as a "mark of public recognition that will call them to order."[3] Behind this impersonal formulation lies Benjamin's conviction that, after a *Habilitation*, his parents would be morally bound to give him more generous financial support.

68

Until then Benjamin, the passionate book collector, thought he could feed himself and his family through the antiquarian book trade. To judge from his recurring complaints in letters to friends, Benjamin's financial circumstances in general were extremely precarious in these months. Thus he writes that he could only rescue himself through "flight from the unpleasantnesses of daily life, which sometimes appear like wolves from all sides"[4]; he makes plans to emigrate to Italy or America. However, since the "economic existence" of his family was based on Dora's work as a secretary skilled in foreign languages, he wanted to make his decision dependent on Dora's opportunities for work.[5]

Benjamin's desperate material circumstances did not however move him—the son of an upper-middle-class family, until then relatively untroubled by financial worries—to give up what he called "the privacy of my existence, which is inseparable from my being."[6] Despite all external pressures he thereby maintained an attitude of distance, enabling him to observe impartially the social situation of postwar Germany, and to attain the insight that his problems were not strictly individual but, rather, characteristic of a whole social group.

"Whoever is doing serious intellectual work in Germany today is threatened by hunger in the most serious way," he wrote to his friend, the writer Florens Christian Rang, thus portraying the impoverishment he himself was experiencing as exemplifying the fact that the bourgeoisie, in times of economic crisis, views the work of the intellectual it has produced as a dispensable luxury.[7] On his trips to Heidelberg and Frankfurt images of the country disrupted by inflation and the Ruhr occupation thrust themselves on him, provoking him to his first current inventory of and critical confrontation with the fundamental social abuses of the time. "These last days journeying through Germany have again brought me to an edge of hopelessness and permitted me a glimpse into the abyss."[8]

Benjamin wrote his "Thoughts toward an Analysis of the Condition of Central Europe," in the first months of 1923 and gave it in the form of a scroll to his friend Scholem in September on the occasion of the latter's emigration to Palestine. In it he makes clear, before knowing anything of Marxism, the contradictions in which he sees bourgeois society enmeshed and which point to its ultimate collapse. In this perspective, inflation appears as the visible culmination of the rule of the commodity in relations between human beings, whereby their humane quality is destroyed. "Number became all-powerful, causing language to disintegrate."[9] The social effects of the permanent crisis and general impoverishment present themselves to Benjamin as the subjection of people and things to crude economic necessities, hence the loss of a protective distance that is indispensable both to open human association and to the process of intellectual cognition. Gripped by panic, the bourgeois loses a sense of social orientation and is afflicted by "uncertainty, indeed perversion of the instincts essential to life, coupled with a feeling of helplessness and decay of the intellect. This is the mental state of the entirety of the German citizenry."[10]

To this accurate diagnosis Benjamin appends a therapeutic suggestion, which is the very opposite of radical: "But the individual must never make peace with poverty, when it casts its immense and enigmatic shadow across his people and his house. Then he must keep his senses alert for any humiliation that befalls them and must impose discipline on them until such time as his suffering has ceased to pursue the diversionary road of hatred and is climbing the rising path of prayer."[11]

In these sentences Benjamin seems to want to confine his political action to the intellectual's traditional response, the contemplative restatement of the crisis. At another point in these first, unsystematic political notes, however, he proceeds from historical-semantic lines of thought to a prognosis of the overall social development. His anarchistic conception of revolutionary violence was fruitful even for the present day:

> In the storehouse of clichés in which the way of life of the German citizen, welded as it is into a unity through stupidity and cowardice, daily betrays itself, the cliché of the coming catastrophe (whereby things "cannot go on like this") is particularly striking. The helpless fixation on the concepts of security and possession of past decades prevents the average person from perceiving the very new and quite noticeable stabilities that underlie the present situation. Since the relative stabilization of the prewar years favored them, they believe it necessary to view any situation that dispossesses them as by definition unstable. However, stable conditions in no way need to be pleasant conditions, and already before the war there were social classes for whom stabilized conditions meant stabilized wretchedness. Insofar as a genuine image of liberation is forming among people oppressed in this way, this image may, in the perfection of its own power, become a revolutionary idea and set a time limit to such stabilization. . . . Only a reckoning that clearly perceives the sole *raison d'etre* of the present situation to be its end would be able to get beyond the wearying astonishment at what happens everyday, to the point where the manifestations of decay are understood to be what is truly stable and the only salvation to be an extraordinary event, bordering on the miraculous and incomprehensible.[12]

In such sentences there is articulated the awakening to social awareness of the dispossessed intellectual. Rejected by his own class, Benjamin recognizes his identity of interests with the socially disadvantaged and finds his way to the radicalism, with which from now on he views the social crisis as prefiguring the revolutionary rupture of an eternally recurrent bad state of affairs, namely history as such.

Current public events, experienced by Benjamin as catastrophe, even impel him to envisage possibilities for political praxis. Thus in a letter to his Frankfurt patron Gottfried Salomon at the beginning of 1923, he reacts to the occupation of the Rhineland by French and Belgian troops with a reminder: "I hope that the danger now overwhelming Germany will result in your emerging somewhat from your political reserve and turning to the plan for the organization of intellectuals that made such an impression on me when you outlined it during my last visit."[13] What he here asks of the sociologist—and what was to be, a few years later, the real content of his activity as a critic—Benjamin had already known as a reality in discussion and collaboration with Florens Christian Rang and his circle. This former theologian and government lawyer, whom Benjamin had met through his Berlin friend Erich Gutkind, became for him the most important conversation partner during the writing of his book on tragic drama. Rang's materialist messianism, derived from Nietzsche's images of a world beyond good and evil and irreconcilably opposed to orthodox Christianity, must have seemed as familiar to Benjamin as his conception of a politics based on the moral decision of the individual.

In 1924 Rang summarized his philosophical and political ideas in the lengthy work *German Builders' Tabernacle: Thoughts Addressed to Us as Germans Concerning Possible Justice Toward Belgium and France and Concerning the Philosophy of Politics.* In it Rang proposed the "joining together of a few people into a 'builders' tabernacle,' whose immediate task would be to obey the direct command of conscience and, instead of barricading oneself behind the state and thus concealing one's own passivity, to compensate to the degree possible, by making personal sacrifices, for the damage inflicted by Germans in the neighboring countries to the West."[14]

Although offering some cautious nuances, Benjamin declared his support for this extremely individualistic politicial vision in a supplement that was printed in Rang's book along with statements by Martin Buber, Karl Hillebrandt, Alfons Paquet, and others. Benjamin's public caution has less to do with personal, tactical considerations related to his uncertain plans for a *Habilitation*—he reckoned Schultz's political leanings, with some justification, to be "far right"[15]—than with fundamental concerns about the relationship between Germans and Jews. Protesting against the inclusion of Buber in the *Builders' Tabernacle*, Benjamin argued: "Here if anywhere, we are at the core of the contemporary Jewish question: that the Jew today betrays even the best German cause by lending it his public support; since

71

his public German utterance is necessarily venal (in the deeper sense), it cannot produce proof of genuineness. The secret relations between Germans and Jews can be legitimately expressed only in a quite different way."[16] The word *venal* is used in the sense that public support by a Jew for Germany, the international pariah of the post-World War I period, could only be seen as an attempt to obtain from the Germans tolerance and recognition as a quid pro quo. In contrast, Benjamin believed that his most valuable intervention on behalf of Germany involved rescuing its "spiritual treasures" from falsification and oblivion. In this sense he wanted his work on *The Origin of German Tragic Drama* to be evaluated as a political act in the true sense: "The fact that, and the depth in which, I am involved in things German is never absent from my consciousness. Least of all could I forget it while engaged on my present work, for nothing involves one more profoundly and binds one more inwardly than a rescue of older writing, such as I have in mind."[17] These sentences are directed at his friend Rang, whom he described after his death as the "only legitimate reader" of the book on tragic drama.[18] Working with Rang and for his cause Benjamin declares, in his analysis of this most specific German dramatic form, his opposition to the "obdurate spirit in which this people outdoes itself in prolonging its prison-like solitary confinement; if it doesn't actually bury its spiritual treasures, it gradually lets them become rusty, hard to use and to move."[19] In the collaboration with Rang he believed he had realized anew that "secret" German-Jewish alliance, which previously had defined the essence of his relationship with Fritz Heinle.

After Benjamin spent the summer semester of 1923 in Frankfurt, participating along with the young Theodor Wiesengrund-Adorno in Salomon's seminar on Troeltsch's book on historicism and vainly trying to gain Schultz's support for a *Habilitation* on the basis of his existing writings, he returned in August to Berlin. There he decided, as he wrote to Schultz, to undertake "the study of the form of tragic drama, particularly in the second Silesian school, in which you have particularly provoked my interest."[20] Throughout the winter he worked in the Berlin State Library, becoming familiar with the theme of his *Habilitation*, of which to that point he had known absolutely nothing. By March 1924 the study of sources provided him with a materials collection of "about 600 quotations . . . in good order and providing a clear overview."

> What has piled up over months of reading and constant brooding stands ready now, not so much like a mass of building blocks as like a heap of brushwood to which I must, with some circumspection, transport the first spark of inspiration from some place quite different. The labor

72

involved in the writing, if it is to succeed, will thus necessarily be very considerable. My base is remarkably, indeed uncomfortably narrow; knowledge of few plays; by no means of all the relevant ones.[21]

To advance the difficult task of writing, Benjamin implemented his long-cherished plan of a "flight" abroad. In early May he arrived in Capri and immediately set to work. External circumstances seemed ideal. In early July he wrote enthusiastically of his new apartment that it was endowed "with all the monkish refinement of spatial proportions and with a view deep into Capri's loveliest garden, which is at my disposal. A room in which going to bed seems unnatural, where working through the night makes obvious sense."[22] In mid-September 1924 he could report to Scholem that he had completed "the epistemological introduction to the work, the first chapter on the king in tragic drama and most of the second on tragic drama and tragedy, so that there remains to be written only the third chapter on theory of allegory plus a conclusion."[23] At this stage of the work Benjamin evidently planned an ordering of the material in a classic dialectical triad, whereby allegory would have appeared as synthesis, hence as fulfillment of what was intended in the analysis of the tragic drama. The regrouping during revision into the two definitive major sections–"Tragic Drama and Tragedy," "Allegory and Tragic Drama"–moves allegory into the negative moment of antithesis, thus leaving the study as a whole with an open conclusion. This regrouping, undertaken in December after his return to Berlin, is of decisive importance for the central place Benjamin assigns to the expressive device of allegory, a literary form that, as he emphasized, he sought to retrieve from historical oblivion and to restore to public awareness.

From Capri Benjamin also reports of "dangers" that threatened the progress of his work. At the beginning of the summer he became acquainted with Asja Lacis, "a Russian revolutionary from Riga, one of the most outstanding women I have ever met."[24] Using biblical allusions, which he could assume would communicate readily to the receptive ears of his friend Scholem in Jerusalem, he revealed the fact of his new love relationship: "Something else are the vineyards that belong also to the miraculous manifestations of these nights. You certainly will have experienced the moment when fruit and leaf disappear in the night's blackness and one reaches cautiously–in order not to be overheard and chased away–for the large grapes. But there's a great deal more to it, on which the commentaries to the Song of Songs can shed some light."[25] His love for the Latvian communist, which he hints at here, was felt by Benjamin to be a "vital liberation." But it was not only of private significance. In discussions with her, in which he endeavored to make comprehensible his interest in the remote historical topic

Capri.

of his study, he gained at the same time an "intensive understanding of the actuality of radical communism."[26]

This experience was reinforced theoretically by his reading of Lukács's *History and Class Consciousness*, published a year earlier. Here Benjamin found his own analysis of the decay of German society confirmed and raised to the level of a coherent historical and epistemological system. Lukács, by reducing the economic and social fault lines now evident in Europe's market

Asja Lacis.

economy to the "antinomies of bourgeois thought," interpreted the crisis of the spiritual tradition, which Benjamin had experienced in his own works as an imperative impelling him toward the esoteric, as a sign of the general dissolution of the bourgeois world. At another level Lukács also indicated the way that this very tradition, which was threatening to collapse under its own unacknowledged contradictions, could be transcended, hence rescued: by turning it into the instrument of social progress. This radical blending together of the philosophical and social factors blocking the change toward a truly progressive culture was exactly what Benjamin needed to

75

strengthen his own viewpoints. This is why he frequently stresses in letters at this time "that Lukács, starting from political considerations, reaches epistemological positions that, at least in part although perhaps not so thoroughly as I at first assumed, are to me very familiar and supportive."[27]

In October Benjamin returned to Berlin via Naples, Rome, and Florence, confirming his impressions of the dangerousness of fascism, which he had already formed on the occasion of a visit to Capri by the Duce. He writes from Florence, exaggerating ironically: "In the alliance between loneliness and drizzle there is a third member, fascism, which wherever I am staying is always ready to give of its utmost. This morning, during Victor Emmanuel's state entry into Florence, I came close to being trampled to death under the horses' hooves."[28] On arrival in Berlin he devoted himself exclusively to the completion of the *Habilitation*. At the end of December he was able to tell Scholem of finishing the "rough draft," now conceived in only two main parts, although he was still doubtful "whether 'allegory'– the element I have been concerned above all to rescue–is vividly enough stated, as it were in all its totality." Finally, after a final revision and rewriting of the preface in the spring of 1925 in Frankfurt, he handed it in to the Philosophical Faculty in early May, setting the official *Habilitation* process in motion.

The history of the writing of the book on tragic drama makes it clear that it is a threshold work. On the one hand, Benjamin's intentions are still fundamentally conservative, in that he is addressing in commentary style a historic form of German literature. On the other hand, in its destruction of the symbolist aesthetic as well as in its radical critique of the humanities and its pessimistic view of history, it bears witness to the political experiences its author underwent while working on it. It is thus not only the conclusion of Benjamin's work in the field of German literary history, as he notes in a letter to Scholem, but also the projection of a post-symbolist aesthetic consciously attuned to the deepest historical and cultural forces of the age.[29]

The "Epistemological Preface," whose "boundless chutzpah" Benjamin self-mockingly proclaims in a letter and which he recommends be read last, is nevertheless the indispensable starting point for any involvement with the work, for it contains above all a portrayal of the method the author will follow in his analytical discussion of the materials. As he himself states, the preface is "a kind of second stage (I don't know if it's a better one) of the early work on language . . . with the grooming of a theory of ideas."[30]

Benjamin's view is that, in the everyday use of language, words refer by their semantic content to empirical objects and can lead to a higher knowledge only insofar as concepts can be extracted from them by way of induction. To this Benjamin opposes his own theory of language, which once again makes use of neo-Kantian concepts, filling them with new metaphysical contents. For Benjamin the word can become the name of things and as such absorb into itself their idea, their spiritual essence. Understood thus, language is the one and only medium of truth.

The metaphysical claim, by which this epistemology sets itself apart from the truth-concept of positivistic knowledge, contains a reflection on Benjamin's own historico-philosophical perspective. After the great idealist philosophical systems had become obsolete, as Benjamin had registered already in his essay "On the Program of the Coming Philosophy," he sought to dissolve the inherent opposition between subject and object by taking as the starting point of his thinking *not* the subject but a third element, namely language. This thinking is exemplified in the central discussion of his book on tragic drama: According to the conventional view of language, which defines the traditional method of the historical disciplines, the scholar can derive inductively something like an abstract concept of the tragic drama from studying the multiplicity of historical examples. His goal is thus a historically based genre concept. Benjamin's goal is precisely not a synthesis constructed from historical data, but an immediate experience derived from language of what the tragic drama *is*, of its "origin." This word, used in the work's title, thus signifies for Benjamin not the historical emergence of the genre, but the moment in which the genre "escapes from history," that is, withdraws from it and in the process becomes an idea.

Despite his Platonic vocabulary, Benjamin's epistemological method is in no way ahistorical. Rather, it constitutes a kind of historical extremism in the sense that it seeks to apprehend phenomena not as reductive illustrations of a law, but as unique, limiting cases. The method sets itself the goal of constructing a constellation "from out of the decayed, despised excess material of history." This fixes an image of truth without describing it. The orientation toward the extreme, the detritus of the historical process, saves Benjamin's study from being a history based on "common sense," that is, an uncritical history from the perspective of the ruling class. It is to include history in its totality, as the methodological core sentence of the "Epistemological Preface" makes clear: "Philosophical history as knowledge of the origin is the form that permits the configuration of the idea to emerge from the remote extremes, the apparent excesses of development: the idea in its totality characterized by the possibility of a meaningful coexistence of such opposites."[31] The totality envisaged in this sentence as the goal of cognition is no longer the harmonious totality of the symbolic image of the world, but a whole whose parts are assembled from the most disparate materials, a whole with unconcealed ruptures, into which the world with all its contradictions can enter.

The method outlined in the "Epistemological Preface" is followed very precisely in the textual analyses of the first main section of *The Origin of German Tragic Drama*. In analyzing the hero, place, and time of the tragic drama, Benjamin seeks out the most extreme illustrations of his topic. Thus the king appears as the hero of Baroque dramas in two opposite guises: as tyrant or as martyr. Accordingly, the court as scene of the action is portrayed in two different ways: as the scene of intrigue or as the scene of worldly conviviality. Finally time is also shaped in a double way: as catastrophe or as idyllic paradise, as "acme." In all these extreme manifestations, the world of the tragic drama is revealed as radically immanent. No prospect of liberation from it is offered. From this Benjamin concludes that in tragic drama the historical world is always viewed from the perspective of natural history, from whose cycle of death there is no escape. Hence its lack of metaphysical consolation, the melancholy of its characters, and the mood of mourning in its audience. The tragic drama, Benjamin summarizes, is a "play before mourners," for whom the catastrophic sequence of their own history and that of the history of the world is enacted on the stage before their eyes.[32]

In Greek tragedy, as Benjamin reformulates Rang's highly subjective theory, the hero wordlessly overcomes his fate by means of his death, mutely escaping the world of myth. In German tragic drama, by contrast, no rupture of mythic fate is achieved. This is underscored by the fact that in it, life is always judged from the perspective of existential extremity, namely death. "From the point of view of death, life is the production of corpses."[33] The inescapable end thus causes the entire natural context of life to appear a priori as guilt-ridden and destined to death. This accurate diagnosis of individual existence is transferred by the tragic drama to history as a whole, by displaying "nature's elemental violence within historical events."[34] By exclusively stressing this aspect Benjamin reveals his contemporary historico-philosophical concerns. History, as it is operative in the plots of Baroque tragic dramas, is unmasked by Benjamin as a catastrophic landscape of ruins without metaphysical meaning. This theory of history in the book on tragic drama is full of immediacy, in that it registers, at a specific point in the past, the collapse of objective reason in history, which has only become apparent in the twentieth century.

Benjamin's "philosophical history" of the Baroque tragic drama paints a picture of the metaphysical situation of the past epoch from the perspective of the present in order to demonstrate its essential compatibility with

Benjamin in Berlin, 1926.

the literary form of the drama. Both concept and method of this procedure are adapted from Carl Schmitt's work *Political Theology: Four chapters on the Doctrine of Sovereignty*, published in 1922, to which Benjamin refers several times by citation. In this book the political scientist sought to ground his autocratic concept of the state in the doctrines of the great thinkers of the Restoration, such as Bonald and de Maistre. "He is sovereign who decides what is a state of emergency": the first sentence of the book contains its political program, the basing of the power of the state in the unlimited power of decision and caprice of a single individual.[35] This theory of absolute state power is conceived as a deliberate antithesis to the doctrine of popular sovereignty on which the constitution of the Weimar Republic was based. As Benjamin himself acknowledges in a dedicatory letter to Schmitt of December 1930, this theory is applied in his analysis of the Baroque sovereign without any alteration of content.[36]

More important still is the fact that his thinking is also methodologi-

Carl Schmitt.

cally related to that of Carl Schmitt, who in his "sociology of concepts" proceeds from the premise that all "generative concepts of modern state doctrine . . . are secularized theological concepts."[37] It is Schmitt's goal to reconstruct the connection between the dominant theological metaphors of an epoch and the form of its political organization. Benjamin undertakes to reveal a similar structural analogy, in his analysis of history's extreme manifestations.

Modifying a statement by Carl Schmitt, Benjamin's methodology could be formulated thus: the metaphysical vision of the world, as formed by a particular epoch, has the same structure as what appears to it to be a self-evidently right mode of *literary* expression. The identity of theoretical procedures adopted by the theorist of dictatorship and the critic of German tragic drama fascinated by the concept of revolution demonstrates, more even than the common focus on specific elements of content, to what extent intellectuals of both right and left in the Weimar Republic were at one in their rejection of the secularizing and egalitarian tendencies inherent in a bourgeois democracy.

In the second part of the book on tragic drama, Benjamin drops the method directed at a rescue of extreme and marginal phenomena and instead reconstructs allegory as the central expressive form of Baroque drama. According to this argument–synthetic in direct contrast to the analytic perspective of the first main part–the way in which the dramatist produces a new system of signifiers as a composite of the most heterogenous parts, namely isolated things torn from their "natural" context–this procedure corresponds with formal precision to the discontinuous process of history. Benjamin's insight into his own historical position is also decisive for this rediscovery of allegory. In the "Epistemological Preface," Benjamin makes the end of systematic idealist philosophy into the starting point of his own argument. With comparable immediacy he proceeds, in the second main part, from the recognition that, in the most advanced contemporary literature, as exemplified by the avant-garde movements, nature is no longer actual in its symbolic significance. The upgrading of allegory as a genuine possibility for literary structure points thus to the end of the classic-romantic period of art, in which an unlimited privilege was accorded to the unified, autonomous work. In fact the book on tragic drama was at first understood as an anti-classical aesthetic program. Thus Georg Lukács, in his programmatic 1956 essay "Against Misunderstood Realism," situates Benjamin paradigmatically as the protagonist of modernist literature, as manifested in Kafka's works, in contrast to his own theory of socialist realism, oriented toward Thomas Mann.[38]

There is a certain historical justification in this view of Benjamin's book, even though it overlooks the fact that Benjamin's critique is also directed against the allegorical procedure itself. This error is all the more understandable as Benjamin himself makes ostentatious use of the allegorical method in the second part. In his letters he frequently drew attention to the fact that the first draft of the book on tragic drama consisted "almost entirely of quotations." "It's the craziest mosaic technique one can imagine and would probably seem so alien to works of this kind that I will surely do some retouching here and there in the final draft."[39] Even though the published form of the text no longer consists exclusively of citations, their significance for the construction of the whole is nevertheless unmistakable. Indeed it is an "alien" use of quotations, to "construct" them according to the requirements of allegorical images. Benjamin tears individual sentences or sentence-fragments from their original context and accumulates them into series, so that, like the significant images of allegory, they form clusters, then adds his own thought to them, without binding all these elements into a continuum. They function, rather, in the manner of a Baroque emblem. The quotations occupy the place of the image, hence constitute the pictura to which meaning is added in a caption, as the subscriptio.

A passage from the book's concluding section can serve as an example for this emblematic deployment of the quotation. Benjamin cites several sentences from the art-historical study *Antiquity in Poetics and Theory of Art* by Karl Borinski, in which a particular type of Baroque altar structure is described:

> " . . . What else can be meant by the pervasive references to the strength of the forces that must bear the burden, the monstrous pedestals, the double and triple groupings of forward projected pillars and pilasters, the strengthenings and reinforcings of their mutual support systems, all in order simply to sustain a balcony—what can all this mean, other than to make immediate, through emphasizing the difficulties of support from beneath, the hovering mystery from above. The 'Ponderacion mysteriosa,' the intervention of God in the work of art is presumed to be possible." Subjectivity, which plunges into the depths like an angel, is captured by allegories and held fast in the heavens, in God by means of "Ponderacion mysteriosa."[40]

The sentences from the learned work on the aesthetic theory of the Baroque are detached from their original art-historical illustrative context and used as an image, which the allegorical critic invests in a concluding sentence with his subjective significance.

According to Benjamin's understanding this method is far from being "unscientific." For him, rather, the allegorist is above all the one who possesses knowledge. "The intention of allegory is so resistant to the intention centered on truth that, more clearly in allegory than anywhere else, there emerges the fusion of a pure curiosity, directed at mere knowing, with the arrogant self-isolation of man."[41] Allegorical procedure is thus revealed as one in which the method of the historical disciplines, namely the forcing of subjective contexts of meaning upon the world's discontinuous structures, is transformed to the point where it can be recognized for what it is. Like allegory, therefore, disciplinary knowledge is declared by Benjamin to have no part in truth. "Knowledge of evil—as knowledge it is a priori. It results from contemplation. . . . It is idle talk, in the deep meaning of the term defined by Kierkegaard. That knowledge of evil is the origin of all allegorical contemplation, as the triumph of subjectivity and the onset of the rule of caprice over things."[42]

In Benjamin's negative theology, knowledge and allegory, scholarship and art are, as products of "purely subjective speculation," in league with the devil. But because subjectivity attains in them its utmost extremity, they

82

also stand closest to salvation. That is how Benjamin interprets the final image of the "ponderacion misteriosa," which he cites:

> The allegorist awakens in God's world. "Yes / when the Highest reaps the churchyard's harvest / then I a death's head will an angel's face be." At that moment the mark of what is most fragmented, dead, scattered is dissolved. And with that, allegory loses everything that had most intimately belonged to it: secret privileged knowledge, arbitrary rule in the realm of dead things, the assumed infinity of hopelessness. All is scattered to dust in that single transformation when allegorical contemplation must abandon the last phantasms of the objective and, forced back onto itself, discovers itself to be no longer at play in the earthly world of things but seriously exposed to the heavens.[43]

With these sentences, which themselves commit the error of allegory, the book on tragic drama, at its conclusion, makes an openly transcending movement into the metaphysical. The suddenness of the radical change from rejected allegorical knowledge to salvation within truth represents—like Benjamin's conception of revolution—a rupture with bad reality, which has its model and its justification solely in the sudden, all-transforming appearance of the Messiah.

The negative characterizations of allegory, collected in these sentences, add up to a devastating judgment against scholarship and art as the modern form of absolute subjectivity. Here the critique of academic scholarship, for which Gundolf's Goethe biography had provided the impetus in the context of the essay on *The Elective Affinities*, has been generalized and sharpened through Benjamin's own existential experience. That experience, he notes of his quest for the *Habilitation*, "prevented him ever more conclusively from viewing the contemporary university as a place of fruitful or, above all, of pure activity."[44] To be sure, the hope generated by a radically destructive critique is valid equally for allegory and for scholarship.

The concluding turn of the book on tragic drama, whereby "acknowledged subjectivity becomes the formal guarantor of the miraculous,"[45] returns the critique of scholarship in the second main section to the epistemological level of the Preface. The antithesis, in which allegory is negated and which is not transcended by any synthesis, finds in the Preface its anticipatory resolution. The program outlined at the beginning, of a rescue of phenomena from the margins into the constellation of the idea, points to the transcendence of a death-imprisoned world in the texture of the eternal, which is represented in his negative theology by the figure of the Last Judgment.

The book's epistemology cannot be more precisely grasped than in theological categories. Benjamin, by making himself an allegorist, takes the

83

sin of knowledge upon himself and strives to transcend it, in order thus to set the salvation of earthly phenomena in motion. Only his total identification with this most depraved figure among all those with knowledge can guarantee the reversal that will lead art and scholarship, controlled by the devil of subjectivity in modern times, back to the truth whose image is anticipated in the Preface. Only when the two main sections of the book on tragic drama are understood in this way as thesis and antithesis, with their final solution already sketched out in the preceding epistemological critique, can the formal unity of the work be recognized.

The contradictions in content however remain unsolved. The open ending of the book suggests this, as does the confrontation of allegory with truth, which is understood as the "divine name," but also as the concept of the symbol, once it is emancipated from its historical coding: "Whereas in the symbol, with its transfiguration of ruin, the evanescent face of nature is fleetingly revealed in the light of redemption, in allegory the facies hippocratica of history presents itself to the beholder as a rigidified primal landscape."[46] This sentence from the beginning of the second main section also designates the antithesis between the "sinful" historical procedure of the critic and the philosophical mode of the author of a treatise, who in his introductory doctrine of Ideas outlines a symbolic world of truth. Only in their mutual "discontinuity" can the secret bond between the two worlds be glimpsed. "Every idea is a sun and relates to other ideas the way suns relate to each other."[47] The allegorical critic, a second angelus novus, works toward this structure of truth by tearing things from their natural context and exhibiting them in isolation. Thus at the end only the barely perceptible yet totally decisive messianic power has to come to his aid for him in fact to "awaken in God's world."

Metaphysical dualism, which as the opposition between treatise and critical analysis is deeply embedded in the book on German tragic drama in the formal sense as well, can only be overcome through the leap into truth. In it the contradiction expressed by Benjamin in regard to his own social role finds its objective expression. On the one hand he criticizes the intellectual, whose melancholy ingeniousness is his own, for losing himself in the bottomless profundity, the infinite extension of significant but absolutely subjective images. On the other hand, he sees in him also the truth finder, who in "the activity of naming" reveals "the symbolic character of the word" and thus affiliates himself with Adam, the "father of human beings as the father of philosophy."[48] In this biblical metaphor is expressed the utopian hope that Benjamin links to his own social role. As a philosopher he is himself the "new Adam." Both characterizations, that of the sinner and that of the savior, coalesce in that of the scapegoat, the critic

84

The original edition of *The Origin of German Tragic Drama*.

who takes the "fall" of allegory upon himself, in order to restore the world to its truth.

In the suppressed ten-line Foreword to *The Origin of German Tragic Drama*, which Benjamin composed after the book's rejection by the Humanities Department of the University of Frankfurt, he ironically clothed the messianic claim of his work in a new interpretation of the "Sleeping Beauty" fairy tale. In it he appears in the role of chief cook, who has replaced Prince Charming by giving a resounding box on the ears to the academic kitchen assistant, thus awakening the Princess Truth. This also is a sign of the continuity of Benjamin's sense of destiny. When he told the same fairy tale twelve years earlier, he had called the princess "Youth." Only the rescuer is the same in both cases, the author himself:

> I would like to retell the story of Sleeping Beauty. She is sleeping amid her thorns. And then, after a number of years, she wakes up. But not because of the kiss of a lucky prince. The cook awakened her when he gave his scullery boy a box on the ears which, resounding from the accumulated power of so many silent years, echoes through the castle. A beautiful child sleeps behind the thorny hedge of the following pages. Let no lucky prince in the dazzling armor of scholarship come close to her. For in the bridal kiss she will bite down hard. Rather, the author himself, as master of the kitchen, has reserved to himself the right to awaken her. For too long the box on the ears has been due, which is to resound through the halls of scholarship. Then this poor truth will awaken, who pricked her finger on the old-fashioned spinning wheel when she thought she might, against the rules, weave for herself a professor's gown in the attic.

When Benjamin wrote these bitterly ironic lines, he had, in September 1925, just withdrawn his petition for *Habilitation* at the University of Frankfurt, on the advice of his friends, in order to spare himself formal rejection. Schultz had finally, after long hesitation, refused to grant him *Habilitation* in the field of "literary history" and had referred him to Hans Cornelius, who represented the specialty "general aesthetics." The latter had, after consulting with Max Horkheimer, his assistant at the time, filed a negative opinion in July 1925. Benjamin's always somewhat strained relations with the subsequent director of the School for Social Reserch may thus have been due partly to Horkheimer's secret sense of guilt at having participated, without Benjamin's knowledge, in the wrecking of his academic career. Benjamin, however, had already written to Scholem before the negative response from Frankfurt, that "with my parents' refusal to improve my financial circumstances in the event of a *Habilitation*, with the turn in my thinking toward politics, with Rang's death . . . one reason after another for this undertaking has become inoperative."[49]

The scepticism with which Benjamin had viewed his prospects in Frankfurt from the outset was partly conditioned by his awareness of how ill-suited and reluctant he was, in the given circumstances, to assume the functions of a university teacher. As he was beginning to write his study, he had already formulated in various ways his "inner resistance" to the project. When in the spring of 1925 matters seemed to be shaping up somewhat more favorably in Frankfurt, Benjamin wrote to Scholem: "I shudder at the prospect of almost everything that would accompany a successful conclusion: Frankfurt itself above all, the lectures, students, etc., things that would make murderous assaults on my time."[50] The reasons for this resistant attitude lie not only with the university, although Benjamin was right to deplore its disdainful attitude and desolate spiritual outlook. To him his solitariness as an intellectual, which alone seemed to make possible independence of critical judgment, was more important than institutional affiliation and security. This attitude had actually been radicalized by his political experiences in the previous two years, so that, even before the Frankfurt process was completed, he was making publishing plans: "For me everything depends on how relations with publishers develop. If nothing works out for me there, I will probably intensify my involvement with Marxist politics and—with the prospect of visiting Moscow at least for a while in the foreseeable future—I will join the Party. Sooner or later I will probably take this step no matter what. The horizon of my work is no longer the old one and I cannot artificially confine it."[51]

Benjamin did not take the step mentioned here, namely joining the Communist party. Such a step would ultimately have been as contradictory to his fundamental decision in favor of existential independence and spiritual responsibility as the professorial function. The announcement of his political projects can thus be read only as an expression of Benjamin's deep personal despair.

His publishing plans, however, soon took concrete form, thanks to a testimonial from Hofmannsthal, who in August 1927 gave advance publication, in his *Neue Deutsche Beiträge*, to the third section of the first main part of the book on tragic drama. Before Benjamin left in August 1925 from Hamburg for a sea voyage to Spain, Portugal, and southern Italy, which lasted until October, he signed a contract with the publisher Rowohlt in Berlin, having established contact through his friend Franz Hessel, Rowohlt's director of publications at the time. The contract guaranteed him "a stipend for the coming year" and committed the firm to publish the book on tragic drama, the essay on *The Elective Affinities*, and a planned volume of aphorisms.[52] Further, he contracted with the publisher "Die Schmiede" to "translate Proust's three-volume work *Sodome et Gomorrhe*" in collaboration with Hessel. After the definitive failure of his academic career he had, with these publishing projects, established something like an autonomous professional perspective and could thus give himself over to what he himself called his "fanatical longing to travel."[53]

Upon his return from Naples Benjamin travelled in November to Riga, to visit Asja Lacis who was directing a proletarian children's theater there. "He loved to surprise me, but this time his surprise displeased me. He came from another planet—I had no time for him. . . . Benjamin naturally wanted to see one of my performances. . . . Nothing pleased him except for one scene: a gentleman in a top hat converses with a worker beneath a street-lamp."[54] This description confirms that for the militant communist her relationship with the intellectual, who did not wish to engage in practical political struggle, had lost its actuality.

Benjamin's attitude to his lover had similarly become more critical. *One Way Street*, as the printed dedication has it, is named "Asja-Lacis-Street after the engineer who broke it open within the author." In it one can find concealed, as Benjamin loved to do, in a small detail of the description of Riga his commentary on their quarrel: "On many corners, next to sheds housing fish, boots, and clothing, small business women stand here the whole year round with multicolored paper switches, of the kind that appear in the West only at Christmas time. These switches are like being scolded by the most beloved voice. Multicolored bunches of punishment for a few centimes."[55] This little impression says much about Benjamin's patience in matters of love.

V

Paris, Berlin, Moscow

1926–1929

he year 1924 marked a decisive change in Benjamin's life and thinking. Under the impact of his experiences at that time, he transformed himself from esoteric philosopher to politically engaged writer, from language mystic to dialectical materialist. The extent to which he himself was aware of this caesura can be gleaned from the summary he made in December 1924 in a letter to Scholem:

> In Berlin people are agreed that a clear change has taken place in me. The intensity with which I prepared myself for this change in the spring, via fasting and similar exercises, and struggled to achieve it inwardly and outwardly, not without Dora's keen support—all this was not in vain. My reactions to communism . . . were also at first signs of a change, which aroused in me the desire to stop disguising the actual and political elements of my thoughts in an antiquated manner, and to develop them instead, indeed in an extreme form for experimental purposes. That means of course that literary exegesis of German texts recedes in importance; in this respect the goal that could be achieved was at best to conserve the essential and to restore the genuine over expressionist distortions. Until I gain access, in the commentator's manner that suits me, to texts of quite different significance and totality, I will be using my inner resources to put forward a "politics." And indeed I have again been amazed at the way in which my thinking makes contact at various points with an extreme Bolshevist theory.[1]

Sacha Stone's photomontage for the cover of *One Way Street*.

Fragments of the planned "politics," which Benjamin rightly put in quotation marks, can be found in the short texts that, from 1925 onwards, he published in the magazine sections of the large daily newspapers of the Weimar Republic. He collected them for publication by Rowohlt in 1928 under the title *One Way Street*, the only "non-scholarly" book published

90

by Benjamin in his lifetime. In its typeface and format—a photomontage by Sacha Stone adorns the cover—as well as in its fragmentary style, it is demonstrably one of the most significant products of the German language avant-garde in the 1920s. Its links to contemporary French surrealism are evident, even without such striking adaptations as the eleven short texts collected under the title "Stamp Dealer," which refer to a few pages from Aragon's *The Peasant of Paris*, published in 1925.

Among the mythical places into which, for the Parisian flaneur, shops of the Passage de l'Opéra transform themselves, Aragon pays special attention to a philatelist's display window. The observer reads the little pictures on the stamps as a sign language in which the present declares itself as the remote past, while exotic lands are thrust into the closest immediacy. In this language the fairy-tale, paradisiacal aspect of time and place is revealed. "O philately, philately, you are a most alien Goddess, a slightly crazy fairy, and yet the one who takes the child by the hand when it emerges from the magic forest, where finally Tom Thumb, the blue bird, Red Riding Hood and the wolf have fallen asleep side by side—you are the one."[2] Benjamin translated these sentences into German and published them, with other excerpts from *The Peasant of Paris*, in June 1928 in the *Literarische Welt*. At the same time, in his own book, he radicalized Aragon's reflection on sign language by making stamps into a metaphor for the allegorical images that make up *One Way Street*. Thus discussion of the object of the child's collecting zeal is used playfully as a reflection on his own poetics.

> Stamps are covered with tiny numbers, letters, leaves, microscopic eyes. They are the material of the cell in graphic form. Everything teems and, like the lower mammals, lives on after being cut apart. That is why one can make such effective pictures out of little pieces of stamps stuck together. But in these stamp-pictures life is always marked by decay, a reminder that it has been composed from dead material. Their portraits and obscene tableaux are infiltrated by skeletons and piles of worms.[3]

With the installation of death within fragmented life, as evoked in this passage, short modern prose texts resemble Baroque allegory, and their significance is the same. In these marginal details, then, the central arguments about allegory in the book on tragic drama are rendered actual.

The essence of *One Way Street* is not, as Ernst Bloch claimed, "philosophy in the form of cabaret,"[4] but transformation of Benjamin's own political and social experience into allegorical images. In them Benjamin collected, kaleidoscopically, the insights of the radical author he had become, and thereby translated into literary praxis his aesthetic understanding of the end of the period of symbolic art, as expounded in the book on tragic drama. From the description of the decay of all human interactions in bourgeois society, manifest in the paroxysms of inflation; through the critique of the money economy and the ironic portrayal of the experience of sailors, to whom the entire populated world appears as ruled by the trade in commodities; to the definition of the "true politician"–again and again ingredients of direct political criticism are evident in this panorama of the 1920s, constructed as a "one way street." The straight lines of this street converge perspectivally in the concluding text, entitled "Planetarium," wherein the author develops in just two pages, truly "with the left hand"[5] (as he demands of any text that would achieve impact within modernity), a large-scale theory of history and of the revolutionary subject. In the perspective of this philosophy of history, human happiness, which here as everywhere in *One Way Street* is viewed as the goal of history, can be localized in antiquity as an "ecstatic" experience of the cosmos. Community of human beings with each other and with nature was at that time, in Benjamin's analysis, an unquestioned premise of life. Since the Renaissance, however, this unity is shattered, because humans have undertaken to dominate nature, whereby within society also the tendencies toward isolation and hierarchy have been strengthened. The snapshots in *One Way Street* give a diagnostic image of the impact of this process on all areas of life.

Following the idealist construction of history, modernity is thus contrasted with an idealized antiquity as a time of decline. And just as Friedrich Schlegel interprets the French Revolution, so Walter Benjamin interprets the First World War as the crisis in which the authentic goal of history is glimpsed under the sign of negativity and destruction. "In the nights of annihilation of the last war a feeling shook the physical frame of humankind, a feeling that looked just like the bliss of the epileptic. And the revolts that followed the war were the first attempt of humankind to get its new body under control. The power of the proletariat is the yardstick of its recovery. If the discipline of the proletariat does not penetrate the body's very marrow, then no pacifist argumentation will save it."[6] To the dialectical materialism defined by Benjamin the exploitation of nature appears as the real evil to be redressed. Technology is to be the means to this end, once liberated from the "profit-lust of the ruling classes." Accordingly the rescue of humanity and the rescue of nature are for him indissolubly linked. By thus prescribing to the proletariat what the revolution's goal is to be, namely the "control of the relationship between nature and humanity," Benjamin distinguishes his view from orthodox Marxism, which was exclusively focussed on economic and social processes.

In this most radical political utterance of Benjamin, one rediscovers

Benjamin in Paris, 1927.

only traces of his messianism, specifically in the unmediated reversal whereby the historical catastrophe of the First World War is interpreted as a guarantee of the coming salvation. Messianism also tacitly shapes his conception of the "true politician," whose destiny it is, in the role of the "one who announces the fire," to cut through the "burning fuse" that is the continued rule of the bourgeoisie, a rule endangering "three thousand years of cultural development."[7] From him is demanded not so much political action as recognition of the right moment for redemptive intervention, that is, laying bare the ambivalent character of the crisis, in which extreme danger and the possibility of rescue are equally actual.

Benjamin's "politics" aims to produce this interventional knowledge in its application to the most important spheres of a writer's life. Thus the "privatization of love" in bourgeois existence is confronted with its politicization, which Benjamin as lover experienced through Asja Lacis. "I know a woman who is absent-minded. In the mental space that in me is occupied by the names of my suppliers, the place where my documents are kept, addresses of friends and acquaintances, the hour of an appointment – in her this space is filled by political concepts, party slogans, articles of faith, and instructions."[8] Only from a distance and "without hope" may the lover approach this beloved woman.[9] His true goal is not to possess her, but to follow her as his political guide.

As critic Benjamin agrees with Valéry "that the book in its inherited form is reaching the end of its social existence," and, through a parallel between books and prostitutes, he ironically locates the reasons for this decline in the commodity character they have in common.[10] His response to this is the outline of a poetics of critical writing in short texts, which, even in the age of advertising, may be able to hold their own in the competition for the attention of the distracted reader. Benjamin goes furthest toward politicizing surrealist intentions when he tries to understand even the dream as no longer a private affair but as a historical phenomenon. In the copious reports of dreams in *One Way Street*, where he appears as the exhumer of old times or as Goethe's savior, he advances his own dreams as proof that the "new man" of his age bears within himself "all the essentials of the old forms" of the nineteenth century.[11] By transmuting his dreams into literary "picture puzzles," the author succeeds in using them to achieve intensive self-understanding. At the cost of his own "private existence" he turns himself into an allegory of the new human being. "In the dream I took my own life with a rifle. When the shot rang out I did not awaken but gazed at myself for a while, lying there as a corpse. Only then did I wake up."[12] These lines follow the title: "Closed for Remodelling!" Thus the dream narrative refers as a puzzle image to the method whereby from the surrealist mythmaker and teller of dream stories the new man is "remodelled," having awakened from the dream of the nineteenth century.

At the center of the book, thirtieth in a total of sixty texts, stands the child whom the author himself once was, under the title "Enlargements."[13] The figure, constructed from six frozen moments, contains at the individual level the promise of happiness, which the historian Benjamin of the final text thinks he can read into the connectedness of antiquity with the cosmos. The reader is shown the child who, in the sensual delight of nibbling on sweets, has a foretaste of sexual fulfillment; the child who, in the joy of reading and as collector of oddments, becomes the model of the materialist historian; and the child who, in his protest against school and playful self-liberation from the magically experienced world of the furnished apartment, rehearses the politician's revolt; and at the center of them all the child "riding the carousel," for whom in his harmony with nature "life is a primeval ecstasy of reigning over the cosmos." Thus all the motifs of future salvation are already present in childhood.

The correspondences between the center of *One Way Street* and its perspectival conclusion show that the panoramic multiplicity of its aspects is to appear to the observer, according to its author's intentions, as an assembled unity of extremes. This quality of construction distinguishes the book from *The Peasant of Paris*, to which Benjamin owes the notion of assembling the texts of his book like a row of houses on a street, and places it with the works of George Grosz or John Heartfield as a genuinely contemporary expression of political art. Whereas Aragon's text is organized according to the impressions and associations of the strolling observer, Benjamin constructs his book from the perspective of the messianic revolutionary. The child appears as the latter's official representative: his remembered, hence allegorically fixed, figure is installed as the ruler over the text, in contrast with the "real" person who speaks for the French surrealist. The intentions of this revolutionary subject are just as much present in the idiosyncratic number games, which dictate the ordering of the texts into groups of seven, eleven, or thirteen, as they are in the vanishing point of the whole book, the ecstatic renewal of cosmos and humanity. "My aphorism book has turned into a remarkable organization or construction, a street that opens onto a prospect of such steeply plunging depth – the word is not meant metaphorically – as Palladio's famous stage set in Vicenza: The Street."[14]

As Benjamin wrote in a letter to Hofmannsthal, he found the form of his new book in Paris. He travelled there in mid-March 1926 with the intention of "settling down here in some respects."[15] The impetus and economic guarantee for this plan, which was a very unusual one after the disruption of Franco-German relations through the world war and the occupa-

95

"The Street": Palladio's stage set for the Teatro Olimpico in Vicenza.

tion of the Rhineland, was the prospect of collaborating with Franz Hessel on the translation of Proust's *Remembrance of Things Past*. His Berlin friend, who had already lived in Paris from 1906 to 1914 and moved in the literary and artistic circles of Montparnasse, introduced him to Parisian society, normally closed to outsiders. Through Hessel and his friend Thankmar von Münchhausen, Benjamin gained access to the circles around Count Pourtalès, Princess Bassiano, and Bernard Groethuysen, among the few friendly to Germans at that time. Still more important for his future work than these social connections was the "art of strolling" through Paris, which Hessel,

96

flaneur and connoisseur of the city's secrets, was able to impart to him. Thus already in his first weeks Benjamin could write to Berlin about strolling on the quays, visiting fairs, and about a "wonderful, undiscovered popular dance, which is called here bal musette and is unlike anything in Berlin."[16]

During this first stay in Paris Benjamin was decisively affected by his reading of the newest French literature. Beside the "regular, even though subordinate work" of translating—in 1927 the volume he and Hessel had translated, *Within a Budding Grove (A l'Ombre des jeunes filles en fleurs)* appeared, followed in 1930 by the two volumes of *The Guermantes Way (Le coté de Guermantes)*—Benjamin was occupied above all with "the splendid writings of Paul Valéry (Variété, Eupalinos) on the one hand, and on the other the dubious books of the surrealists. Confronted with these documents I need gradually to learn the techniques of criticism."[17] This sentence, in which Benjamin formulates his new life plan, barely suggests the severity of the break separating him from his previous aspirations. After the failure of his academic career he turned away from the esoteric mode of writing and toward literary criticism in the magazine sections of the large daily newspapers, in order to be able to have an immediate social impact.

Already in July 1925, with his Frankfurt enterprise entering its final stage, Benjamin wrote to Scholem: "I have made commitments of all kinds to a new literary review, appearing in the fall . . . in particular to do a regular report on new French theories of art."[18] He is referring here to the weekly journal *Die literarische Welt,* founded by the Rowohlt-Verlag and initially intended to function, under its editor Willy Haas, above all as a showcase for the authors of the publishing house; however it developed very early on into one of the leading literary organs of its time, oriented "toward the left in the daily war of words" of the consolidation phase of the Weimar Republic.[19] Economically independent after dissolving its ties with Rowohlt, the paper was able to attain a "universalism," despite its unambiguous political posture, making it the authentic location of the ideological debates of the time between left and right intellectuals.

Benjamin was already involved in the planning stages of this most important review journal of the late 1920s and soon advanced, along with E. R. Curtius, Walter Mehring, Franz Hessel, and Axel Eggebrecht, to the status of one of its "principal collaborators."[20] In the literary criticism that flourished here, he was able to formulate his political conceptions openly. Thus in the years between 1926 and 1929 he published an average of thirty contributions a year in the *Literarische Welt,* among them the extensive and important essays on Keller, Proust, and surrealism. His editorial activity is evident in several special issues of the journal. After 1930, when the liberal conception of the paper became endangered by the intensification of ideo-

Title page of the *Literarische Welt* (1926, number 52): caricatures of Ernst Rowohlt and Walter Benjamin, among others, by B.-F. Dolbin.

logical debate to a hitherto unknown sharpness, Benjamin gradually reduced his editorial involvement.

Much more problematic from the outset was his relationship to the *Frankfurter Zeitung*, which represented "left democratic journalism in the public mind." Under the direction since 1924 of Benno Reifenberg, it had built up the most highly regarded literary section in the Weimar Republic.[21] Through Benjamin's connection with Siegfried Kracauer, one of its editors, with whom he had become acquainted during one of his earlier stays in Frankfurt, there appeared in April 1926, under the title "Small Illumination," the first of the short prose texts that later were collected in *One Way*

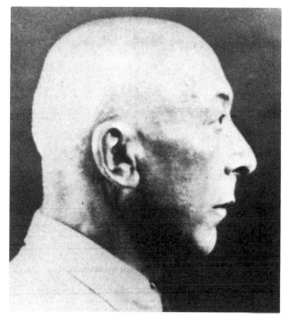

Franz Hessel.

Street. However Benjamin could never manage to achieve any kind of official collaborative status, among other reasons because there was a marked rivalry between the *Frankfurter Zeitung* and the *Literarische Welt*, and he himself, with his specialization in French literature, encroached on the interests of Reifenberg and others. Thus, even in the early 1930s when the *Frankfurter Zeitung* published an average of fifteen contributions from him annually, Benjamin remained dependent on Kracauer's personal goodwill.

In his private life the year 1926 plunged Benjamin into a deep crisis. His still uncertain career prospects may have contributed to it, but personal problems were decisive. Already in April he wrote from Paris in a letter to Jula Cohn that he had spent the last weeks "in terrifying depressions." The reasons can be gleaned from hints he let drop in the same letter. A short while before, Jula Cohn, whom he still loved passionately, had married the friend of his youth Fritz Radt: "I'm thinking of you a lot and above all I often wish you were in my room," he wrote her.[22] In July 1926 Benjamin's father died. Concerning the summer months, which he spent in Agay on

Siegfried Kracauer.

the Cote d'Azur, partly in the company of Jula Cohn, he wrote that they had "turned out badly": "As the soothing phrase has it, I experienced a nervous breakdown: more precisely, I had one after another."[23]

In this precarious situation his journey in early December to Moscow, to visit Asja Lacis, seems to have been a kind of escape from his current tribulations. Once again, and for the last time, his longing for the beloved woman who had taught him the living political power of Marxism, provoked him to break out into new circumstances. At the time Asja was staying with her lifelong companion, the director and critic Bernhard Reich, at a Moscow sanatorium, recovering from the consequences of a nervous breakdown. On 6 December 1926, Benjamin arrived in Moscow, a city unfamiliar to him, where he did not speak the language and had no connections at all of the kind that would have been essential for his work as a critic. For all professional and private undertakings he was thus dependent on Reich's support, which led to constant tensions and quarrels among all three people involved.

Benjamin was fully aware of the extraordinarily difficult situation into which he was placing himself. In his diary, which he kept daily throughout his two-month stay, he noted already on 20 December: "I am confronting an almost impregnable fortress. To be sure I tell myself that simply to reach the fortress, Moscow, represents an initial success. But any subsequent success, any success with consequences, seems almost impossible to achieve. Reich's position is strong, because of the evident successes he has scored here one after the other, during an extremely difficult six months, not knowing the language, feeling cold and perhaps hungry too."[24] The comparison of the strange city with a fortress, an image that is then also fluidly transferred to the beloved woman denying herself to him, indicates the secret motives for Benjamin's obstinate, almost desperate wooing of her. The woman and the city are both experienced by him as inaccessible; the lover, equipped only with his power as reader, tries to approach them anyway. Like a difficult text they demand from the interpreter intense concentration. "And Asja demands undivided, totally devoted attention such as I simply cannot produce without any kind of encouragement and friendliness on her part."[25] Again, Benjamin tries here to practice "love at a distance," that is, to be close to the beloved in a situation where everything combines to distance him from her. It is the utopian attempt to make her into an object of study like a favorite text.

The failure of these efforts was inevitable. Benjamin's diary entries complain ceaselessly about quarrels, humiliations, jealous confrontations. With cutting irony Asja Lacis exposed the absurdity of his behavior during a scene about one of her flirtations: "Are you going to play the role of the constant companion even opposite the red General? Perhaps he's as stupid as Reich and won't throw you out. I'd have nothing against it."[26] Until the time of departure Benjamin's feelings remained profoundly ambivalent. In his heart of hearts, however, he knew he could not attain his goal. Thus the diarist conversant with psychology reports at length on the scene with the key, which took place on the morning of his departure. In order to buy something sweet for Asja he separated from her briefly and found her on his return sitting in the lobby of his hotel." I said: 'Why didn't you go in? The key is there!' And I was struck by the strange friendship in her smile as she answered 'No.'"[27] Secretly Benjamin was already clearly aware that the separation was final. Although Asja Lacis later came for an extended period to Berlin and even lived with Benjamin for two months, his stay in Moscow led him to the decisive experience that what he sought in his love relations with Jula Cohn and Asja Lascis was impossible in life. In the future only love for the text was to be important to him. He noted: "At any rate it appears that the coming period will differ from the one just past in that the defining power of the erotic will diminish."[28] This insight governs the dreamlike image with which *Moscow Diary* closes: "With the large suitcase on my knees I drove weeping through the darkening streets to the station."[29]

The one fortress had proved to be impregnable, not however the other, the city itself. From his first day in Moscow Benjamin wandered through its streets, attended theater and film events under Reich's knowledgeable guidance, and satisfied his tireless collector's passion by tracking down hand-crafted toys. Despite his awkward personal situation, despite cold weather and language difficulties, he managed to capture, with the flaneur's perspective, a vital image of Moscow in the years of upheaval of the New Economic Policy. In the essay he wrote after returning for Martin Buber's journal *Die Kreatur*, he tried to actualize the central tendencies of the era through the city's multiple facets, thus beginning an enterprise that later, in the *Arcades Project*, was to become the chief object of his efforts as a writer. As he wrote to Buber: "I want to construct a portrayal of the city of Moscow at this moment, in which 'everything factual is already theory' and which thus refrains from all deductive abstraction, all prognostication, indeed, within limits, from any kind of value judgment."[30] Thus in the essay observations of beggars, children, or street vendors are juxtaposed with notes on traffic, advertising images, church construction, and theaters, the whole framed and interwoven with analyses of the general economic situation, of the social function of the intellectuals, and of the relation between money and power under the new regime. At the end an image of Lenin as revolutionary is programmatically presented, "his gaze to be sure focussed on what is distant, but the tireless care of his heart focussed on the moment."[31]

Benjamin's journey had nothing in common with the tourism of the revolution customary at the time among intellectuals. He came upon its traces in the presence in Moscow of Ernst Toller and Joseph Roth. For him Lenin's city became a place that demanded an existential decision. He notes in his diary:

> It's becoming ever more clear to me that for the near future I need a firm scaffolding for my work. For that, of course, translation is wholly inadequate. The precondition for its construction is, again, political engagement. What restrains me from joining the German Communist party are exclusively external considerations. For the very fact that membership in the party may be only an episode for me means that it is wrong to postpone it. But the external considerations remain. Under their pressure I ask myself whether an outsider's position on the left could not be, through intensive work, designed strategically and economically in such a way that it would assure me the possibility of wide-ranging critical production within my established spheres of work.[32]

"An outsider's position on the left" is the precise definition of the social posture Benjamin was to assume in the future. The end of the "bourgeois era of art," which he had diagnosed on the basis of his own experience in the book on tragic drama—a diagnosis confirmed in his eyes by the newest literary production in France—meant for him also the demise of the intellectual in his traditional social role. In post-revolutionary Russian society Benjamin discovered the intellectual engaged on a new task, which he presented to his German readers in a very prominent place, an illustrated lead article in the *Literarische Welt* of 11 March 1927. The title of his essay, "The Political Grouping of Russian Writers," already implies that, in the new society, it is political and no longer aesthetic affinities that generate group formations among writers.[33] Benjamin connects the three most important tendencies—leftist cult of the proletariat, rightist Poputschki, and the All-Russian League of Proletarian Writers (WAPP)—to the fundamental social forces of the time: heroic militant communism, renewal of bourgeois strength under the NEP, and dictatorship of the proletariat under the party's direction. This materialist analytic method renders comprehensible the amazing fact that Benjamin does not identify with the left-wing avant-gardists, who stand closest to his own literary intentions, but with the "new Russian naturalism" of the WAPP. This means that a clearly political point of view is underpinning his literary-critical statement. He concludes from the praxis of the WAPP that it is the function of literature in a revolutionary society to produce an "absolute public realm." In this he sees a development underway toward its goal, which had only been very partially realizable within the liberal communicative model of literature. In his view literature in the Soviet social order is no longer functioning as the medium for self-understanding of a bourgeois elite, but is serving the cause of "rendering literate" the masses now being summoned to political maturity.

As he often does in his reviews, Benjamin compresses the argument of his text into a concluding image: "The best Russian literature, if it is in fact fulfilling its destiny, can thus only be the colored illustration in the primer from which the peasants are learning to read in Lenin's shadow."[34] With this comparison the pedagogical function of political mass art is urgently formulated. The new Soviet literature must first create its public, but in doing so it is simultaneously working on the structure of a new society. In this didactic-political system of communication the free-lance writer has no further justification for existence and, as Benjamin notes, is thus economically and ideologically "bound to the state apparatus in one or another form . . . and controlled by it as an official or in some other way."[35] With the neophyte's enthusiasm he idealizes a system in which the intellectual's outsider position, experienced by Benjamin as painful, no longer exists. To

Page one of the *Literarische Welt*, 11 March 1927.

be sure he knows that the Soviet model is not transferrable to Western social structures; to be sure the "absolute public realm" of the revolutionary formations is wholly alien to his own inmost desires—his most frequent complaint during his Moscow stay is that he can never be "alone" with Asja. Nevertheless, from the experience in Russia of a concrete social function for the writer, Benjamin receives the impetus to set a practical goal for his own critical activity as well.

In the critical pieces and reviews Benjamin wrote after his return from Moscow, he is always concerned to analyze the role and function of the author in the social crises of his time. His texts thus appear as self-reflections structured through literary techniques, in which he strives, as a critic, to become certain of his social identity. Beyond that, however, they address themselves to a public affected similarly by the problems they discuss, to the intellectuals who constituted the essential readership of both the *Literarische Welt* and the literary section of the *Frankfurter Zeitung*. To this audience Benjamin wants to reveal clearly the "decay of the 'free intelligentsia'"—

the formula stands in explicit opposition to Karl Mannheim's definition of a "socially free-floating intelligentsia"—and the intellectuals' growing social and economic dependence. Thus through the example of recent French literature Benjamin shows how it expresses "the subterranean communication of the intelligentsia with the dregs of the proletariat," whereby the traditionally autonomous status of the intelligentsia is destroyed and the need to side with one of the two parties involved in the class struggle rendered unavoidable.[36]

Benjamin also applied to historical texts the model he had derived from current literature, as is shown by his 1927 essay on Gottfried Keller, which inaugurated his series of major essays in the *Literarische Welt*. In this commissioned piece he used the critical review of a complete critical edition of the Swiss author's works as the occasion for bringing into play his own historical-theoretical viewpoint. As he himself put it retrospectively in a 1931 letter to Max Rychner:

> In this essay too it was my precise aim to legitimate my insight into Keller by testing it against my understanding of the true state of our present existence. Historical greatness is defined by the way in which any understanding of the work turns into the philosophical-historical— not psychological—self-understanding of the reader; that may be a very unmaterialist formulation, but it is an experience that still links me more to the bizarre and crude analyses of, say, Franz Mehring, than to the most profound transcriptions of the realm of ideas, such as emanate today from Heidegger's school.[37]

These sentences define the method of Benjamin's materialist analysis of Keller's work. The Archimedean point, from which the critical project emerges and to which it returns again as its goal, is the critical subject itself. The critical subject's social experience defines its perspective; the goal is to achieve understanding of that experience through the medium of the similarly produced yet fundamentally different experience of the historical author.

As a materialist critic Benjamin first describes the material and ideological support received by Keller from the bourgeoisie of Zurich, his hometown. He explains the thoroughly unusual—for the 1850s—identity of interests between bourgeoisie and intelligentsia in terms of Switzerland's special development, which "retained for the longest time features of the pre-imperialist bourgeoisie in its higher social strata."[38] To the social identification of the storyteller still close to the "craftsman's mode of production" with the milieu of his origin there corresponds, in his work, the sensuousness of the descriptions, the love of concrete detail, in short, the realistic narrative style. Keller, so Benjamin argues, takes all things seriously in their earthly concreteness, which gives his writings their antique, unsentimental character. His world has been "reduced to a 'Homeric Switzerland.'"[39] In these words Benjamin attributes genuinely epic qualities to the nineteenth century storyteller, that is, homogeneity, organic structure, and sensuous fullness, such as were, according to Lukács's *Theory of the Novel*, characteristic of the Homeric epic.

Despite its historical and social precision, Benjamin's interpretation of Keller reveals itself as a nostalgic utopia. He invokes a harmonious condition, which has long since vanished in the confusions of the intensifying class struggles, indeed whose visions of material happiness were possible, even in the nineteenth century, only on the basis of the old-fashioned Swiss patriarchal system. The distant images of Keller's work stand—as Benjamin says, using the metaphor of a Keller poem—in the clear light of the "evening sun."[40] The melancholy that erupts into the critical text in such sentences, as well as the brilliant colors by which the realistic epic style is transfigured, testify to the longing of the intellectual outsider for social integration.

By grounding literary criticism in both materialist theory and the philosophy of history, Benjamin gives it a new function. For him it is no longer an element of the literary marketplace, nor is it a method of aesthetic evaluation; it is the place where he can accelerate the "politicization" of the writer, through the discussion of his or her task and function in the present day.[41] In terms of substance he achieves this end by imparting his own experiences in the social sphere. Thus when, in his great essay of 1929 on surrealism, he traces the awakening of its political consciousness and its engagement on behalf of proletarian revolution, he is speaking primarily of the history of his own politicization, which had received tangible expression in *One Way Street*. As a German intellectual he has, through the destruction of his privileges, reached a posture of opposition to bourgeois society and has "had to experience in his own life the totally exposed position between anarchistic *Fronde* resistance and revolutionary discipline."[42] But this experience enables him to unmask and destroy "the space made one hundred percent from images," in which in his view all social activity takes place. In contrast to the party political engagement of the surrealists, Benjamin's definition of the intellectual's task remains purely negative: the intellectual is "to organize pessimism" and to undertake the "dialectical destruction" of false images, from the projections of which social space is constituted.

With such formulations Benjamin transcends the localized political actionism of the surrealists, in order to identify the form of existence peculiar to the intellectual, his lonely thinking and critical self-awareness, as a political one. The destruction of false consciousness, which such an existence involves, is understood by Benjamin entirely in the spirit of his negative

Walter Benjamin.

theology in the book on tragic drama: as a power engaged on the overcoming of the world's bad, fallen temporality and the installation of a new one. To be sure, the object of Benjamin's critique is now no longer the symbolic work of art, but public consciousness itself, shaped by the intellectuals and leaving its residue in their writings. Thus the critic no longer sees his work as a preparatory meditation on death as an individual closing out of the fallen natural state, but as the furthering of revolution, that is, as the attempt to change, through solidarity and organization, the social condition whose sickly discharge is false consciousness. But, as Benjamin indicates by occasionally calling his revolutionary concept a "purification," his vision is quite other and more radical than that of orthodox Marxism: not the fulfillment of history through internal social change – but its messianic end, its closure.

The essay "Surrealism" was conceived as "a screen in front of the 'Parisian Arcades'"[43] the work that occupied Benjamin most intensively during the years 1927 to 1929, the time of his "elliptical life-style between Berlin and Paris."[44] He was still receiving powerful provocations from Aragon's *The Peasant of Paris*, a book which, as he once wrote, he could never read without his heart beating faster[45]; in response, his work on the *Arcades Project* was an attempt, in a "dialectical fantasy,"[46] to generate, somewhat as in the Moscow essay, a historico-philosophical perspective on his own time through a materialist description of the city's appearance. With the methodological premise that the streets were "the residence of the collective,"[47] he and Franz Hessel collected materials in Paris from April 1927 onward, for what was initially planned as a newspaper article. In the process Paris became more and more his true spiritual focal point: "Whereas, with my goals and interests, I feel quite isolated in Germany among people of my generation, there are specific phenomena in France – Giraudoux and especially Aragon as writers, surrealism as a movement – in which I see my own concerns at work."[48] Benjamin was indeed correct in identifying his own peculiar stance as that of an avant-gardist; his judgment was confirmed by the fact that only in the 1960s, in the wake of an intensive renewal of interest in surrealism, did the German literary public recognize the particular quality of Benjamin's work.

From the outset the essay on the arcades, which was to form the synthesis and conclusion of the materialist cycle begun with *One Way Street*, aimed at a new theory of history.[49] Starting from the disappearance of "one of the oldest arcades," the Passage de l'Opéra – the demolition of which had already inspired Aragon's book – and the solemn opening of a new one on the Champs-Elysées, Benjamin proceeds in his notes to describe these architectural forms, typical of the appearance of the nineteenth-century city, as

The Cairo Arcade, Paris.

secret temples in honor of the commodity.[50] In the process of uncovering the economic base of capitalist society in the image of the aging, glass-covered passages, he attempts simultaneously to render certain insights into the psychoanalytic interpretation of dreams fruitful for his own concept of history:

> The Copernican revolution in historical perception is this: people saw the "past" as the fixed point and the present as trying to adapt its own cognition to this given reality. Now the relationship is to be inverted, and the past is to be stabilized dialectically through the synthesis that the act of awakening accomplishes with the contrasting dream images. Politics receives priority over history. Indeed the historical "facts" become something that has just happened to us: to establish them is the task of memory. And awakening is the exemplary form of remembering.[51]

In these extremely compressed formulations Benjamin crystallizes for the first time thoughts that were to be of extreme importance for his entire later work. The historical manifestations of human society are conceived by him as dream images whose displacements it is the historian's task to decode. Like the Messiah at the end of time, the historian must rearrange the "demented" images and thereby endow the world with its true meaning.

The methodological difficulties involved in adapting this new conception to the more traditional mode of materialist analysis proved to be insuperable at this stage of the work. Hence its completion was repeatedly delayed. In May 1928 Benjamin reported from Berlin, where he had returned in November 1927, on the reasons why he could not leave the city at that moment: "First of all there's my room—and it's a new one, for I'm living for the moment not in Grunewald but deep in the Zoo District—in the Tents—in a room with nothing but trees looking through both my windows. . . . The work on the Paris arcades looks at me ever more enigmatically and insistently and howls through my nights like a small animal, if I haven't given it to drink from the most remote sources during the day. God knows what havoc it will wreak if I release it one day."[52] Towards the end of the year he had to acknowledge that the whole thing had expanded into a "philosophical Fortinbras, who will claim the legacy of surrealism. In other words: I am postponing very significantly the conclusion of the project."[53] Finally at the turn of the year 1929–30 he broke off the work altogether, taking it up again only in exile.

The *Arcades Project* had competed since its initial conception with Benjamin's quite different goal of learning Hebrew and going to Palestine. In August 1927 he had had a reunion in Paris with his friend Scholem, who had emigrated in 1923. Scholem had in the meantime become a lecturer in Jewish mysticism at the newly founded Hebrew University of Jerusalem and was currently visiting European libraries. He introduced Benjamin to Jehuda Leon Magnes, first rector of the University of Jerusalem. In the course of a lengthy conversation, Benjamin expressed, as Scholem recalls, "his desire to explore the great texts of Jewish literature through the medium of Hebrew, not as a philologist but as a metaphysician, and declared himself ready to come to Jerusalem for this purpose, either temporarily or permanently."[54] Looking back, Scholem himself confesses that he had been "surprised by the clear and decisive form in which Benjamin developed this thought. It was a living espousal of the chances of rebirth, which I like so many others hoped to bring about in the land of Israel, and only here, for the Jewish people and for Judaism, which I was then incapable of separating."[55] In retrospect one has to regard this project as nothing less than wishful thinking on Scholem's part and self-deception on Benjamin's, the latter having let himself be blinded by the enthusiasm, the outward success, and the spiritual consistency of his younger friend.

In the following months the project became defined more precisely in an active correspondence between Berlin and Jerusalem. Benjamin was to master the Hebrew language, studying first in Germany, then in Palestine. In March 1928 the plan had progressed to the point where Benjamin could write to Hofmannsthal: "The University of Jerusalem intends in the foreseeable future to set up the structures of an Institute for the Human Sciences. And in fact the plan seems to be to offer me the professorship in modern German and French literature. The condition is that I gain a solid understanding of Hebrew in two to three years."[56] The hope he expresses here for an academic career, which would have compensated him for his failed plans in Frankfurt, may have contributed to his taking this project seriously. Another factor was the prospect of a stipend to assist him in his Hebrew studies, which Magnes opened up during a second meeting in Berlin in June 1928. And in fact Magnes did indeed, to Scholem's dismay, have the whole amount of the promised support—said to have been several thousand dollars— transferred to Berlin in October, without Benjamin having begun his language studies. Benjamin kept postponing his agreed upon departure for Palestine, pleading work still to be finished: the arcades essay and a lengthy article on Goethe from a materialist perspective, which he had promised the editors of the Great Soviet Encyclopedia, and which he completed in October 1928.[57]

Moreover Benjamin's personal circumstances at this time were becoming unfavorable to his emigration plans. In November 1928 Asja Lacis returned to Berlin, where she worked in the film section of the Soviet trade mission. When Benjamin lived with her for a while, relations with his wife,

Dora Benjamin and son Stefan.

having been tense for a long time, shattered completely. During the year 1929, lengthy divorce proceedings were "conducted with the greatest bitterness on both sides,"[58] causing such physical and psychic pressure on Benjamin that in October he experienced another breakdown. "I could not telephone, could not speak, let alone write to anyone."[59] When the divorce became final in April 1930, Benjamin was ordered to pay Dora's substantial dowry back to her; according to Scholem it amounted to forty thousand marks.[60]

This separation from his own family took place at the same time as his final, long-delayed emancipation from his parental home. One can glimpse the entanglements binding Benjamin to his origins when one reads his essay on Julien Green, written in 1929, about which he writes to Scholem: "Your mention of Green gave me all the more food for thought, in that for some time I have been conscious that the constellations, at least in the family I come from, have a striking relationship to those one encounters in Green's novels. My sister can compete with his most unlovable female characters."[61] In his essay he identifies "the trauma of the sight of the parents in its double figuration as primal and as historical phenomenon" as "the recurrent motif of this author."[62] Many symptomatic aspects of Benjamin's own life suggest that he lived for a long time under the spell of the animal terrors haunting the inhabitants of "the house of the fathers, which stands in the double darkness of the immemorial and the barely past."[63] With his wife and child he continued to live in the parental villa until he was almost forty. His manic addiction to travel, his gambling passion, and the psychic breakdowns to which he frequently refers essentially constitute his despairing attempts to break this excessively strong tie. In February 1929, Benjamin's mother became seriously ill; she died on 2 November 1930. Her death finally gave her son the freedom to emancipate himself from his dependence on the parental home. One can regard it as a truly symbolic conclusion of his family ties that he found himself compelled to "hand over" his entire inheritance, in order to reduce the financial burdens resulting from the divorce.

This definitive breach with the past meant on the one hand even more material uncertainty: "it is not easy to stand on the threshold of one's forties, without possessions, job, dwelling, or resources."[64] But on the other hand it also meant his final release into the way of life for which he had shaped his existence from the outset: that of the outsider, living as an isolated individual exclusively through and for writing. Thus it is not surprising that he interpreted the events of 1929–30 as the "beginning of a new life."[65]

Under these circumstances Benjamin's involvement with Hebrew, for which in any case he could find little time because of his own writings, was completely pushed into the background. To be sure, in May 1929 he began daily language lessons with the Zionist rabbi Max Mayer, whom Scholem had recommended. He wrote to Jerusalem shortly thereafter: "As I said, I am taking two hour-long classes daily and have the grammar book with me at all times. For now, our home is in the grammar, but Mayer intends to move to reading material soon."[66] But already at the end of June he put it more narrowly in a letter to Hofmannsthal: "For two months I've finally been taking my plans seriously: I'm learning Hebrew. But it proved impossible to make this hiatus in my work into a completely symbolic change of life, as you so convincingly advised me to do in our first conversation. I could not leave Berlin. . . . In general the only difficult thing about the present situation is the alternation between studying and literary activity."[67] A few weeks later he left abruptly on a trip to Italy with the writer Wilhelm Speyer, letting his language studies drop completely and never again resuming them.

The decisive elements in Benjamin's hesitation and final abandonment of his plan were probably not so much the external circumstances stressed by Scholem, but rather, inner inhibitions. After all, his refusal to commit himself to Palestine strikingly echoes his refusal of Zionism in 1913, as outlined to Ludwig Strauss, and his plea for an establishment of the spiritual values of Judaism in the context of European culture. Scholem's disappointment at Benjamin's withdrawal was naturally great. He was also much affected by the fact, to him unforgivable, that his friend had accepted money from a Jewish organization, without fulfilling the promised commitment. Years later in the extreme existential menace of exile, Benjamin begged Scholem to facilitate his immigration to Palestine; the latter answered evasively and finally refused to support the move of his endangered friend.

Benjamin was thoroughly aware of the false situation in which he found himself in relation to Scholem. In the fall of 1929 he announced his arrival, one last time, for November, and once again failed to follow through. After an embarrassed three-month silence, he wrote on 20 January 1930 a letter of apology in his somewhat idiosyncratic French, attempting to give an account of the goals of his work for both himself and his friend:

> Dear Gerhard, you will doubtless think me crazy; but I feel such immense difficulty in breaking my silence and writing you about my projects that perhaps I'll never manage it without finding a sort of alibi, which is what French is for me. . . . I think I have to give up definitively the hope of learning Hebrew so long as I am in Germany; the work and the requests for work coming at me from all directions are simply too pressing, and my economic situation is too precarious for me to evade them completely. I am in the process of looking over the last two years, the time of my absence from Paris, and reckoning up what has been done during these months. Two things in particular, from what I can see. First I have established a situation, albeit a modest one, for myself in Germany. The goal I had proposed for myself is not yet fully realized, but at last I'm getting close to it. That goal is to be regarded as the premier critic of German literature. The difficulty is that, for more than fifty years, literary criticism in Germany is no longer seen as a serious genre. To make oneself a situation as a critic means basically

114

to recreate criticism as a genre. On this path serious progress has been made—by others, but above all by me. . . . But then by far the most important project is going to be my book on the Paris arcades. And unfortunately, for everything that concerns the book (which is in truth the theater of all my struggles, all my ideas), conversation seems to be the only viable communication. . . . What today seems to me an established necessity is that for this book, as for the one on tragic drama, I will not be able to do without an introduction on the theory of knowledge—and this time it will concern above all the theory of historical knowledge. It's there that I will find Heidegger in my path, and I anticipate some sparks to be given off by the impact of our two very different styles of conceptualizing history.[68]

Only during his exile could Benjamin return to the tasks sketched here. They held him in thrall until his death.

115

VI

Crisis and Critique: The End of an Era

1929–1933

In the last years of the Weimar Republic, which were overshadowed by the world economic crisis and the resultant rise of National Socialism, Benjamin was in fact able to assume the position to which he aspired: to be one of the outstanding critics in the German language. Not only did he succeed in publishing regularly in the two most important literary journals of the time, he also was increasingly faithful to his own precept, that the literary critic should function as a "strategist in the literary struggle." By utilizing his Paris and Moscow experiences for the analysis of German conditions, he raised the status of the ephemeral genre of book review, transforming it into a small-scale literary text that could serve to reveal the antinomies of public consciousness. Following the principle he himself had established in "Thirteen Theses on the Critic's Technique," he sacrificed "objectivity to the partisan spirit, when the subject of the struggle makes it worthwhile to do so."[1]

One target of Benjamin's critical polemic in these years is thus conservative and fascist theories of culture and society. In *Die literarische Welt* he disputes, under the title "Against Masterpieces," Max Kommerell's programmatic work, imbued with the spirit of the George circle, on "The Poet as Leader in German Classicism"; not without justice he sees in this a "magna carta of German conservatism."[2] In the social democratic periodical *Die Gesellschaft* (Society), he subjects the "theories of German fascism" to a withering critique, using as his example Ernst Jünger's mystique of war.

Surprisingly, his attack on the positions of the left intellectuals is if

116

anything more vehement than that against the right. To be sure he concedes that the radical bourgeois left has seen through the "impossible position" of intellectuals in the intensifying social conflict;[3] but he then makes the serious charge that the left is selling its insights for the mere amusement of a decadent public, instead of deploying them in the interest of social change. The polemic against the left intellectuals culminates in the review of Erich Kästner's poems entitled "Leftist Melancholy," scheduled originally for the *Frankfurter Zeitung*, but rejected by its editors because of its extremely aggressive tone. It was not published until 1931, in the periodical *Die Gesellschaft*, which was oriented toward the Social Democrats. Starting from an analysis of the readership of leftist poetry, which locates the readers in the intermediate class of upper-level officials and new-rich philistines, Benjamin categorizes the author Kästner's political position as "to the left of anything possible." Instead of making a contribution to the process of reaching fundamental social decisions, Kästner, typically for all the "radical left publicists of the stamp of Kästner, Mehring or Tucholsky," is accomplishing with his poems nothing but the transformation of the political struggle "from the urgency of decision into an object of pleasurable titillation, from a tool of social production into a consumer commodity."[4]

Benjamin's own position can be gleaned from these negative judgments. As he sums up, in exile in 1934, his experiences from the "literary struggle" of the Weimar Republic, literature is "to have an organizational function as well as and ahead of its character as a work."[5] This is particularly the case with literary criticism, which could thus become the instrument of social self-understanding on the part of those who write. In his review of Siegfried Kracauer's study *The Employees*, which appeared in 1930 in *Die Gesellschaft* under the title "The Politicization of the Intelligentsia," Benjamin comes the closest to fulfilling his functionalist intentions. In his elaboration of Kracauer's procedure, he demonstrates that the latter's analysis of employment structures in Berlin has the goal of unmasking false consciousness. For Benjamin the discrepancy uncovered by Kracauer, between the employees' proletarianized economic situation and their consciousness dominated by the obsolete cultural models of the bourgeoisie, signifies the extent of their self-alienation.

With this argument he translates Kracauer's situational analysis into the conceptual framework of Lukács's book *History and Class Consciousness*, in order thereby to ascribe a new function to it. Kracauer had wanted his book understood as providing information about an "unknown sphere" of social reality, as a "diagnosis" of bad conditions aimed above all at those directly affected—employees, employers, sociologists—having as its goal changes in the areas investigated through provocation of "public discussion."[6] Benjamin,

117

on the other hand, argues bluntly: "This study will have to renounce all hope of political impact as it is currently understood, which means demagogic impact." Instead he sees in it "a constructive theoretical indoctrination, directed neither at the snob nor at the worker, but consequently in a position to achieve something real and demonstrable: the politicization of the author's own class."[7] Behind this assertion lies the accurate awareness that literature, especially the sociological kind, is read only by intellectuals, hence can only achieve an impact by advancing the social self-understanding of these readers.

For Benjamin the author of the study of employees represents the "typical embodiment of the unhappy consciousness."[8] Behind this sociological mask, Benjamin the melancholy author of *The Origin of German Tragic Drama* is again discernible, dialectically extracting cognitive possibilities from his unhappiness at a marginal existence without practical impact. As an outsider who has lost his unquestioning identification with the class of his origin, he is able to assume the role of analyst of the general neurosis. As in the *Arcades Project*, "contradictory" social consciousness is understood "according to the schema of repression."[9] The intellectual, as expert interpreter of collective "image production," has to uncover the mechanisms of repression, in order thus to help society as a whole toward self-identity.

Benjamin's review, outlining the social character of the intellectual, becomes condensed in its last sentence into an image that captures its message as in a prism. The author appears as "a ragpicker in the gray early morning, poking with his stick at the ragged ends of speeches and scraps of language, then tossing them, grumbling, stubborn, a trifle intoxicated, into his barrow, not without mockingly letting one or another of these bits of faded cotton, such as 'humanity,' 'inwardness,' or 'depth,' flutter in the morning wind. A ragpicker, early–in the gray dawn of the day of revolution."[10] What Benjamin described elsewhere as "subterranean communication of the intelligentsia with the dregs of the proletariat" appears here as an allegorical image, in a motif from Baudelaire's poem "Le vin des chiffoniers" ("Ragpickers' Wine"); the possibility of such allegory is based no longer on metaphysical structural homologies, as in the book on tragic drama, but on class relations. The ragpicker can represent the author because, like him and like his object of investigation, he has fallen out of the two great class groupings, bourgeoisie and proletariat.

The multiple levels of Benjamin's critical prose can only be fully comprehended, however, when one becomes aware that, even in the sociological allegory, theological overtones can still be heard. The ragpicker is presented as a critic of language, similar in his gestures to the "Angelus Novus" whom Benjamin has repeatedly invoked in his texts since 1920; history

Benjamin, ca. 1931.

hurls its rubble at the angel's feet, but the storm from paradise is caught in his wings. This emblematic analogy suggests that the critic Benjamin, even in the most extreme secularization of his language, adheres secretly to the eschatological conception of revolution and the revolutionary's task.

By becoming sociologically concrete, allegory for its part acquires a political dimension. By equating intelligentsia and rag-picking proletariat, Benjamin is negating the central dogma underpinning the cultural work of the German Communist party in the league of proletarian-revolutionary writers. In the formulation of Johannes R. Becher, in his 1928 statement of principles, "The Party and the Intellectuals," the intellectual must, through daily political organizational work and submission to party discipline, turn himself into a proletarian, in order to be able to write revolutionary literature.[11] Benjamin contradicts this explicitly, although without naming his target, when he insists "that even the proletarianizing of the intellectual almost never produces a proletarian. Why not? Because the bourgeois class endowed him from childhood with a tool of production in the form of culture (*Bildung*), which impels him, on the basis of cultural privilege, into solidarity with his class and, perhaps more important, makes the bourgeois feel solidarity with the intellectual."[12]

Behind this opposition to the official party line stands an extremely precise analysis of the actual political situation. It is striking that the review speaks exclusively of those social groups most vulnerable to seduction by national socialism: the ever-increasing mass of people driven out of the bourgeoisie and the proletariat, namely the "Lumpenproletariat": the unemployed, the intellectuals, certain groups of employees. To enlighten these groups concerning their social status, to tear them away from self-alienation, hence to save them from the threatening self-abandonment to national socialism: this is the task Benjamin assigns to the revolutionary intellectual. Even if, in the circumstances, these proposals could not be translated into practice, they are yet based on an illusion-free grasp of the situation and reveal Benjamin's ability, well before 1933, to see through the self-deceptions of official Communist politics. Already in October 1931 he writes with amazing perceptiveness to Scholem:

> Germany's economic order has a base as stable as the high seas, and the emergency measures cut across one another like the crests of waves. Unemployment is about to make the revolutionary programs as antiquated as is already the case with the economic-political ones. For it appears that, with us, the de facto representatives of the mass of unemployed are the National Socialists; the Communists have so far not found the necessary access to these masses, which alone could make possible revolutionary action. In every concrete sense the representation of worker interests, because of the existence of the fantastic army of the unemployed ("Reservearmee"), is becoming more and more a reformist undertaking and presumably could hardly be managed any differently by the Communists than it is by the Social Democrats.[13]

In the intricate mixture of sociological insights with reflections on reception and indicators of political action, the Kracauer review exemplifies Benjamin's journalistic production in these years. The same elements are present more or less markedly in all the reviews and give them a density unique to occasional texts of this kind. That applies also to his radio scripts, which he had been writing several times a month since August 1929 for the Berlin radio and the Southwest German Radio in Frankfurt, often producing the presentation himself. In Berlin until spring 1932 and in Frankfurt until January 1933, that is, until the political infiltration of the radio stations by the Nazis, Benjamin produced a total of eighty-five broadcasts, among them radio plays; a series on the city of Berlin conceived for young listeners; lectures on Hebel, George, Brecht, and Kafka; and the "practical radio pieces": (*Hörmodelle*) conceived jointly with the journalist Wolf Zucker. In these latter the listener was offered practical guidance for everyday life by means of a dialogue situation.[14]

Benjamin's activity as a radio journalist was far from being merely an extra job for the purpose of making money. As one of the pioneers in this new medium, he may have gained here the experiences that enabled him, in the great essays written in exile, to formulate a theory of non-auratic art. In his practical pieces and radio plays, even in his literary lectures, he tried to use the technical apparatus of reproduction to work against "the limitless spread of a consumer mentality" and to provoke the listener, through the way he presented his broadcasts, to a productive autonomy.[15] A broadcasting system refunctionalized as a medium of dialogue would fundamentally "overcome the separation between broadcaster and public," thus becoming the model for a new "people's art."[16]

The enlightenment tradition in which he was placing himself with these "Reflections on Broadcasting," is evident in one of Benjamin's earliest radio scripts, a 1929 portrait of the writer Johann Peter Hebel. He characterizes the popular writer of calendar stories as an "actualizer," in the process describing his own attitude as a journalist. As Hebel tells his stories in such a way that "the anecdotal, the criminal, the comic, the local fact as such becomes a moral theorem," so Benjamin also strives to tie his political morality to everyday situations "in which people must discover it for themselves." Thus the transformed broadcast becomes for him "the continuation of the epic by other means," in an age over which Hebel's "Goddess of the French Revolution" no longer hovers but which exists in the shadow of that far more radical goddess glimpsed directly by Benjamin himself during his visit to Moscow in the winter of 1926–27.

The attempt to transform an apparatus dedicated to entertainment and distraction into a communicative instrument that would advance the self-enlightenment of the public was then, as now, a utopian dream. However, it was a utopia whose social significance was even more undeniable than that of the didactic plays through which Bertolt Brecht was simultaneously trying to endow the theater with an enlightenment function. Benjamin's work in journalism and media politics in these years is in fact increasingly defined by his intensive exchange of ideas with Brecht. He had become acquainted with Brecht in May 1929 through Asja Lacis. Brecht had at that time just gained notoriety as the enfant terrible of the Berlin theater world through the success of his *Threepenny Opera*. In June Benjamin wrote to Scholem: "You will be interested to hear that very friendly relations have recently developed between Bert Brecht and myself, based less on what he has done, of which I know only the *Threepenny Opera* and the ballads, than on his present plans, in which one cannot but be interested."[17]

The "plans" to which Benjamin is referring are the first volumes of Brecht's new periodical *Versuche* (Experiments), in which the earliest didactic plays, some Keuner stories, and the Fatzer fragment were published. Here the critic Benjamin saw for the first time, in the medium of avant-gardist poetic texts, the confirmation and implementation of his theory of a functional literature. Thus it was not surprising that he repeatedly recommended Scholem to read these volumes as an index of current conditions of literary production in Germany. To the uncomprehending silence from Jerusalem he finally responded with the admission that to talk about them was "especially significant because these texts are the first, of a poetic or literary kind, to which I give as critic an unreserved (public) endorsement; because part of my development in recent years has been governed by my interactions with them; and because they, more than any other texts, give a penetrating insight into the spiritual context within which the work of someone like myself is carried on in this country."[18]

Benjamin's public comments on Brecht refer thus primarily to the first volume of *Versuche*. In a lecture broadcast on June 27, 1930, on the Southwest German Radio in Frankfurt, he introduced to his listeners "Bert Brecht, the educator, politician, and organizer," with the latter's alter ego, Herr Keuner, being the archetype of the "leader" (*Führer*). "He is simply quite different from what one usually imagines as a leader; not at all a rhetorician, demagogue, producer of effects, or tough guy. His chief concern seems infinitely distant from what one might think would preoccupy a leader today. Herr Keuner is in fact a thinking man."[19] The confrontation of the literary figure with the political seducer appealing to the instincts, whose actuality could not have escaped any listener in 1930, generates, in Benjamin's view, the political application of the Keuner stories. They are to provoke ques-

Walter Benjamin at the time of his first meeting with
Bertolt Brecht.

tions, questions about the defective thinking of politicians and the political interests of thinkers, in short, as Benjamin puts it, "robust questions." By offering a formulation of these questions, the critical text fulfills the task of bringing the poetic text's productive intentions into the open, thereby placing the public in the "disquieting position of having to think for itself." This radical inversion of the communicative situation is Benjamin's response to a political state of affairs that threatens to rob the individual of all autonomy.

The other two texts on Brecht from these years also stress the political dimensions of his work. In the "Brecht Commentary," of which parts were published in the *Frankfurter Zeitung* for 6 June 1930, a poem from Brecht's *Fatzer fragment* is linked to political conditions in the Soviet Union. The

Bertolt Brecht, 1929.

essay "What Is Epic Theater?" provides, on the occasion of the 1931 Berlin performance of *A Man's a Man*, a first theoretical balance sheet on Brecht's new dramatic form and performance practices. In the process Benjamin recalls the arguments of his book on tragic drama, when he assigns Brecht's didactic theater and his un-tragic hero to a tradition, whereby "straight through the sublime but sterile immensity of classicism the legacy of Medieval and Baroque drama has come down to us."[20] In this historical projection Benjamin expresses both his knowledge of the obsolescence of the autonomous artwork and his awareness of being the first to have grasped theoretically this secular rupture.

Insisting on the "literary transformation of the theater," whereby it will develop its organizational function, Benjamin even sees the advent of the end of criticism:

124

If the theater's aesthetic ceases to be in the background, if its forum becomes the mass public, and its yardstick not its quantum impact on the nerves of individuals but the organization of a mass audience, then criticism in its current form is no longer ahead of this mass audience but remains far behind it. In the moment when the mass differentiates itself in debates, in responsible decisions, in making reasoned arguments; in the moment when the false, masking totality "the public" begins to disintegrate, revealing at its center the division into political parties that corresponds to genuine social relations—at that moment criticism experiences the double misfortune of seeing its function as mediator disclosed and at the same time rendered superfluous.[21]

This argument is clarified when one remembers that the utopia of criticism's self-transcendence is based on the model of the "political association of Russian writers." What Benjamin had experienced in the Soviet Union as the effect of the proletarian revolution, he anticipates in Germany from the dialectical-materialist renewal of the theater, whereby paradoxically he in fact renews the "idealist misery" into which German classicism had escaped in the face of the French Revolution. On the other hand, this ideological overestimate of literature's impact also retains its element of historical truth: through the secret correspondence between his own times and the historical conditions prevailing in Germany at the end of the eighteenth century, it becomes comprehensible that Brecht could subsequently attain the status of something like a "classic of modernity."

The intensive collaboration between the author and the critic led in 1930 to the project of a journal, the program of which Benjamin had worked out "together with Brecht in long conversations." It was to bear the characteristic title *Crisis and Critique*.[22] Surviving notes from these conversations reveal that the two men were at one concerning the basic function of criticism: "to teach interventionist thinking," hence to restore "theory to its productively justified role."[23] As the notes categorically phrase it: "Criticism is to be understood in such a way that it would be the continuation of politics by other means."[24] However, whereas Brecht wanted the critical function of thinking to be tied to "what can be achieved in a given society," Benjamin insisted that there had "always been movements, in earlier times primarily religious, which like Marx instigated a radical destruction of society's icons." He therefore suggests "two research methods: 1. Theology. 2. Materialist dialectic."[25] This remark makes it clear that the politicization of Benjamin's thinking, which found its most visible public expression in his endorsement of Brecht, in no way involved renouncing his "theological genius," as several of his friends, especially Scholem, feared. Rather, in his collaboration with Brecht he continued on a new level that sequence of ex-

125

emplary relationships, which had begun with his friendships with Fritz Heinle and later Florens Christian Rang, and in which a central concern was always also the confrontation between German and Jewish thinking.

In November 1930 he announced to Scholem: "When I next write you will receive the manifesto and guidelines of a new journal called *Crisis and Critique*, which is to be published bimonthly by Ihering at Rowohlt-Verlag, and will appear for the first time on January 15 with myself, Brecht, and two or three others named as co-editors. It will fill you with ambiguous satisfaction to see me listed as the one Jew among nothing but goyim."[26] However, because of financial and organizational difficulties, above all because of disagreements among the editors about conceptual questions, the paper did not survive the project stage. At the end of February 1931, Benjamin resigned as co-editor, justifying his move in a letter to Brecht: "The journal was planned as an organ in which specialists from the bourgeois camp were to portray the crisis in scholarship and art. The purpose of the undertaking was to show the bourgeois intelligentsia that the methods of dialectical materialism were mandated by necessities peculiarly their own – necessities of spiritual production and research, necessities of their very existence."[27] When it appeared that the first contributions received did not correspond to these, his most committed intentions, Benjamin, with uncompromising consistency, resigned his editorship.

The misunderstandings that repeatedly afflicted Benjamin's relations with Brecht as well as with Scholem derived from his exceptionally daring enterprise of unifying in his critical thinking the extremes of Judaism and dialectical materialism. Whereas in his journalistic writings – which he dictated rather than wrote out by hand, implying their lesser status in his mind[28] – he presented himself primarily as a materialist historian and politician, he strove in the great literary-critical essays of these years for a synthesis of theological and materialist dialectic.

In April 1930 he signed a contract with Rowohlt for the publication of a volume that would collect his most important essays, thus documenting for a wider public his claim to be the second founder of literary criticism in Germany.[29] The planned book was to contain among other work his essays on surrealism, Keller, Proust, Green, and Brecht. In late 1930 and early 1931 he wrote what was to be its centerpiece, the essay on Karl Kraus, which among his Weimar writings represents the most radical attempt at a synthesis between early theological and materialist thinking. It received advance publication in March 1931, in the literary section of the *Frankfurter Zeitung*. However the planned book publication was not to be. In 1931 the Rowohlt-Verlag had to stop all payments after the collapse of its bank, and the newly founded holding company, controlled by Ullstein, implemented only financially profitable ventures,[30] something Benjamin's books had never been.

When Benjamin sent the essay on Kraus to Scholem in February 1931, he himself pointed out the links of this text with his early writing: "Here is a draft of 'Karl Kraus,' on which I have worked an immensely long time, almost a year and, during the last month, to the complete exclusion of all personal and material commitments. You will see rising before you all kinds of concepts from a period which, God knows, we can perhaps already call our 'youth.'"[31] Among these concepts are those expressed by the titles of the three dialectically related parts of the essay. In the first part Kraus appears as "cosmic man," because he possesses the capacity "to treat social relations, without deviating from their reality, as natural relations, indeed even as paradisiacal," thus restoring the degraded human creature to its original condition.[32] In the second, antithetical part, Kraus is invoked as "demon," insofar as he himself is in league with nature, and nature's ambiguity overshadows his writing, as suggested by the polarity in his work between "mere spirit" and "mere sex." Finally he is categorized as "Non-Human (*Unmensch*)" because, in his satirical quotations and in the role playing of his readings of operetta, he tears language out of the ambiguity and fraudulence to which it is subject in the newspapers and daily business of culture, thus elevating himself far above merely natural humanity.

This synthesis is to be understood in the terms of Benjamin's negative theology, whereby the critical strategy of citation, like the allegorical process described in the book on tragic drama, is a metaphor for an event in the history of redemption. The quotation "summons the word by its name, wrenches it from its context and, in doing so, calls it back to its origin. . . . In the word thus emancipated is mirrored the language of the angels wherein all words, shaken out of the idyllic context of meaningfulness, have become mottos in the book of Creation."[33]

However, at a further level of meaning, the critic gives a materialist foundation to this theology of pure naming through an analysis of economic and social circumstances, delivering the following charge against Kraus: "That human dignity is not viewed as the destiny and fulfillment of liberated nature—nature changed by revolutionary rupture—but rather as a given element of nature understood as archaic and ahistorical in its unbroken primal being: this sets his idea of freedom and humanity in an uncertain, uncanny light. This idea is not emancipated from the realm of guilt, which he has traversed from pole to pole: from spirit to sex."[34]

Benjamin's critical text compensates for what he diagnoses as the reason for this defect, Kraus's lack of insight in the "sociological realm," by no longer accepting the linguistic decline and general decay of the bourgeois

Karl Kraus, ca. 1930.

world, which Kraus rails against in his journal *Die Fackel* (The Torch), as something given in nature; rather, it can be shown to be the consequence of the prevailing social organization. Benjamin demonstrates that the newspaper language so bitterly fought against by Kraus necessarily results from the discrepancy between the extraordinarily increased possibilities for technical reproduction and the social structuring of these possibilities in the interests of private capital. Benjamin interprets the writer and the whore, who embody "mere spirit" and "mere sex" in Kraus's work, as allegorical figures, enabling the reader to perceive the transformation of the human being into a "manifestation of the exchange of commodities."[35]

From this materialist analysis, which for the first time in his work draws expressly on Marx's early writings, Benjamin concludes that "genuine humanism," as opposed to "classical" humanism, can only be achieved through revolution.[36] This insight remained inaccessible to Kraus: "But that the emergent human being comes into true existence, not in the natural realm but in the realm of humanity, the realm of freedom; that he is recognizable by the response which the struggle against exploitation and need exacts from him; that there is no idealistic but solely a materialist emancipation from myth; that it is not a pure state which stands at the origin of creation, but a purifying event—all this has left traces in Kraus's genuine humanism only in its very latest phase."[37] In the more clearly materialist manuscript version of the essay the concluding phrasing is more accurate: " . . . has left no traces at all."[38] The difference between the two versions suggests that, in the form of the essay, Benjamin is also criticizing his own earlier thinking. It is above all in his own work that the "materialist emancipation from myth" has left traces only in its later phase.

But even this materialist approach is not Benjamin's final word. The concept of "purification," which here as in the early "Towards a Critique of Violence" designates the social function of revolution, points to a further horizon of meaning. Using the example of the newspaper degraded by "high capitalism," Benjamin argues that one should expect from "a force overcoming capitalism" neither the renewal of classical style nor "a new blooming of cosmic, paradisiacal humanity." "From the present ruling class the new one will be quite distinct, in that it will put the ideals which the rulers have degraded out of operation."[39] In contrast to Marx, revolution is thus the negation of the already lived, the rupture of a bad history. Benjamin gives an idea of the horizon that would make this meaningful, in the final passage of his text: "Neither purity nor sacrifice have been able to master the demon; but when the originary and the destructive find one another, at that point his rule is over. His conqueror stands before him as a creature that is both child and cannibal: not a new human being but a Non-Human, a new angel. Perhaps one of those who, according to the Talmud, are created anew in countless numbers every instant, only to cease existing after they have raised their voice before God, and to dissolve in nothingness."[40] Here again, and not for the last time, Klee's picture and Jewish legend are fused in order to mark that critical point in Benjamin's thinking at which the revolutionary destruction of the existing order can be interpreted as messianic preparation of a new age free of domination.

In Benjamin's Kraus essay all the motifs of his previous work are assembled in a kind of summary. He demonstrates how the profane text can be read as a sacred one, by driving its worldly elements into their extreme form, into the sheerly material, in order thus to rescue them theologically. Hence the compression of interwoven motifs, the multiplicity of overlapping levels of meaning, the magisterial certainty with which language is addressed and everything assigned its name. Kraus's reaction to the essay was disappointing. He dismissed it polemically, with ostentatious incomprehension, as "psychoanalysis."[41]

Scholem in contrast was provoked by the essay to argue, in several long letters, with Benjamin's materialism, of which he declared that it stamped on Benjamin's "production at this time the mark of adventurousness, ambiguity, and sleight of hand."[42] Against these furious attacks from Jerusalem, Benjamin advanced tactical considerations:

> But I ask you, as I sit here in my little writing factory in the middle of Berlin's western district, do you really want . . . to prevent me, with the argument that it's nothing but a piece of fabric, from hanging the red flag out my window? Even if one writes "counter-revolutionary" pieces—as you call mine, quite correctly from the party's point of view— must one go further and expressly place them at the disposal of the counter-revolution? Shouldn't one rather denature them, as one denatures alcohol—at the risk of making them foul tasting to everyone— make them definitely and reliably foul tasting to the counter-revolution?[43]

However, he hinted at his real intentions, which are to be understood as disguised perpetuations of Jewish traditions, in a letter to his acquaintance Max Rychner, editor of the *Neue Schweizer Rundschau*. Referring directly to the Kraus essay, he wrote: "I have never been able to think or do research except in what might be called a theological framework—namely in accordance with the Talmudic doctrine of the forty-nine levels of meaning in every passage of the Torah. Now: in my experience the stalest communist platitude has more levels of meaning than current bourgeois profundity, which always possesses only the one level, apologetics."[44]

Benjamin himself viewed the few years between the onset of the world economic crisis and the Nazi seizure of power as the high point of his life. Not only had he consolidated his professional situation and, for the first time, fulfilled his vocation as a critic working in Brecht's circle, he had also, after emancipation from all familial entanglements, found his way to a personal life-style that suited him. An important element of this was his occupation of his own studio apartment in October 1930, at 66 Prinzregentenstrasse in Wilmersdorf:

> As to my study itself, it's not yet fully equipped, but it is beautiful and livable. All my books are here and even in these times they have increased over the years from 1200 to 2000—and I certainly haven't kept all the old ones. This study has its peculiarities: for one thing it has no desk; in the course of time, because of a variety of circumstances, not only my habit of working a lot in cafés but also certain associations

haunting the memory of my old desk-writing ways, I have reached the point of writing only while lying down. From my predecessor I inherited a sofa of the most wonderful qualities for working–for sleeping it's pretty useless.[45]

To this picture of new-found existential security belongs also the quest for new experiences, which Benjamin sought in smoking hashish since 1927 and with special intensity in the years 1930–31. Under the scientific supervision of two doctors, Ernst Joël and Fritz Fränkel, and sometimes in the company of Ernst Bloch or other acquaintances, he would take a previously fixed dose of the narcotic and note down his sensations during the intoxication. These notes, on the basis of which he planned to write a book on hashish, try to crystallize the "cognitive yield" from absorption and trance, and reveal vividly traits of an aesthetic mode of existence such as was characteristic of Benjamin's life-style at the time.[46]

Happily he notes the fluid connectedness engendered by intoxication, in which he knows himself to be "at the center of all excesses": "People and things relate to each other at such times like those elderwood props and elderwood figures in a glassed-in tinfoil box, which have become electric through rubbing of the glass and now, with every movement are propelled into the most bizarre juxtapositions with each other."[47] The person at the center of these narcotic images experiences his own being as that of an omnipotent essayist with the world at his disposal, ceaselessly projecting new configurations in the kaleidoscope of his text.

> To come closer to an understanding of the joy of intoxication, one must re-think the story of Ariadne's thread. . . . We are going forward: but as we go we not only discover the bends in the cave into which we are penetrating, but experience this joy of discovery only on the basis of that blissful counter-rhythm which consists in the unwinding of a skein. Such certainty about the ingeniously woven skein, which we are unwinding–is that not the joy of all productivity, at least in prose form? And in smoking hashish we are prose beings enjoying our existence at its highest potency.[48]

The feeling of professional and emotional independence finally achieved leads Benjamin to an admission surprising for someone almost forty years old: "I could say–and certainly material difficulties have their part in this–that I seem to myself to be an adult for the first time in my life. Not only no longer young, but adult, in that I have virtually realized one of the many forms of existence that were latent within me."[49] But the image of the intellectual who has found peace after outward storms and lives only for his work–this image is deceptive. The extent to which the delight in hashish-

Portrait of Benjamin by B.-F. Dolbin.

smoking has to be seen against a dark background can be gleaned from a sentence written in the state of hashish intoxication on 18 April 1931: "No one will be able to understand this intoxication, the will to awaken has died."[50] The deep longing for death expressed here can be found also in diary entries Benjamin made in May and June of the same year on a trip to the Cote d'Azur in the company of the popular author Wilhelm Speyer, later also of Brecht and his circle. At the very beginning of his notes written at Juan-les-Pins, he speaks of his increasing readiness for suicide. As reasons he names the German political situation, his "war weariness on the economic front," but also the feeling of having lived a completed life. In conversation with Speyer and his cousin, the doctor Egon Wissing, he mentions the "three great love experiences" of his life, meaning the relationships with Dora, Jula, and Asja, which, he feels, nothing comparable could follow.

Shortly afterward he begins further notations under the title "Diary from August 7, 1931, until the day of my death": "This diary promises not to be very lengthy. Today came Kippenberg's refusal of the offer to take over the essay volume; thus my plan acquires the immediacy which only hopelessness can give it. . . . But if anything can increase still further the resolve, indeed the peace with which I contemplate my intention, then it is the intelligent, dignified use of the last days or weeks."[51] These words suggest a resolution of the contradiction between the relaxation evident in Benjamin's attitude in these years and his secret longing for death. As he already indicates in the essay on *The Elective Affinities*, death destroys on the level of the individual the bad condition of the world, in the same way that he expects revolution to accomplish the destruction on the cosmic level. Hence he feels drawn to death, anticipates it in joyful guise through intoxication and through writing, both being ways of turning away from life, through which life is at the same time given back to the subject in a purified and intensified form.

The distance from his previous life was manifest in still another fashion: Benjamin began to write down memories of his childhood. The impetus came from a contract signed in October 1931 with the *Literarische Welt*, wherein he committed himself to deliver "a Berlin chronicle of between 200 and 300 lines for each quarter of a year."[52] During the winter spent in Berlin in distracted and generally unproductive activity, the first notations "that concern the history of my relationship with Berlin" came into being.[53] In April 1932 he broke away from the situation in Berlin, which he found less and less satisfying, and boarded a freighter from Hamburg to Barcelona, from where he journeyed to Ibiza for a stay of more than three months. Here he continued his work on the autobiographical notes. The completed parts of these memoirs, which remained fragmentary and were edited for publication by Gershom Scholem for the first time in 1970 under the title *Berlin Chronicle*, contain a continuous narrative of events from Benjamin's childhood and school days, and from the time of the Berlin youth movement.

The stay at Ibiza, were he could "live under tolerable circumstances in a beautiful landscape for no more than 70 or 80 marks per month," was for Benjamin something like a voluntary anticipation of exile. It seemed to him a "commandment of reason to honor the opening ceremonies of the Third Reich through absence."[54] At the end of July 1932, shortly after his fortieth birthday, he returned to France from the island, in order to put into effect, in a hotel in Nizza, the long-considered plan to commit suicide. The final impetus for this resolve probably came from the fact that, because of the gradual takeover of power by the Nazis, particularly since Papen's coup d'état in Prussia on 20 July 1932, opportunities for work were increasingly closed to him. In a letter to Scholem of 26 July, he spoke of "the deep tiredness" that had overcome him. His works, he said, were "victories in details to which, however, correspond defeats in important matters"; in the

133

latter category belonged particularly the uncompleted books *Parisian Arcades, Collected Literary Essays*, and "a highly significant book on hashish." These constituted "the real site of the ruin or catastrophe" of his life.[55]

A day after this despairing inventory Benjamin drafted his will, in which he bequeathed all his manuscripts to Scholem. In a letter he named Eugen Wissing as his executor and wrote short farewell notes to Ernst Schoen, Franz Hessel, and Jula Cohn, the people who had been closest to him in life. In the letter to Jula Cohn he says: "You know that I once loved you very much. And even at the moment of death, my life has no greater gifts to offer than those provided by the moments of suffering through longing for you."[56]

It remains unclear why, after these declarations and detailed preparations, he did not carry out the deed. Some light may be shed by the final sentence of a brief notation written a year earlier: "The destructive character lives on the feeling, not that life is worth living, but that suicide is not worth the trouble."[57] In any case immediately after this crisis Benjamin began the revision of the *Berlin Chronicle* into *Berlin Childhood*. In early August he travelled to the Italian spa Poveromo, where together with Wilhelm Speyer, he worked until mid-November on a detective drama. The first short prose texts, characteristic of his autobiography in its published form, were produced on the side. On 26 September he wrote to Scholem about his new book (although Scholem had spent the summer in Europe, Benjamin, despite protestations to the contrary, had avoided meeting him): "It is not only a slim volume, it is one made out of small pieces: a form to which I am constantly driven both by the materially endangered, precarious character of my production and by concern for its marketability. . . . You will have noticed that these childhood memories do not at all constitute a chronological narrative, but represent individual expeditions into the depths of memory; I am hopeful that they will be able to appear as a book, perhaps with Rowohlt."[58] These lines clearly express the tendency that dominates the revision of the text from *Berlin Chronicle* to *Berlin Childhood*. The resulting work is discontinuous, seeking to emulate, in its brief sections, the mystic rapture of the single moment, the remembered moment of childhood as well as the lived moment in which the remembering adult gains power over his past.

After his return to Berlin in the winter months of 1932–33, Benjamin continued to work on his book. In February 1933, just after the Nazi seizure of power, he sent the completed manuscript, containing thirty texts, to Scholem in Jerusalem; this too was a symbolic gesture, an attempt to rescue his threatened childhood from the assault of those who had definitively destroyed its historical basis.[59] At the same time he sold it to the

Wilhelm Speyer, 1930.

Frankfurter Zeitung, which published three series, totalling twelve pieces, in February and March 1933, with six further single texts appearing under pseudonyms between then and August 1934. In the first year of his exile he added further sections to the planned book, and then in 1938, with renewed hope of publication, revised it again "thoroughly," reducing it once more to thirty texts.[60] The longed-for publication in book form of this, his most personal work, did not, however, occur until after his death, in an edition produced by Theodor W. Adorno in 1950.

The proximity of the basic experience shaping *Berlin Childhood* to the experience of death is clear, even if Benjamin had not specifically drawn attention to it in his "Lecture on Proust, delivered on my fortieth birthday," in which he says of the "mémoire involontaire" (involuntary memory): "And it is in fact the most important images, those developed in the darkroom of the lived moment, which it enables us to see. And that completed life which, as we often hear, passes before the eyes of the dying or the person in danger of dying, is composed precisely of these tiny images."[61] Benjamin

135

gives in these sentences the most exact historical location of his own remembered images. They are inspired by Proust's *A la Recherche du Temps Perdu* (Remembrance of Things Past). But the narrative continuity that is guaranteed by Proust's bourgeois identity and hence guarantees his identity as an author, is shattered in the extreme situation of threat to the individual's life and of threat against whole classes and racial groups. In the face of death the author awakens to the truth of his absolute abandonment in the historical world and situates the totality of his past life in the constellation of childhood memories grasped in momentary flashes.

The desperate historical situation in which Benjamin found himself at the time of writing *Berlin Childhood* is traced backward in the book's texts to its beginnings in his earliest childhood, for example in the third-from-last piece "The Moon." There he takes up the penetrating sketch of the child awakening in the night, with which Proust opens *A la Recherche*, and rewrites it. In both texts we read of the boy's frequent awakening and resultant terror in the middle of the night. But however similar the two scenes are in themselves, their outcomes differ significantly. Proust's youthful protagonist at first feels "more helplessly exposed than a caveman" and finds in "his soul in its most primitive form that sense of simply existing which an animal may feel at the center of its being." But he succeeds in collecting himself with the return of consciousness, thus strengthening his own identity: "In a second I traversed centuries of civilization, and out of vague images of petroleum lamps and shirts with open collars my individuality gradually recomposed itself with its original features."[62] On Proust, then, human history appears as the organon with the help of which the narrator's subjectivity assures itself of its unity. The story of Benjamin's child awakening in the moonlight ends otherwise. Not only does the world sink into "non-being," the child's existence becomes profoundly questionable as it is thrown back upon itself. Through the destruction of the child's sense of his social integrity, the text characterizes the author's own precarious situation and attributes Benjamin's social alienation to his childhood experiences.

Thus in every text of *Berlin Childhood* the author is doubly present—at the beginning of his life and in the historical moment of his writing. In the preface of the planned book edition of 1938, Benjamin asserts that "the images of a big city childhood are perhaps capable of containing, preformed within themselves, later historical experience. It is evident in these images, at least I hope it is, to what extent the remembering persona later forfeited the security which had been granted to his childhood."[63] The doubling of the authorial self, wherein the self is both divided into the extremes of the beginning and the virtual end of life and projected in its underlying unity, is mirrored objectively in Benjamin's method in these memoirs, of dissolv-

Benjamin in Ibiza, 1932.

ing the ambivalent twilight of the historical world into the extremes of light and dark. Nature appears in the paradisiacal light of an imagined childhood and simultaneously in the "ashen light" of this world in its disintegration – this formulation occurs in the "Imperial Panorama."[64] In "The Victory Column," history reveals itself both as the "hell" of the defeated and as the festival of peace of an "eternal Sunday."[65]

This Janus face of experience, its simultaneity of futility and utopia, is given expression both in the realm of the child's experience and in that of the adult. Boxes of bricks, sheets of sticky paper, and toys are evoked as allegorical images of a better world; funny postcards and children's verses as images of guilt and death. On the other hand Benjamin cites the reading experiences of the cultured bourgeois, for example Dante's *Inferno*, in order

137

to illustrate the darkness over which the victory column is raised. In a rhythmically structured sentence at the end of "The Victory Column"– "Creatures of such blissful caprice were the people above in the light"– Benjamin covertly echoes the classical formulae of the emancipated life, from Goethe's "Song of the Fates" to Hofmannsthal's poem "Some there are . . . " ("*Manche freilich . . .*").[66] Yet these apparently irrefutable meanings, sanctioned by the classical tradition, are secretly undermined by the child's repeated self-identification with the oppressed and defeated, and his consequent actions contravening the canonized values. In the text "Christmas Angel," the child, in solidarity with the poor courtyard dwellers, only feels close to the Christmas tree when it is lying in the courtyard without leaves or decorations; in its "glory" it was alien to him.[67] And the Christ child, whose return is invoked in a carol, conceals the coming of the angel who could transform history. Under the child's anarchic gaze what is socially sanctioned appears as negative, what is despised and forgotten as the bearer of hope.

The attempt to construct a unity from extremes is revealed to be the structural principle in the volume's penultimate text, which bears the programmatic title "Two Brass Bands" and in which Benjamin gives his method a philosophical justification. The "dehumanized, shameless" music of a "military orchestra" near the zoo is confronted with "another music," to which the boys skated in the winter on the New Lake.[68] Here, where an artistic medium of expression is at issue, the spheres are clearly separated from the outset. On the one hand music is aligned with "natural" nature, mingles with the rutting cries of the animals in the nearby zoo, and forms the background for the guilt-ridden awakening of sex. On the other hand music inspires the movements of the young skaters, as they describe their circles on the pure ice surface. It is characteristic of the treatment of music in *Berlin Childhood* that this positively invoked music not only is experienced "much earlier" in the boy's life, but also is recalled in a manner that is again inseparable from literary echoes. The very name "Rousseau Island" evokes a utopian nature in the innocence of childhood; and the description of the New Lake reinforces this effect by conjuring up, through a merging of the seasons, a timeless idyll.

Finally Benjamin alludes here too to classical texts, to Klopstock's odes "The Ice Race" and "Winter Joys" and to Goethe's celebration, referring to these odes, of ice-skating in the twelfth book of *Poetry and Truth*, where he praises the "ever-renewed vigor" that it imparts to the body.[69] To be sure, in contrast to the classical optimism that art could achieve conciliation between human being and absolute, Benjamin insists on art's ambiguities. As long as art remains in thrall to nature, it can have no humanizing impact.

138

Only when it is interwoven with the playful world of early childhood does it generate that image of utopia, which has been distorted shamelessly into its commodified antithesis in the daily life of the adult world. Only to that "other music" does Benjamin ascribe the power to reconcile the whole human being, body and soul, with nature. "From the island the music accompanied me a little of the way homeward": in this, the text's last sentence, the word *homeward* alludes, in a variation of Ernst Bloch's well-known remark, to that home toward which we are all forever travelling but in which none has yet lived.[70]

The later version of *Berlin Childhood* reveals that the work as a whole is also structured through binary oppositions. The polarity controlling the entire book is enacted in the first text "Loggias" as a poetological introduction. Here the child appears as ruler of the courtyards. He is at home in this place of poor people, where nature and art are perceptible only in a residual state. Enthroned above the courtyard in his loggia he feels "as if in a mausoleum which had long been assigned to him."[71] These words anticipate the ambiguity of the remembered childhood; for the mausoleum embodies both death and royal dignity. Furthermore, being empty, it is a mere sign and as such expresses the specific quality of allegorical images, out of which *Berlin Childhood* is constructed. These images renew the allegory of the randomness of human existence and the subjectivity of all projections of meaning.

The book that follows such an overture collects primarily at the outset the texts stressing the happiness of childhood, its paradisiascal character, while toward the end the experience of nothingness becomes ever more pronounced. This sequence characterizes the historical development. At the beginning those texts dominate that present the security of late-nineteenth-century society as dreamlike yet not overtly threatened. The conclusion however, to cite the title of one of the later texts, is filled with "Misfortunes and Crimes." One cannot help perceiving, in the ghosts and outbreaks of fire, in the bands of robbers and murderers who at the end loot the parental home with the adults looking on helplessly, the child's presentiment of the destruction of the bourgeois world by national socialism.

But even this negative experience does not represent the last word. In Benjamin's world the condition of radical danger is ultimately the only possible salvation. This messianic paradox is frequently formulated in the texts themselves: biographically, when the tardiness and failures of the schoolboy are interpreted as guaranteeing his later existence as an outsider; sociologically, when, to the child as "ruler of the courtyard" in his alliance with the poor, the angel of history appears; mystically, when the child, contemplating his postcard collection, sees light breaking out of the darkness. For Benjamin's messianism, what is despised and wretched is transformed into its opposite and becomes the bearer of hope. It is in this sense that one must also read the "texts of destruction" constituting the work's conclusion. The multiple aspects of destruction function for the author as guaranteeing the possibility of that paradise that could be glimpsed in anticipation in earliest childhood.

Thus negativity and positivity are fused in this book through a structure of "dissonant harmonies." And it is altogether characteristic of Benjamin's dialectical materialism that, at the end, the antithesis stands without conciliation. As in most of his writings, most clearly in the book on tragic drama, one can discern in *Berlin Childhood* a two-stage dialectical structure, whereby the transcendence of the contradiction in a synthesis is withheld—left open as the reader's task.

The five texts following "Loggias" amplify the ambivalence of the introductory text by contrasting the infernal and messianic moments of the child's life-world. They are organized in a circular sequence, with the text "The Telephone," which evokes as the central childhood drama the oedipal confrontation with the father, placed in the center of the group. The child experiences the telephone as his "twin brother," with the same fate in store for it as for himself. Both are initially subjected to the father's violence: a second Zeus, he threatens the whole world with thunder and lightning through the medium of the telephone. However the telephone, at first banished to the darkest corner of the hallway, "like a legendary hero exposed to die in a ravine . . . makes its regal entry into the cleaner and brighter" rooms of a younger generation; and the son too succeeds in eluding the father's domination, by allying himself with the new technology.[72] He abandons himself willingly to the voice from the telephone. It nullifies all "consciousness of time, duty, and purpose." Like Kafka's land-surveyor K., who on the evening of his arrival in the village telephones the castle and hears mysterious sounds that cast a spell on him, so the author of *Berlin Childhood* lets himself be lured out of everyday life by the telephone. His confused escape from the order of the paternal world certainly leads to his failure in practical life, but also guarantees the hope for a "regal entry" into another, better life.

Around this center are grouped the texts "The Victory Column" and "Butterfly Chase." If in the first of these the child's experience of world history is thematized and broken down into its eschatological poles, in the second the same is true of his experience of nature. The child's pleasure in the butterfly chase becomes an allegorical image for the closeness of all nature to death. The child, in his hunting and collecting zeal, is subjected to it also, as the "spirit of the creature dedicated to death" enters into him.[73]

The Victory Column (in winter) of which Benjamin wrote:
"O Victory Column, baked to perfection, ornamented with the sugar of
winter out of the days of childhood."

Thus he experiences the basic law of all unredeemed nature, which is ruled
by "delight in killing." Following his own philosophy of language derived
from the beginning of Genesis, Benjamin compresses the utopian counter-
world within the name of the vacation spot, a name drenched, for the
remembering author, in the blue air of his childhood summers. This air contains a promise: "Hence the Potsdam of my childhood is enveloped in blue
air, as if its Camberwell Beauties or Admirals, its Orange Tips and Peacock
Butterflies were scattered over one of the gleaming Limoges enamel plates,
on which the turrets and walls of Jerusalem stand out from the dark-blue
background."[74] More openly than virtually anywhere else the eschatological content of the early experience is named in terms of the ancient promise
to the Jews, but again not directly, only in the mirror of a sacramental art,
which redeems nature and transfigures it as primal model of a better world.

The outer ring of this group of five is formed by the texts "Imperial
Panorama" and "Tiergarten" (Zoo District). The first text evokes, through
the memory of the widely accessible panoramas at the turn of the century,

The Tiergarten in Berlin (in summer) at the end of the nineteenth century.

the space of an imaginary childhood in Aix-en-Provence. Even these dreams of travel, provoked by the painted scenery, summon the child "homeward," then suddenly reverse their meaning, when through a lighting change "the landscape lost its color," and offer a glimpse of the nothingness of the world. The description of the technology of these old-fashioned "arts" provides a poetological linkage to Benjamin's own procedures.

> There was no music in the Imperial Panorama. But for me a tiny, actually disruptive effect seems superior to all the fraudulent magic. . . . That was a ringing that started a few seconds before the picture was moved off backward, opening first onto a gap, then onto the next picture. And every time it resounded, a profoundly melancholy mood of departure bathed the mountains down to their foot, the cities with all their windows blank as mirrors, their remote, picturesque inhabitants, the railway stations with their yellow smoke, the vine-clad hills down to the smallest leaf.[75]

The sobriety of Benjamin's own writing style is characterized here, as is the meaning of the book's construction, its brief texts separated from one another by "gaps." These neutral intervals are the places where the author, who otherwise refrains from all sentimental or psychological commentary, surrenders to his "nostalgia" and endeavors to communicate to the reader an insight into a past irretrievably lost because of social change.

To these journeys into an imaginary world there corresponds in the final text of the group a journey to the end of the world, marked by the pillars of Hercules. The child gets there however only after he has traversed Western history in the Tiergarten and in the old Western district, where Benjamin grew up. By articulating time as compressed into a child's experiential space, hence immobilized, the text enables the child to contemplate simultaneously, in multifaceted images, the myth-realm of the ancient Gods, the cold beauty of the aristocratic world and the work ethic of the bourgeoisie. A second Theseus, guided by the red thread of Eros, the child penetrates into the labyrinth, into the primal vision of the world that opens before him in the grounds of the Tiergarten district. The child gains his first aesthetic experiences from the statues of King Friedrich Wilhelm and Queen Louise, as well as from the small flowering paradise in which his fellow student Louise von Landau lives until her early death and which later becomes a cenotaph to her memory. Work, finally, which for the child takes place at school, confronts him in the stairwell of the parental home in the allegorical figure of a woman who translates the promise contained in the visions of love and beauty into tenets appropriate to the bourgeois era: "Work is the citizen's adornment / Blessing is his toil's reward."[76] But like the worlds of myth and art, work also fails to keep its promise. Like everything else it is overshadowed by death and it is thus understandable that the child holds himself apart in all of these worlds, identifying with none of them. This distance enables the author, on his return to Berlin thirty years later, to rediscover the utopian surplus contained in the images of his childhood and to reformulate it as text. Thus "Tiergarten" ends with the transformation of its landscape into the ancient garden of the Hesperides, the timeless paradise from which Hercules, model of the suffering and laboring human being, is able to extract the golden apples of promise.

In the text Benjamin's materialist messianism is realized within the picture-puzzle of the child's imaginative capacity and at the same time transcended. With extraordinary methodological awareness, the historical origin for this transformation of history into myth is also fitted into the text.

> When, thirty years later a person experienced in these fields, a peasant of Berlin, took an interest in me and returned to the city with me after we had together spent a long time away from it, his path traversed this garden, in which he sowed the seed of silence. He went down the steps

143

> ahead of me, and every one was steep to him. They led downward, if not to the mothers of all being, then certainly to the mothers of this garden. His steps caused an echo in the asphalt as he stepped onto it. The gas illuminating our pavement cast an ambiguous light upon this ground.[77]

The peasant of Berlin, with whom Benjamin had lived in Paris at the end of the 1920s and subsequently returned to Berlin, is Franz Hessel. Benjamin borrows his honorific name from Aragon's book *The Peasant of Paris*, which was so important to him and where the "capital of the nineteenth century" is portrayed as a "labyrinth without a minotaur." A double historical context is thus established. First, Hessel is accurately named as a mediator of the surrealist tradition in Germany. At the same time Benjamin also places himself in the ranks of those who have learned the "fine art of the flaneur" in Paris in order to practice it as dream-walking in the far coarser atmosphere of the capital of the German Empire.

If the figure of the father stands at the center of the first five texts, which show the child in his epoch, the following seven, in which the child emerges in his developing individuality, are unmistakably defined by the figure of the mother. At the middle of this group is placed the text "At the Corner of Genthiner and Steglitzer Streets," in which Benjamin's ancestors on his mother's side, represented by his old aunt Lehmann, and their places of origin in Brandenburg and Mecklenburg are evoked. In this maternal world, work becomes a game for the child, an object of contemplation, as in the model of a mine constructed in the Biedermeier style, through which the child grasps the social meaning of work and at the same time its "mystical" content, such as the Romantics had ascribed to the figure of the miner. Against this bourgeois mystique the child reacts at the text's end with an open expression of solidarity with the old serving women: "They were mostly . . . more massive and powerful than their mistresses, and it seemed to me that the parlor itself, despite mine work and chocolate, had less to say to me than the vestibule where the old helper, whenever I came, took my coat from me as if it were a great burden and, whenever I left, pressed my cap onto my forehead as if she wanted to bless me."[78] In "Tiergarten" blessing had been both announced to the child in the stairwell—and withheld from him, by the allegorical image of Work; here he receives it from the archaic, motherly figure of the old servant.

The three texts preceding this humanization of work within the mother's zone make visible the child's gradual emancipation from the realm of paternal domination. This realm is defined above all as the school, where the teacher rules as substitute father. "Tardiness," the title of the first of these seven texts, designates the child as an outsider in this paternal world. His name is "taken" from him by the teacher and he has to "labor" without it until the end of the hour. "But there was no blessing in it."[79] Thus the child loses, through not fitting in at school, what had been promised him at the end of "Tiergarten"—to rediscover it, transformed, in the mother's friendlier world.

The matriarchal principle, cryptically heralded in the last text of the first group of five, where Hessel led the author onto paths that brought him "if not to the mothers of all being, certainly to those of this garden," now becomes increasingly the decisive aspect. "Boys' books" are now for the child not only the beloved "trashy novels" from the school library, enabling the boy to continue the exotic journeys begun in "Imperial Panorama"; more particularly, they are the strange books that he encounters in dream. "To open one would have led me into the middle of the womb, where a dim and changing text was clouding up, pregnant with colors. They were seething and evanescent, but always turned into a shade of violet that seemed to emanate from the entrails of a slaughtered animal."[80] Reading, absorption in a book, is here a return to the maternal womb from which, in the seething colors of primal chaos, the world is given birth. The child, familiar with the scene from dreams, escapes into it, is at home there. At the same time there may be concealed in this description of dreambooks an allusion to the source of such cosmological imagery, which may have reached Benjamin through the books he read by Ludwig Klages in the early 1920s.

In third text of the group, "Winter Morning", the attributes of the maternal world are equally unmistakable. The scene is dominated by the figure of the nurse, who elsewhere is given the archaic name of "maiden" (*Magd*). She appears as guardian of the fire, on which the boy gazes from the secure hollow of his bed. The promise hidden in this scene is concentrated in the aroma of the baked apple, which, "familiar and yet changed," becomes the child's consolation on his path into the cold world.[81] The despair endemic to that world then overwhelms him with full force at his school desk. With this motif, the negative realm of the first text of the group is recalled. In general, all the texts are secretly linked through such thematic interweaving. The apple, ancient attribute of the mother goddess Demeter, had previously been granted to the exemplary laborer Hercules; here it has taken on the quality of the messianically transformed world. With a slight textual shift, such as will befall the world on its last day, it can become a sign of utopian hope.

The concluding twist, whereby this childhood memory is interpreted as the desire "to be able to sleep late," a desire fulfilled in the insecure position of the free-lance critic, brings once again a mother figure into play:

the good fairy who fulfills all wishes, thus prefiguring the following text: "At the corner of Genthiner and Steglitzer Streets," where the aunts appear as "fairies whose influence pervades a whole valley, although they never descend into it."[82] The child knows he is protected by them, in their care he escapes the anonymity and work pressure of the paternal world.

In the texts analyzed here Benjamin makes his own biographical actuality transparent by means of a primal history defined as gynocratic. As in Bachofen's writings, with which he had early become acquainted through Klages, but read more intensively only in 1934, the archaic maternal world is presented as a counterimage to the work-obsessed, achievement-oriented society, which is perceived as a threat to the self. This society's principles are again represented by the school in the text "Two Enigmas": the school's essence is actualized allegorically in the figures of two teachers. From the consonants in the name of Fräulein Pufahl, the catalogue of virtues of bourgeois society is read off in the manner of Hebrew writing: "The P with which the name began was the P of duty (*Pflicht*), punctuality (*Pünktlichkeit*), and top student (*Primus*); f meant obedient (*folgsam*), industrious (*fleissig*), and absolutely correct (*fehlerfrei*); and, as regards the l at the end, it was the figure of pious (*lammfromm*), praiseworthy (*lobenswert*), and studious (*lernbegierig*)."[83] Against this the child, with his intricate dialectic, erects a symbol of death at the center of the life perverted by school, namely the cenotaph of his dead schoolmate Louise von Landau. The other teacher, Herr Knoche ("Mr. Bones"), glorifies death in battle through a recitation of Schiller's "Horseman's Song." And against the death thus equally perverted he erects a symbol of life through the misunderstanding of an expression from Schiller's poem: "das gewogene Herz." In the context of Schiller's poem, it means "the heart put to the test in battle," but the child understands it as "the affectionate heart." The child's symbols, both marked by love, are "two enigmas to which life will continue to owe me a solution," signs of a different world order that remains unrealized.[84]

In the next to the last text of the group, entitled "Market Hall" (*Markthalle*), the reference to Bachofen is most overt. As the child's distortion of the name into "Mark-Thalle," evoking the Greek word for *sea (thalassa)*, already implies, the principal Berlin shopping center on Magdeburg Square is transformed in this text back into a primal "swamp world." There the market women appear as "priestesses of the commercial Ceres, sellers of all fruits of tree and field, of all edible birds, fishes and mammals, procuresses, untouchable colossi in woolen knit dresses."[85] In these mythological invocations the allusion to the condition of hetairism is unmistakable: the critical point of the text is that this condition is installed in the heart of commodity capitalism itself. When Benjamin states in his 1934 essay on Kafka that "he did not consider the age in which he lived as an advance over the beginning of time,"[86] the statement applies equally to himself. "An experience penetrating more deeply than that of the average citizen," namely the experience of the child, reveals the mythic structures still present in even the most advanced social forms. That enlightenment has not yet taken place at all is the virulent conceptual core of this critique of capitalism.

The group of seven texts concludes with "The Fever," which binds together and intensifies all the preceding motifs. Here the child's illnesses are understood as an escape from everyday existence; in them he develops and exercises his saturnine patience. In this exceptional situation, mother and child are especially close. As storyteller she acquires almost magical healing powers. She tells the child stories about the body, and the child reenacts them in his shadow play under the bed covers. With a clear allusion to the image of the cave through which Plato articulates his doctrine of ideas, Benjamin suggests the continuity of those shadow images that constitute *Berlin Childhood* itself. Like the storyteller in a preindustrial society, the mother hands on to the sick child "the life story of an ancestor, grandfather's rules for living."[87] She thereby overcomes the generational barriers erected by death and creates a tradition in which the narrator of *Berlin Childhood* still views himself as standing. His place in life is of course quite different from his mother's naive one. As the child causes shadows to be silhouetted against sheets and wall, fixing things in their outline while cancelling their living substantiality, so the narrator of his Berlin childhood conjures up a realm of the dead. It is at the cost of life itself that he succeeds in making visible the essence of his historical epoch, in the context of the primal history that still prevails.

Thus the child's self is already playing the role of "world destroyer," which only fully becomes part of the adult through the function of the critic as "destructive character." In this context, then: "incipit vita nuova," a new life began for me, as the author puts it, alluding to Dante's famous programmatic text. The social meaning of this new life is revealed to the child at the end of his illness, when the beating of carpets, reaching his ears from the courtyard, becomes the music of the new age. Here, as in other texts of *Berlin Childhood*, it is identified as the "idiom of the underclass": The critic's future work is thus assigned its social location.[88] The text's final ironic twist, wherein the many school hours missed because of illness are reckoned as equally many "medals of honor" for the child, simply expresses his rejoicing at having so often outwitted the paternal world of the school. In this text, then, which concludes the book's first part, a shadow world is constructed under the protection of the mother; as negation of natural life, this world corresponds to Benjamin's deepest intentions.

By inserting after the thirteenth text in the Paris typescript version the two pieces "Sexual Awakening" and "The Carousel," which are not listed in the table of contents, Benjamin drew attention to the compositional principle dividing the two parts of the work. Depending on how they are counted, the seventeen or nineteen texts that follow can also, when read closely, be seen to divide into groups of five or seven shaped by parallel motifs and structural repetitions. The final two texts, "Two Brass Bands" and "The Little Hunchback," stand alone, in symmetry with the opening text, as syntheses of the method and content of the whole.

"Work on good prose has three steps: a musical one on which it is composed, an architectonic one on which it is built, finally a textile step on which it is woven," writes Benjamin under the attention-catching title "Watch Out for the Steps!" in *One Way Street*.[89] The author did indeed carry out, in *Berlin Childhood*, the method thus prescribed. The work is not only carefully composed, with a constant recurrence and variation of a few specific themes; it also follows a structural plan, which can be shown to sustain the meaning of the whole. Thus the first double grouping of five and seven texts, making with the introductory piece a total of thirteen, is balanced by an exactly comparable sequence at the end: first a group of five arranged around "Crooked Street" as centerpiece, then a group of seven with "Misfortunes and Crimes" at its center, and finally "Two Brass Bands" standing alone, raising the work's fundamental polarity to a conscious level and thus closing out the series.

The "woven" quality of the whole becomes evident in that the pieces positioned at a given point in the second sequence in many cases stand as polar opposites to their equivalents in the first. Thus "Crooked Street" situates sexual awakening in relation to reading as that activity in which the youthful self has found its own identity and hence has eluded the domination of the paternal world to which it had been subject in "Telephone." The peacefully enclosed zone of the bourgeois house, which in "At the Corner of Genthiner and Steglitzer Streets" enveloped the child in security, is shown, in "Misfortunes and Crimes," to be inwardly endangered. The transformation of the world into a shadow realm, presented in the final text of the first sequence under the aegis of the mother in the fullness of her positive potentiality, reveals in the final text of the second sequence its total negativity under the aegis of the moon. World and self have fallen equally into the void. Thus the "world-destroyer," as the self of the first part had recognized himself to be, is himself extinguished. Only when one views this event in its relation to the whole structure, as negation of the negation, can one glimpse in it that possibility of hope it doubtless possessed for Benjamin.

Between the two sequences of thirteen, Benjamin placed a group of five functioning as a hinge. At the center of these is again an emblematic text, "The Otter," the animal that symbolizes the lightning eruption of memory from the undersea realm of myth. Grouped immediately around this core are "The Carousel" and "Peacock Island and Glienicker," two texts displaying the child in his dynastic, hierarchical function, thus recalling the dominating images of the first part. Finally another pairing is formed by the first and last pieces in the group, "Sexual Awakening" and "News of a Death," which anticipate central motifs of the second part.

"Thirteen: I experienced a cruel pleasure at stopping on this number." This sentence of Marcel Proust served Benjamin as a motto prefacing a sequence of thirteen short texts in *One Way Street*.[90] It could also preface *Berlin Childhood*, which, in its Paris version, is structurally dominated by the number thirteen. As the frequent changes in the order of texts during the book's composition testify, the author was not guided by any kind of chronological, sequential outline. Rather, he gave himself over to an aleatory procedure, by means of which he playfully rearranged the existent text material in constantly varied sequences, resembling the multiple orderings of his early sonnets. To these constellations based on number games can be applied what Benjamin said in the *Arcades Project* concerning the composition of Fourier's and de Sade's works: "One must understand that Fourier's harmonies do not depend on any inherited numerology, like those of Pythagoras or Kepler. He spun his numbers completely out of himself and they give the harmonies something remote and hermetic: They surround the harmonies like barbed wire. Le bonheur du phalanstère est un bonheur barbelé."[91] The envisioned happiness of *Berlin Childhood* is also "remote and hermetic." It is of little importance that one can decode, in the number thirteen, the meaning ascribed to it in apocryphal Jewish tradition: namely that the Twelve and the One are contained in it, meaning the present-day world to which the Messiah is added as the element that revolutionizes it. "Out of thirteen comes redemption."[92]

The reader should however recognize that in such idiosyncratic constructions Benjamin was armoring himself against the dissolution threatening him in the time of rising fascism; at the same time he displayed his threatened subjectivity, giving the readers a suggestion as to how they could defend themselves against a comparable dissolution. The ambivalent structure of the whole, corresponding to the ambivalent imagery of every individual text, signifies to readers that they—like the child and the author renewing himself through the child—can and must free themselves from the dream of their own epoch through working productively on themselves, extracting the constructive elements from the given textual material, in

149

order to awaken in the true space of history. Benjamin's autobiographical texts thus summon the past at the moment of extreme historical danger, when the bourgeois epoch is dissolving into the National Socialist era, in order to gain for himself from the past the strength to resist, as one individual, the truly terrible present.

VII

Emigration:
The Theory of Non-Auratic Art

1933–1937

On 17 March 1933 Benjamin left Berlin on the urging of Gretel Karplus, later Theodor W. Adorno's wife. After a brief stay in Paris with Jean Selz and his wife, with whom he had become acquainted the summer before on Ibiza, he sought out his old island refuge. He felt driven to this flight not by direct physical threats, but by the cultural-political consequences of the Nazi seizure of power, which meant for him the end of all opportunities for work and publication. From Paris he wrote soberly and realistically about his circumstances:

> The situation is better understood in terms, not of individual terror, but of the overall cultural state of affairs. Concerning the former it is difficult to be sure of anything absolutely reliable. There are unquestionably numerous cases in which people have been dragged out of their beds at night and mistreated or murdered. . . . In my case it is not this situation, which has been more or less predictable for a long time, that has brought the decision to leave Germany, conceived only a week ago and without any definite shape, to such rapid fruition. Rather, it was the almost mathematical simultaneity with which from all the relevant places manuscripts were returned; pending, sometimes almost completed, negotiations were broken off; inquiries were left unanswered. The terror directed at any attitude or mode of expression that does not completely correspond to the official one has reached a virtually unsurpassable level.[1]

Benjamin in Ibiza, in a drawing by Jean Selz, 1933.

On Ibiza Benjamin resumed his old way of life. He lived in the simplest circumstances, with acquaintances or in an unfinished rough brickwork house, toured the island in the company of a young man, Paul Gauguin's grandson, flirted with a woman whom he even thought of including in his "angelology," and, among other projects, worked with Jean Selz on the French translation of *Berlin Childhood*.[2] As soon became clear, the boycott of his writings in Germany was less total than he had feared initially. Thus both the *Vossische Zeitung* and the *Frankfurter Zeitung*, the latter as late as 1935, published his reviews and short prose, of course under various pseudonyms. From this income and also from the sale of an extensive autograph collection, transacted by an old acquaintance in Berlin, he was able to finance his extremely frugal way of life on the island. Only toward the end of September when, weakened by the "depressing food" and a feverish inflammation, he returned to Paris with an acute case of malaria, did the wretchedness of exile strike him with full force. As he wrote to an acquaintance on 20 October:

> In the meantime I have conquered the fever, and the exhaustion . . . leaves me with just enough strength to become aware of the bleak situation, but in no way enough to overcome it: I cannot even climb the stairs of the cheap hotels among which I must select my place of residence. What is done here by and for Jews can perhaps best be described as negligent charity. It combines with the hope of alms—seldom fulfilled—the highest degree of humiliation, and it provides constant food for thought, for former members of the bourgeois class, to study the outposts of that class concerned with Jews.[3]

A stipend of 700 francs per month, granted him from February to April 1934 by the Alliance Israelite, was all that Benjamin received from this quarter.[4]

His central concern from this time on was to open up new possibilities of publication, hence of earning income. If from the outset he judged the "chances of work in France" to be very dim, events were to prove him only too correct.[5] A cycle of lectures on "L'avantgarde allemande" (Kafka, Bloch, Brecht, Kraus), which he planned to give by subscription in March 1934 in a private Paris salon, had to be cancelled at the last moment.[6] The essay on Bachofen, which he wrote in French in early 1935 for the *Nouvelle Revue Française*, was finally rejected by the journal that had commissioned it.[7]

The exile press turned out to be equally inaccessible. His review of Brecht's *Threepenny Novel*, already set in type for *Die Sammlung*, was returned without comment by Klaus Mann, when he dared to ask for an honorarium of 250 francs instead of the 150 offered. Only near the end of the 1930s did he succeed in placing a few reviews and a sequence of texts from *Berlin Childhood* in Thomas Mann's journal *Mass und Wert* (Measure and Value). Here too his analysis was confirmed, to the effect that in exile "the disorganization of the market-place . . . has left only belletristic writing with some chances of success."[8]

Benjamin had placed greater hopes in the Communist press. He had, to be sure, set aside in early 1934 a study on Baron Haussmann planned for the party newspaper *Le Monde*, because of the "all too unreliable impression" that the editors made on him.[9] However that did not prevent him from inquiring a year later, through Asja Lacis and Egon Wissing, about the possibilities of work in the Soviet Union. Above all it was his opinion that the Communist public constituted the real forum for part of the work he was doing at the time. Thus he had hopes that his programmatic essay, "The Work of Art in the Age of Mechanical Reproduction," could, through

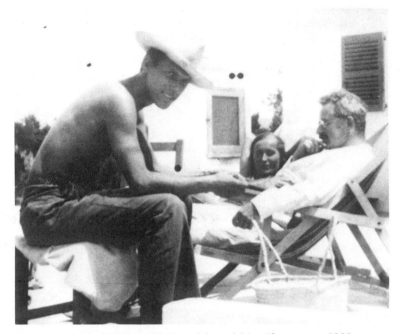

Benjamin in Ibiza with Jean Selz and his wife, summer 1933.

Bernhard Reich's mediation, be printed in the German edition of the Moscow journal *Internationale Literatur*.[10] It was his desire to make the essay known as his contribution to the discussion of Marxist aesthetics being conducted at the time as a "debate on expressionism" (*Expressionismusdebatte*). When the editors of the journal, sworn to defend socialist realism, rejected his contribution, Benjamin had to admit with resignation that the essay would "accomplish the least in the place where it really belongs, in Russia."[11] Only in 1936 did he succeed, through Brecht's intervention, in placing the first part of the *Paris Letters* in the Moscow organ of the Popular Front, *Das Wort* (The Word). However the second part, commissioned by the editorial board, to which Brecht belonged, was not printed, and all Benjamin's efforts to place the second version of his "Work of Art" essay or his Brecht commentary with the journal remained unsuccessful.

Hardly more effective were Scholem's attempts to instigate publication opportunities for his friend-in-need with Jewish publishers and journals. He did succeed in persuading Robert Weltsch, editor-in-chief of the *Jüdische*

Rundschau, with a circulation of 40,000 the largest German-Jewish publication after 1933, to commission from Benjamin a commemorative article on the tenth anniversary of Kafka's death. To its author's great disappointment however, the article, which he felt formulated a central theme of his thinking, was printed only in excerpts. In the fall of 1934 Benjamin had to inform Scholem: "When I tell you that Weltsch deemed it appropriate to pay me an honorarium of 60 marks for the fragmentary (cut by half) printing of the Kafka essay, you will understand that for me the intensive involvement with purely literary subjects has probably come to an end, given the fate of the Kafka essay."[12]

No further works by Benjamin appeared in the Jewish press. Weltsch had expressed his reservations from the start since, as Scholem reported his opinion, "'not a soul' among the readers would understand you, thus it could only be a piece for a small circle (which to be sure exists) of people willing to make an effort linguistically and intellectually."[13] Equally fruitless were Scholem's efforts to have his friend employed as author or editor with Schocken Books or to interest the publisher Schocken in the book publication of the complete Kafka essay.

Thus, Benjamin's standpoint outside all political parties and ideological camps had the consequence that in exile his always-difficult working conditions as an author became radically worse. The only serious work opportunity remaining to him was his link with the Institute of Social Research, directed by Max Horkheimer. Early on the institute had transferred its endowment capital to Holland and in 1933 had emigrated from Frankfurt to Geneva, and a year later to New York. Before his exile, in late fall 1932, Benjamin had already met with Horkheimer. The impetus came from Adorno, one of the few younger intellectuals to have recognized Benjamin's philosophical importance early on. At this first discussion with the director of the institute, Benjamin had agreed to write "a sociology of French literature" for publication in the newly founded *Zeitschrift für Sozialforschung* (Journal for Social Research). This essay, which Benjamin wrote with a bare minimum of source material available during the summer of 1933 on Ibiza, appeared in the journal's first 1934 issue, under the title "On the Present Social Position of the French Writer." In each of its subsequent volumes until 1937, Benjamin is represented with a substantial essay and several reviews. In the last edition to appear in Europe, the double issue 1/2 of the 1939–40 volume, his last essay "On Some Motifs in Baudelaire" was published, together with his introduction to Carl Gustav Jochmann's "On the Regression of Poetry."

For the very reason that in exile Benjamin was almost exclusively dependent for work on the Institute of Social Research and its organ of publica-

Max Horkheimer.

Theodor W. Adorno.

tion, tensions and differences of opinion arose with its directors in New York. Out of concern for the institute's difficult position abroad, Horkheimer instigated numerous alterations and cuts of entire sections in Benjamin's essays; the latter protested vehemently every time. The publication of the three completed chapters of the Baudelaire book was denied by Horkheimer and Adorno without possibility of compromise because of fundamental philosophical and methodological reservations; Benjamin thus had to undertake a completely new version. In spite of the annoyance and the humiliations to which he thus found himself exposed, he always sought to absorb the editors' objections, in all essential points, into his own thinking. "To me your suggestions are of course authoritative," he responded on 29 March 1936 to Horkheimer's proposals for cutting the "Work of Art" essay.[14] A decisive element in this attitude was probably his solidarity with the theoretical and political positions of the inner circle of members of the institute. For him as for them, the key task was to rescue the European cultural tradition, threatened as it was by destruction, by transcending it through an unorthodox, materialist style of thinking. Moreover during the years of exile Benjamin's friendship with Adorno, nourished by the latter's help in practical matters, above all in financial dealings with the directors of the institute, and by his involvement in theoretical questions, had deepened to the point where for a time he was Benjamin's only serious intellectual counterpart. In March 1937 Benjamin writes: "Given the isolation in which

156

I find myself here, not so much in my life as in my work, these visits from Wiesengrund (Adorno) are doubly valuable for me." Similar sentiments are found frequently in his letters. There were thus many good reasons for paying close attention to the objections reaching him from New York.

Nevertheless a certain mental reserve on Benjamin's part is perceptible. Thus he concludes the discussion with Horkheimer on the "Work of Art" essay with this assurance: "And when I say I am ready to make amends for the misunderstanding, I hold firmly to the hope . . . that a misunderstanding is really all that is involved. . . . Let me conclude with the hope that the loyal image, which you hitherto had of my relations with you and with the institute, may be fully restored without any blurring from these events."[15] This almost servile apology suggests that, in regard to the institute, Benjamin found himself hard pressed. For one thing he had learned by bitter experience to make concessions in order to achieve publication of his texts, which for him was absolutely the first priority. Thus he commented in a letter to Brecht on Klaus Mann's rejection of his review of the *Threepenny Novel* in 1935: "I would of course have accepted Mann's unreasonable demand, had I anticipated the result. I have shown myself to be not shrewd enough for this world, at the very moment when shrewdness would have been very valuable to me."[16] Subsequently he indeed became more shrewd and yielded to the objections of the institute's editors, in order not to endanger his publications.

In addition he became financially ever more dependent on the institute, as other sources of income became closed to him. In the first years of exile he was compelled to live an absolutely minimal material existence. For periods of time he lived with his sister Dora, who had also emigrated to Paris, or as a tenant with other émigrés. Beginning in spring 1934 he received a "monthly stipend of 500 francs" from the institute, as well as "supplementary funds" for trips, book purchases, and the transfer of his library.[17] This sum did not however suffice for him to live continuously in Paris, which he much preferred; the Bibliothèque Nationale remained his "most longed for place of work."[18] Thus in the winter of 1934–35, he lived for almost five months in San Remo, returning later from time to time, in the boardinghouse run by his divorced wife Dora, where he was cut off from all intellectual tools and conversation partners. Even in his decision to spend the summer months of 1934 and 1935 in Brecht's Danish place of exile, Skovsbostrand, financial considerations played a role that should not be underestimated.

Between 1935 and 1937 Benjamin wrote hardly a single letter to New York that did not contain a complaint about his economic distress. For example, in June 1937, when the institute was paying him 1,000 francs

The reading hall of the Bibliothèque Nationale in Paris.

monthly, he set his "minimal living costs" at 1,500 francs.[19] Still more oppressive was the constant uncertainty as to whether the institute was prepared to continue its support at all. It must therefore have been a considerable relief to him when, in the fall of 1937, after delivery of the essay on Fuchs that the institute had commissioned a long time earlier, Friedrich Pollock, the director responsible for finances, offered him a monthly stipend of eighty dollars—still a much smaller sum than that received by the regularly employed contributors in New York—and at the same time promised him "the position of a research fellow of the institute."[20]

Poverty resulted in Benjamin losing contact more and more with his earlier friends and conversation partners, with Brecht's circle in particular. He writes from Paris in January 1934, in what was to be a common refrain of his letters in exile: "I have hardly ever been so isolated as here. I could of course seek out opportunities to sit with émigrés in cafés, they are easy to obtain, but I avoid them."[21] Instead he devoted his time almost exclusively to study, to reading the most remote sources, and to commenting on them for his chief work, the *Arcades Project*, which he had taken up again in the winter of 1934–35 in San Remo. When he remarks to Horkheimer that "the years and life circumstances" had resulted in "work taking up an ever-increasing amount of space in the schedule of my life,"[22] he is outlining a form of existence toward which his life had already long been tending, but which had reached its radical realization only under the oppressive circumstances of exile.

Thus Benjamin's experiences as an intellectual in the Weimar Republic take on now an extreme form. His response to this intensification is to formulate a theory of non-auratic art, which he articulates in the great essays of the early years of exile. In the first essay written for the Institute of Social Research, he sums up and radicalizes the sociological theory that underlay his earlier critiques and reviews. He investigates the "social position of the French writer," from the rightist conservatism of a Barrès through the bourgeois liberalism of a Julien Green to the communist engagement of Gide, Malraux, and the surrealists, and concludes that the "death of the free intelligentsia, brought about decisively if not exclusively by economic factors" is the theme that unites recent French literature.[23] The intellectual, Benjamin argues, neither stands for the "most humane interests" of the bourgeoisie, as he did in the time of undisputed bourgeois rule, nor can he fully assimilate himself to the proletariat. "Hence there developed the mirage of a new emancipated condition, a freedom between the classes, that is, the freedom of the Lumpenproletariat. The intellectual mimics proletarian existence without being in any way tied to the working class."[24]

This insight, wherein Benjamin conceptualizes his own social situation, is the clear sign, in his view, of a world historical crisis in which the redemption or death of humanity is being decided. In this crisis art and the artist must assume a new function. Thus in his speech "The Author as Producer" (1934) and in the programmatic theses of the essay on "The Work of Art in the Age of Mechanical Reproduction" (1936), Benjamin works out the categories of an aesthetic theory that definitively turns its back on the traditional concept of the artwork. In his temporal framework, which moves in millennia, art from antiquity to the present is defined through its origin in religious ritual. As an autonomous entity apprehended through contemplation, the work of art in its uniqueness has always preserved the theological implications that structured it from the outset. Benjamin gives this condition the name of *aura,* defined as "the unique phenomenon of a distance, however close it may be."[25] He includes in this formula all traditional art as what it has always been—but not always understood to be: the manifestation of the divine, however secularized, however obscured. Against this, Benjamin's theses, starting from an analysis of the newest aesthetic pro-

159

ductions, such as Brecht's epic theater and Chaplin's grotesque film comedies, attempt to understand art as a wholly secular medium, that is, as a medium of political revolution.

However revolutionary this theory may sound, it is still sustained by the Enlightenment optimism that art remains the privileged instrument of social transformations. Using the example of film, whose form and content are the first to be wholly defined by the means of technical reproduction, Benjamin analyzes the radical rupture in the ways of producing and apprehending art. The film is produced as a collective effort, the actor no longer faces a public directly but plays his role as a "form of testing" in front of "mechanical equipment," behind which a group of experts is concealed. "Thus, for contemporary man the representation of reality by the film is incomparably more significant than that of the painter, since it offers, precisely because of the thoroughgoing permeation of reality with mechanical equipment, an aspect of reality which is free of all equipment."[26] In the "simultaneous collective reception," which characterizes the viewing of a film, Benjamin finds in the "laughter" and the "shock effect" indications that the public "organizes and controls itself in its reception." And to this process he ascribes directly the impact of a political catharsis:

> When one calculates what dangerous tensions the rise of technology and its consequences have generated among the masses—tensions that at critical stages can take on a psychotic character—one realizes that this same intensified technology has also produced the possibility of psychic immunization against such mass psychoses, in the form of certain films; in these films a forced and artificial development of sadistic fantasies or masochistic delusions can prevent their natural and dangerous maturation among the masses. Collective laughter represents the anticipatory and preventive outbreak of such mass psychoses.[27]

If one interprets these and similar sentences as a diagnosis of the actual impact of Chaplin's films, then their illusory character is obvious. But it would be a misunderstanding to read them only as findings based on actual aesthetic phenomena. Rather, Benjamin explicitly insists, in the first section of the essay, on the "prognostic value" of his theses. It is his purpose, in a situation of historical rupture, to establish "theses about the developmental tendencies of art under present conditions of production."[28] In the collective, rationally controlled production, as in the active, therapeutically functioning reception of technically reproduced artworks, he sees a double development instigated that, in the infinity of a utopian condition, would culminate in the intersection of the two parallel lines. This condition he defines, in his lecture "The Author as Producer," as "the literary structuring of life relations, which can master the otherwise irreconcilable antinomies." He illustrates this ideal through the example of columns by worker-correspondents in the Soviet press:

> The death of creative writing in the bourgeois press reveals itself as the formula for its restoration in the Soviet press. As writing gains in breadth what it loses in depth, the distinction between author and public, maintained in a conventional way by the bourgeois press, begins to disappear in the Soviet press. There the reader is always ready to become a writer, namely a writer of descriptions or even prescriptions. As a person with knowledge, if not professional knowledge, then knowledge of the position he holds in society, he gains access to authorship.[29]

Benjamin transfers this enthusiastic description of the practice of worker-correspondents to the utopian core of the "Work of Art" essay, while to be sure suppressing the references to the Soviet Union, which had been openly stated in the lecture intended for the leftist Institute for the Study of Fascism.[30] In his programmatic statement on aesthetic theory, he formulates it quite generally: "[T]here is hardly a gainfully employed European who could not, in principle, find an opportunity to publish somewhere or other comments on his work, grievances, documentary reports, or that sort of thing. Thus, the distinction between author and public is about to lose its basic character. The difference becomes merely functional; it may vary from case to case. At any moment the reader is ready to turn into a writer."[31] Only in this new version is the utopian quality of the idea fully revealed: that everyone should be able to write, meaning that the social antinomies, as also the exploitative opposition between humanity and nature, should no longer be decided violently but in the rational medium of writing. Thus the theological hope for a paradise free of violence has found its most extreme, radically secularized form in the elaboration of the work of art's organizational function.

In June 1936, referring to the "Work of Art" essay, Benjamin sees the "continuity" of his work as consisting in his having "sought to articulate an ever more precise and uncompromising conception of what a work of art is."[32] In this he is interpreting the programmatic theses also as a critique of his own earlier aesthetic theory, which tried to formulate the theological content of a work of art all too directly. Yet here too his theory remains strictly linked to his own existential situation. The outline of a society in which everyone can communicate his experiences without hindrance, and the associated hope of being able thus to revolutionize society without violence: this is not only the recapitulation of a dream that has inspired intellectuals at least since Romanticism, it is also the precise mirror image of

Leni Riefenstahl on the set of *Reichsparteitag*, 1936.

the isolated intellectual threatened in his very existence, which was Benjamin's condition in exile. Thus what he says of the heroes of Malraux's novels applies also to himself as author of "revolutionary demands in the politics of art": "They live for the proletariat; but they do not act as proletarians. At least they act far less from class-consciousness than from the consciousness of their isolation."[33]

Nevertheless Benjamin was no mere political dreamer. His image of the worker-writer is the militant yet nonviolent counterpart of the idealized figure of the worker-soldier, as portrayed by the propaganda literature and art of fascism. His stress on the "shattering of aura" was designed to counter the fatal production of aura for the Führer and the masses hypnotized by him, as instigated by the fascist radio and even more by the weekly news films and the works of Leni Riefenstahl. His insistence on the politically progressive tendency of the most advanced artistic techniques was to prevent their cooptation for an "aesthetics of war," such as futurism advocated. In this sense the innovations of literary technique he proposes have a precise political function: "An author who teaches nothing to writers, teaches nothing to anyone. The decisive element in literary production is its character as model, provoking other producers to the act of production and also generating an improved set of tools for them to use. And the quality of these tools is recognizable by the extent to which they lead consumers toward production, are able, in short, to turn readers or audiences into collaborators."[34]

In this formulation is concealed a second polemical thrust, that against socialist realism. Benjamin held no illusions concerning the gloomy prospects of a Western Europe threatened by fascism and a Soviet Union ruled by Stalin, as is attested by statements in letters from the summer of 1936.[35] Nevertheless he advocated worker-correspondences and reportages as progressive literary forms; he thus gave theoretical weight to literary practices that, after Lukács's attacks in the Soviet Union and in the context of the Popular Front dominating Communist cultural politics in Western Europe, had long been outlawed. Hence his insistence that his essay was really directed at the debate within the Soviet Union. Hence his fruitless attempt to publish it in the Moscow journal *Das Wort,* where at just this time the so-called expressionism debate was having a decisive impact on future Marxist aesthetics. Hence the unusual project of having his theses debated in the Paris "League of German Writers" where, as he drily noted, they were "boycotted by the party members among the writers."[36] In his efforts to intervene in the discussion concerning a materialist literary theory, he was finally abandoned even by Brecht, whose creative practice had primarily inspired his theory of a non-auratic work of art. When in summer 1938 in Svendborg he gave Brecht the work to read, the playwright noted in his "Work-diary": "Everything is mystical, despite an anti-mystical attitude. In such a form does he adapt the materialist theory of history! It is rather horrible."[37]

Thus Benjamin remained dependent, for the dissemination of his theses, on their French translation by Pierre Klossowski, which in 1936, after lengthy preliminaries, appeared in the *Zeitschrift für Sozialforschung.* However, not only did it lack all the politically relevant concepts, the programmatic character of the whole was further obscured by the omission of the first section, vital for the political and historical grounding of the theory. Horkheimer justified these changes, which he instigated, by his endeavor "to preserve the journal, as a scholarly organ, from being drawn into political discussions in the press."[38]

With his characteristic obstinacy Benjamin, a year later, took the essay, "Eduard Fuchs, Collector and Historian" (1937) commissioned by the Institute, as a pretext, using the example of this pioneer of a materialist "cultural history," for attacking the undialectical premises of such arguments—and of socialist realism in general. Again he advanced the claim, both self-conscious and provocative, that he himself had achieved in his analysis of the conditions of aesthetic production what Marx had accomplished in the economic sphere. Accordingly, Benjamin argued, he was the first to have formulated a revolutionary aesthetic dialectically, that is, in the "acceptance of extremes."[39] In this case too the New York censorship functioned remorselessly. With knowledge of the extensive relevant materials, one has to conclude that here also the stronger party—in the nature of things, the editors in New York—imposed their point of view and, in so doing, they deprived Benjamin's program for a politically functional aesthetic of its audience, hence of any immediate impact.

Adorno criticized this most extreme development of Benjamin's dialectical materialism by return of post as "a highly sublimated residue of certain Brechtian motifs."[40] Yet the extent to which Benjamin actually grounded his theory in mystical thinking, as Brecht correctly observed, can be gauged by the fact that, between April and July 1936, thus immediately following the "Work of Art" essay, he wrote "The Storyteller," which complemented the materialist theses by revealing the messianic goal of the future aesthetic. In this treatise-like text, which takes a review of Nikolai Leskov's stories as the occasion for fundamental considerations, Benjamin imposes a three-stage dialectic on co-existing epic forms and interprets story, novel, and information as forms of communication that succeed each other in the context of specific historical conditions of production.

Thus storytelling represents for him "an artisan form of communication, as it were."[41] That means above all that it is bound to a pre-industrial society, to the life of peasants, artisans, merchants, in whose work places and domestic rooms, not yet equipped with electric light, stories are told. It also means that the stories themselves have the quality of handcrafted art. They are passed down from generation to generation. Experience accumulates in them, is supplemented by the storyteller's own experience, and finally is handed on as "counsel," as the moral all stories contain. Like a valuable tool, the story is thus not created by an individual artist; the collective experience of whole populations enters into it.

It is clear that this idealized description of a past narrative form gains its intensity from the contrast with the currently dominant epic form, the novel. According to Benjamin the novel, in comparison with the story, is already the expression of "profound perplexity." The technical advance making possible its dissemination, the invention of printing, not only ensures a gradual dying out of the art of storytelling, it also means that the reader becomes an isolated subject. This comparison renders comprehensible the nostalgic tone in which Benjamin mourns the disappearing narrative mode and which he has in common with one of his sources, Goethe's novel *Wilhelm Meister's Years of Wandering*. In this late work of Goethe, as Benjamin notes in his 1928 article for the *Great Soviet Encyclopedia,* "the 'humanists' from the *Apprentice Years* have all become artisans."[42] This comment refers to the novel's third part, where a society basing itself on manual forms of production is described in detail; storytelling, psalmsinging, and oral transmission of useful advice are still directly integrated into the work process. In Goethe's novel this idyllically portrayed life is already a backward-facing utopia, wherein an older social form is to be preserved from what is called in the novel itself the "threatening power of the machine."

Benjamin provides the story with such a positive emphasis because the tradition survives intact within it. He defines tradition as the overcoming of generational barriers, which death represents, and actualizes this process in the biblical image of Jacob's ladder: "A ladder extending downward to the interior of the earth and disappearing into the clouds is the image for a collective experience to which even the deepest shock of every individual experience, death, constitutes no impediment or barrier."[43] These words evoke the theological model in which tradition has its origin: the handing on of the revealed Word whereby the people of Israel maintains God as present and finds its special identity confirmed from generation to generation. In the description of the handcrafted form of the epic this Word is secularized, reimagined as a mystical concept.

But Benjamin does not stop there. In his dialectical construction where, just as in Georg Lukács's *Theory of the Novel,* the novel functions as the antithetical moment, there appears as synthesis a third epic form, "information." "With the full control of the middle class, which has the press as one of its most important instruments in fully developed capitalism," information plays a role for the first time.[44] However the bare definitions Benjamin assigns to information–that it "supplies a handle for what is nearest" and "lays claim to prompt verifiability"–seem hardly adequate to demonstrate its status as the epic form of the future. Only if, as the text's dialectical structure demands, one were to project certain central characteristics attributed to the story into the moment of synthesis, which is consciously left blank in the essay, would information become intelligible as the new epic form, maintaining storytelling's mystical quality while doing justice to present-day conditions of production. Such a transfer is suggested above all by the central theoretical passage of the "Work of Art" essay, where the practice of worker-correspondents is invoked as the example of the new function of information. In the utopian image of a proletarian literary society is thus to be found the actual reference point for the definitions that, in "The Storyteller," Benjamin ascribes to storytelling in a society of manual workers. In both hypothetical constructs there is virtually no distinction between authors and audiences in the communicative process; in both the

Benjamin at the Bibliothèque Nationale, 1935. (Photo Gisèle Freund.)

specific forms of the epic are interpreted as the medium of a public profoundly involved in its everyday life. Still more important, even in this literary form, which presupposes a proletarian revolution in society, the mystical qualities of the epic are preserved. In it there occurs the transmission of a collective experience, and by it the collective constitutes itself as such: the theological name for this is tradition.

"The Storyteller" gains its complex structure from the fact that the dialectical, tripartite philosophy of history is overlaid by a bipolar system, which is based on the distinction between myth and liberating truth. From this perspective the epic forms enumerated in the essay's second part share a common aspect: "natural," hence death-dominated life is overcome. The fairy tale, for example, confronts myth with "liberating magic." This magic, it is argued in the essay's sixteenth section, "does not bring nature into play in a mythical way, but points to its complicity with liberated man."[45] Chronicle and legend resist natural history in principle, with their explicit orienta-

166

tion toward redemptive history. The story, finally, transcends death through the continuity of the generations of narrators speaking through it.

This enumeration of genres has as its purpose – the central speculative purpose of the essay – a simultaneous survey of all historically existent epic forms. In a metaphor used already by Benjamin in his essay on *The Elective Affinities,* where he acknowledges its source in Goethe's theory of colors, this mystical core of his text is invoked: "Any examination of a given epic form is concerned with the relationship of this form to historiography. In fact, one may go even further and raise the question whether universal history does not constitute the point of creative non-differentiation between all forms of the epic. Then written history would be in the same relationship to the epic forms as white light is to the colors of the spectrum."[46] The esoteric meaning of these sentences is vividly illuminated when one juxtaposes them with a 1939 note linked to the very late "Theses on the Philosophy of History," in which Benjamin no longer adjusts his text to publication needs:

> The messianic world is the world of all-sided and integral immediacy. Only there is universal history possible. But it would be not a written, but a festively enacted history. This feast is purified of all solemnity. It knows no festival hymns. Its language is integrated prose, which has broken the shackles of writing and is understood by all human beings. . . . The idea of prose is inseparable from the messianic idea of universal history (the genres of creative prose as the spectrum of the prose of universal history – in "The Storyteller").[47]

In this text, written under the direct and mortal threat from Hitler's troops, the mystical hope breaks through, which, as "white light," already illuminates "The Storyteller." In meditations that pick up strands of early Romantic thinking, Benjamin expands the theological language theory of his youth into a mystical theory of epic forms. Just as the many existing languages will one day dissolve into the one adamic language of unmediated cognition, thus overcoming the Babylonian confusion of tongues, so the many forms storytelling has assumed in its interaction with history will ultimately dissolve into the one integral prose, which is what messianically liberated history actually is.

The essay anticipates the end of the epic's journey through history, which will be complete only at the moment of history's destruction, by assembling the forms of the epic within itself and calling them by name. This mystical vanishing point, toward which the essay is directed, appears remote from the concrete social-historical dialectic that defines its surface.

Nevertheless the two are identical in Benjamin's understanding, in that he cannot conceive of social revolution otherwise than as messianic redemption of the world. This formulation does not indeed resolve the paradox of Benjamin's thinking, but provides insight into its power and extreme elasticity. The multiple levels of meaning that a reading of the essay uncovers prove that, here too, he has written "in accordance with the talmudic doctrine of the forty-nine levels of meaning in every passage of the Torah." The result is a multi-dimensional textual space whose fascination for readers may well derive from those dark corners into which their understanding cannot penetrate.[48]

Benjamin came closest to the synthesis between materialist and messianic thinking in the text where he could interpret the writings of an author spiritually akin to himself, namely in the essay on Franz Kafka for the *Jüdische Rundschau,* of which he himself said, "this topic has all the potential of becoming a crossroads in my thinking." "The reason why is evoked by the image of the bow: here I am dealing with two ends at once, namely the political and the mystical."[49] With justification Benjamin speaks of the mystical pole of his thought, not of the theological; for in the Kafka essay the latter is completely subsumed in negativity. Emphatically and frequently he argues against the prevailing theological interpretation of Kafka, propagated by Max Brod: "Kafka was neither mantic nor the founder of a religion."[50] Nevertheless he locates the Prague storyteller's work explicitly in the context of traditional Jewish religion when he remarks that "his prose pieces [do not] belong entirely in the tradition of Western prose forms; they have, rather, a similar relationship to doctrine as the Haggadah does to the Halakah."[51] If Kafka's stories are thus to be understood in the context of the parable-like illustrations that in the Talmud accompany the doctrine as commentary, then it is only with the all-important reservation that no doctrine corresponds to them any more.

In this way all categories that Benjamin borrows from the Jewish religion to characterize Kafka's narrative procedure are deprived of their theological content. So it is with the "postponement," which Kafka's figures gain through storytelling, delaying the judgment upon them. So also with "remembering," whereby the epic writer resists the distortion of the world through forgetting. And it applies above all to "studying," to which the hopeful figures in Kafka—animals, assistants, and students—tirelessly devote themselves. For what is here studied with such indefatigable diligence is no longer the sacred texts, but rather the profane world of the bureaucracies and excessively powerful social organizations of the twentieth century. "Profane illumination": the goal Benjamin had ascribed to the writing of the surrealists becomes the precise conceptualization of what he rediscovers in

Kafka's texts. This world is profane indeed; in it the technocratic accoutrements of the twentieth century are mixed in unholy confusion with the hetairic "swamp world" of the "destiny which appears here in all its ambiguity."[52] Thus Benjamin uncovers the false bottom of Kafka's corrupted cosmos, rediscovering in his texts the actuality of the primeval within the administered society.

Kafka's work can claim political relevance in this interpretation, since it is read, in the spirit of Marx's early writings, as characteristic "of maximum alienation of men from one another, of unpredictably intervening relationships which have become their only ones."[53] Benjamin's meditation on this condition of the world, as embodied in Kafka's texts, traces reification in the most intimate human realms. "For just as K. lives in the village on Castle Hill, modern man lives in his body; the body slips away from him, is hostile toward him. It may happen that a man wakes up one day and finds himself transformed into vermin. Exile – his exile – has gained control over him."[54] Only when Kafka's parables are read in this way, literally and radically, as images of the modern condition of the world and human beings, does the necessity of the "reflections without end," which in Kafka's work are tied to the parables, become unmistakable.

In these reflections the interpreter Benjamin discerns the work's mystical quality and adds his own reflections to the existing sequence. His activity thus appears as a conscious continuation of the processes begun in the work itself. Interpretation understands itself as a judicial procedure directed at the world, wherein to be sure no acquittal is in sight; but the verdict of the vengeful fathers is postponed indefinitely, because the trial is incomplete, indeed is fundamentally incapable of completion. Consequently the Kafka essay, unlike almost all of Benjamin's major texts, is not dialectically constructed, but opens itself in its fourth part to an apotheosis of studying.

With his definition of the writer's task, linking its mystical hope precisely to the elimination of content from the writing process, Benjamin is also speaking of himself. He places himself in the ranks of the students and writers and claims for his own writing the redemptive power he ascribes to learning. For him it is "a cavalry attack against [the] tempest that blows from the land of oblivion." "Reversal is the direction of learning which transforms existence into writing." "The gate to justice is learning."[55] The constantly re-experienced failure of his writing, manifested in the Kraus essay for example, in the impossibility of mediation, or in the merely aesthetic mediation of theological and materialist categories – this endless Sisyphean labor is thus endowed with a sacred quality. The meaning of these sentences is not, however, confined to the ascetic imagery of writing as a turn-

Gershom Scholem.

ing away from the world's violence. Its mystical core is concealed in the phrase about the "gate to justice." This is the gate through which, at the end of time, the Messiah will enter to redeem the world. The critic has secretly inserted himself here into the role of the Messiah—of course, a thoroughly materialist and nihilist Messiah.

Benjamin took steps to ensure that his text, of which the *Jüdische Rundschau* published only the first and third parts, was made accessible to his friends, and on the basis of their reactions he drafted a "dossier of others' objections and my own reflections" for a later "revision."[56] In this he showed consistency in stressing the fundamental openness of his writing process. In the file that has survived there are reflections by Werner Kraft and Theodor W. Adorno, as well as objections from Scholem and Brecht, prominently placed. Benjamin's project was in fact inspired in many ways by Scholem's cabbalistic studies, above all by the latter's mystical conception of God as

170

Nothing, most concisely formulated in a didactic poem sent in response to Benjamin's essay:

> Thus alone does revelation
> Permeate the age that rejected You.
> Your nothingness is the only experience
> The age may have of You.[57]

Benjamin's more radical nihilism, however, charging worldly actions with religious meaning while at the same time destroying religion's theological content, was too much for Scholem in the one decisive respect, the denial of God's existence. Thus he indignantly imparted theological instruction from the holy city of Jerusalem to the worldly thinker in Paris: "The incompleteness of revealed truth is the point at which, most precisely, a correctly understood theology and that which gives the key to Kafka's world become as one. Dear Walter, it is not the absence of theology in a pre-animistic world that is its problem, but rather its incompleteness, the impossibility of consummating it."[58]

Brecht's reaction, coming from the opposite direction, was equally emphatic. Benjamin had given him the manuscript to read during his stay at Skovsbostrand, without Brecht making any comment at the time. Only after weeks of silence did an argument develop, in the course of which Brecht charged the Kafka essay with "encouraging Jewish fascism. It intensifies and extends the darkness surrounding the figure of Kafka, instead of dispersing it."[59] In his diary Benjamin carefully recorded the ensuing discussion, in which Brecht interpreted Kafka as the typical petit bourgeois, who confronts the complex and opaque mechanisms of capitalist society, not with a heroic response in the fascist manner, but with questions like a sage. Against this crudely polemical, "relevant" approach Benjamin defended himself cunningly by making the "interpretation of the individual detail" into the criterion for judging the various approaches, and by demonstrating his conception of the messianic power of memory through the temporal distortions of Kafka's story "The Next Village." But he already secretly portrayed himself as the victor in this dispute, when he cited Brecht as ending an early conversation about this story with words epitomizing his own mode of thinking: "'One would have to study it carefully,' he [Brecht] observed. Then the conversation broke off; it was ten o'clock and the radio news came from Vienna."[60]

Benjamin was his own severest critic. Under the dramatically worsened historical circumstances of 1938 he repudiated, in a long letter to Scholem,

171

the central point of his Kafka study in the *Jüdische Rundschau:* "What I like least about this essay today is its apologetic character. To do justice to the figure of Kafka in its purity and special beauty, one must never forget one thing: it is the figure of a failure."[61] Again, when Benjamin speaks of Kafka, he is speaking of himself at the same time. His study was an "apologetics" above all in the sanctification of his own writing. In the face of the imminent destruction of Europe, a court against whose judgment no stay of execution could be obtained by writing, Benjamin looked directly at the possibility of real, tangible failure engulfing his life's work. In this he must have known himself to be again at one with Kafka, who in 1922, shortly before his death, complained in a letter to Max Brod: "I have not purchased my freedom through writing."[62]

The shortened version of the essay, published in 1934 in National Socialist Berlin, concludes with a quotation from the children's song that is also quoted at the end of *Berlin Childhood:*

> "My dear child, I beg of you, / Pray for the little hunchback too." So ends the folksong. In his depths Kafka touches the ground which neither "mythical divination" nor "existential theology" supplied him with. It is the core of folk tradition, the German as well as the Jewish. Even if Kafka did not pray—and this we do not know—he still possessed in the highest degree what Malebranche called the "natural prayer of the soul": attentiveness. And in this attentiveness he included all living creatures, as saints include them in their prayers.[63]

This identification of Jewish and German "folk tradition" contains, in its conscious adoption of the by-then Nazi-tinged term, a reminder of the better Germany toward which Benjamin felt a strong obligation.

In 1936, when official Nazi Germany was celebrating its triumphs at the Berlin Olympiad, Benjamin publicly invoked this other Germany one more time. Through the mediation of the socialist and theologian Karl Thieme, he succeeded in publishing *German People* with the publisher Vita Nova in Lucerne. It is a series of twenty-six letters by well-known German writers and philosophers from the years 1783 to 1883, which Benjamin had already published, together with his own commentary, in 1931–32 in the *Frankfurter Zeitung.* The motto with which he prefaced this collection of documents from the bourgeois century suggests the political actuality of his book, published for the German market under the pseudonym Detlef Holz: "Of honor without fame / Of greatness without grandeur / of dignity without pay." Against the deadly displays of fascism he wants, through the testimony of a bourgeoisie actively defending human rights, to invoke once more the "inner relationship between a bare, limited existence and true humanity."[64]

At the same time however these texts and the commentary on them offer the most precise mirror image of Benjamin's own existence. All the motifs of his own life as he perceived it are alluded to here: the "wretchedness of the German intellectual" in exile, articulated through letters of Forster and Büchner; the central role of hope and the necessity of renouncing love; and the "religion of unconditional, eschatologically grounded world-negation," of which he speaks in connection with a letter from Overbeck to Nietzsche.[65] The humanistic values of the bourgeois era, now that they have definitively receded into history, are thus invoked once again through an actualization of his own fate. In his commentary on the first letter Benjamin names the leitmotif that governs this quest for values: "All these letters have one thing in common: they bring into focus that attitude which may be termed humanistic in the German sense, and which it now seems all the more appropriate to evoke, the more decisively it is abandoned by those who hold power in Germany today."[66]

Nowhere did Benjamin's vision of a European culture permeated by the metaphysical genius of Judaism achieve a more convincing form than in this self-portrait, built from fragments expressing the distress and creative power of the bourgeoisie. In it the occasional writings of Germans from the eighteenth and nineteenth centuries are annotated with the devotion normally accorded to a sacred text. He thus rescues them from the deluge of fascist barbarism by hiding them at the center of the Jewish tradition, in what he openly called, in the copy dedicated to his sister Dora, his "ark constructed on the Jewish model."[67]

173

VIII
Parisian Arcades

1 9 3 7 – 1 9 3 9

In March 1934, when Benjamin had barely dealt with the first difficulties of emigration, he already resumed work on the *Arcades Project* which had been interrupted at the beginning of 1930. In the following years this project formed the center of his endeavors and meditations, binding him to Paris and to Europe even when staying on the continent had long since become a mortal risk for him. In his hope of completing this work, the lonely and exiled Benjamin ultimately saw "the real, if not the only reason not to give up in the struggle for existence."[1] During his stay at San Remo in the winter of 1934–35, he set himself to work "sytematically" through the material gathered thus far, in order to amplify it, on his return to Paris, through excerpted passages and illustrations from the inexhaustible resources of the Bibliothèque Nationale. In May 1935 he drafted an expository essay outlining, for the first time, a plan for ordering the whole mass of citations and commentary and sent it to the directors of the Institute of Social Research in New York, in order to obtain funding for the project.

In the spring of 1937, having fulfilled all his obligations by sending in the long-postponed Fuchs essay, Benjamin could finally, with the institute's approval, resume work on the subject on which he had focussed attention for so many years. Even at this stage there were again problems with Horkheimer. On the basis of a discussion with Adorno, Benjamin planned to develop the epistemological foundations of his own project

174

through a critique of C. G. Jung's doctrine of archaic images. Horkheimer opposed this undertaking, principally because it infringed on the territory of other institute members, specifically Erich Fromm and Herbert Marcuse; he suggested instead that Benjamin work out the Baudelaire chapter of the planned book. After Benjamin had spent the summer absorbed in "Jung's psychology—authentic devil's work which one has to fend off using white magic," he finally agreed in the fall of 1937, with some hesitation and regret, "to postpone the Jung critique in favor of Baudelaire."[2]

The *Arcades Project* had been conceived initially in 1927 as an essay for the journal *Der Querschnitt;* during its subsequent long period of germination its epistemological premises were drastically revised. "The saturnine tempo of this whole thing had its deepest cause in the process of revolutionary change, which had to be undergone by a mass of thoughts and images dating from the long past time of my metaphysical, indeed theological style of thinking, in order for this material to nourish my present outlook with its full strength."[3]

In a letter to Scholem Benjamin articulated the substantive meaning of this distinction between the originally planned "dialectical fantasy" and the book sketched in the 1935 essay, to be called *Paris, Capital of the Nineteenth Century.* He compared the plan of the new work with the "inner construction" of the book on tragic drama: "And I can tell you that here too the working through of a traditional concept will play the central role. Where before it was the concept of tragic drama, now it will be the fetish character of the commodity."[4] At this stage of the work, then, Benjamin is concerned to show in what way the social and cultural forms of expression and organization in the nineteenth century are, in all their manifestations, distorted by the basic structure of capitalist society, as diagnosed in the early work of Marx and in Lukács's *History and Class Consciousness.* This he does as a dialectical critic, with the aim of overcoming these distortions in his own historical construction, thereby summoning up the past in its purified form in order to combat the false historical tendencies of the present.

In the concluding section of his outline for the book, Benjamin formulates this linkage in terms of psychology applied to the collective subject of the nineteenth century:

> From this era derive the arcades and interiors, the exhibition halls and panoramas. They are residues of a dream world. The realization of dream elements at the moment of awakening is the textbook example of dialectical thinking. Thus dialectical thinking is the organ of historical awakening. Every epoch not only dreams the next one but, in the process of dreaming, propels itself towards awakening. It bears its own

Benjamin at the "Decades de Pontigny," 1937.
(Photo Gisèle Freund.)

ending within itself and—as Hegel already recognized—makes it manifest through cunning. With the shattering of the social order based on commodities we are beginning to recognize the monuments of the bourgeoisie as ruins even before they have disintegrated.[5]

Benjamin planned six chapters for his book: "Fourier or the Arcades," "Daguerre or the Panoramas," "Grandville or the World Exhibitions," "Louis Philippe or the Interior," "Baudelaire or the Streets of Paris," and "Haussmann or the Barricades." In this sequence was to be delineated the rise of historical consciousness to the moment of awakening, which had taken place in the struggle of the Commune on the barricades, the moment when the collective subject finally achieved an understanding of its historical task.

Just as the texts of *Berlin Childhood* portray the awakening of the child's self from the dream of the nineteenth century through the consciousness of the author mature in his own identity, so the texts of the *Arcades Project* present the awakening of the proletariat in the dialectical construction of the historian fully conscious of the dangers he incurs in the very moment of writing. Taking up his earlier distinction, derived from the Judaic tradition, Benjamin grounds the historian's methodology in the "doctrine of the

176

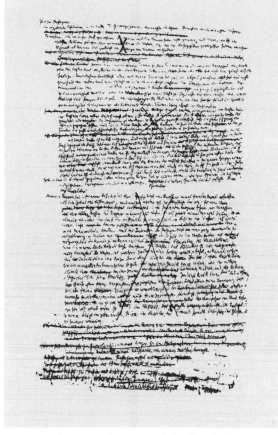

A manuscript page of the first draft
of the *Arcades Project*.

historical dreams of the collective," whereby he endeavors to transcend Freud's
"doctrine of the natural dream." For Benjamin all cultural expressions, all
social and economic forms of organization are merely dream images, phantasmagoria, since old and new elements appear in them all mixed up together.
"The century was unable to respond to the new technical possibilities with a
comparably new social order."[6] This ongoing contradiction, most clearly
manifest in the commodity, determines all forms of expression of the nineteenth century and makes them appear displaced as in a dream.

The Princes Arcade, Paris.

To understand humanity's history in this way as its dream means, in effect, that although the true desires and longings of human beings, for fulfillment and happiness, do achieve expression, they only do so in a displaced, censored, repressed form. Such dream work keeps humanity from the awakening that would signal an end of history and the onset of the messianic kingdom. The "doctrine of the historical dreams of the collective" thus restores to historical phenomena their ambivalent aspect, reveals them as forms expressing simultaneously the failures and the chances of history. "In the dream wherein to every epoch its successor appears in imaginary form, these images of the future are blended with elements of primal history, that is to say of a classless society."[7]

To render visible this utopian element, which already permeates the material of history, is the task of the materialist historian. This is what Benjamin defines, citing Bloch's terminology, as "'not yet conscious knowing' about the past; securing this knowledge has the structure of an awakening."[8] In order not merely to reproduce the dream, which would mean to remain within the myth like Aragon and the surrealists, it is essential to analyze the dream, that is, to recognize and thus to dissolve the "expressive link" between the economic order of the nineteenth century and its social and cultural structures; the utopian element concealed within that expressivity can thus be brought into the open.

The instrument of this analysis is the dialectic, its methodology is "literary montage."[9] The historian's analytical strength is thus to be manifested in the dialectical structuring of materials that, uprooted from the illusory continuities of the period, have become quotations. However, the collective dream images will only become legible to him if, unlike the distanced, "neutral" psychoanalyst, the historian includes within the analysis his own endangered situation. "The legible image, that is, the image that has become recognizable within actuality, bears to the fullest extent the mark of the critical, dangerous moment that underlies all acts of reading."[10]

These methodological reflections of the materialist historian have their objective correlative in his concept of "apocatastasis," the "universal ingathering."[11] Deriving from late Judaic apocalyptic thought and neo-platonic-gnostic speculations, this term designates the restoration of the original paradisiacal state, which is to be expected from the Messiah's advent. All things would accordingly return to their correct relationship with one another, dissolving the condition of displacement determining the existent dream state of the world. Destruction of the prevailing context that defines and confines cultural expression, and restoration of the primal context of being: these are the goals of "cultural-historical dialectics" as outlined by Benjamin in his 1935 draft. In his essay on Goethe's *Elective Affinities,* Ben-

179

jamin the critic had forced the dimension of the "expressionless" into the open by shattering the classical work of art into the "torso of a symbol"; as materialist historian he now seeks to construct that negation of expression from the material of history itself. The argument of the 1935 draft thus ends logically in the optimistic assumption of an awakening into the true historical context, at the very moment when the economic foundations of the nineteenth century appear destined for definitive oblivion.

It was not only external circumstances that made it impossible for Benjamin to implement this grandiose plan. For there persisted within it, from his original conception, a phantasmagorical element. "Paris as Goddess": with this inscription he labelled the emblematic image at the beginning of his review of Marthe Bibesco's novel *Catherine-Paris* in 1928, at the time of his earliest labors on the "dialectical fantasy."

> The Goddess of France's capital city, in her boudoir, resting dreamily. A marble fireplace, molding, swelling cushions, animal skins adorning divan and plaster floor. And knick-knacks, knick-knacks everywhere. Models of the Bridge of the Arts and the Eiffel Tower. On the pedestals, to keep alive the memory of so rich a past, the Tuileries, the Temple, and the Château d'Eau in miniature. In a vase the ten lilies of the city's coat of arms. Yet all this picturesque bric-a-brac is heightened, trumped, buried by the overwhelming multitude of books in a thousand formats—sextodecimos, duodecimos, octavos, quartos, and folios of every size and color—presented to her by airborne, illiterate amoretti, poured out by fauns from the cornucopia of the portieres, spread before her by kneeling genies: the homage of the whole planet in its literary production.[12]

This evocation, labelled by the author himself as a "bibliographical allegory," shows Paris as the capital of the nineteenth century surrounded by its historical memories, which have receded into their most phantasmal form, that of knick-knacks such as filled the high bourgeois salons of the age. But they are present for a second time, in no less phantasmal form, in the books with which the poets of the civilized world honor their goddess. In this tableau the emotional investment that the bibliophile Benjamin brings to books as objects is transferred to the city. At a deeper level, however, an allusion is made also to the sources of writing about Paris. The image of Paris portrayed in Benjamin's text includes the material of history only in its phantasmal form, the shape of texts preserved in books. The book to be written about Paris accordingly has its origin in already written books. For the author Paris thus becomes "a large reading room, a vast library, through which the Seine flows."[13] In the image of the river, this sentence certifies the futility of the author's undertaking. Hence: "Paris is the city of mirrors."[14] What was implied in the embodiment of the city as a goddess is openly stated in these sentences. Paris is unapproachable, the products of textual labor fall at her feet like a second, idyllic nature, without touching her. But she is also the revered woman whom the author, as saturnine lover, pursues in his study, without ever reaching her.

In his essay on *The Elective Affinities* Benjamin introduced, through a metaphorical comparison, woman and truth as polar opposites: "As a word of command is able to draw the truth out of a woman's evasion, at the precise point where it breaks off, so the 'expressionless' compels harmony, in its precarious trembling, to halt, capturing the vibration for eternity through its impact."[15] The dialectic of enlightenment is at work in this imagery. Against the will of its author, the metaphor reveals the violent character of all interpetation of art, insofar as it reduces beauty to being the mere shell of a metaphysical truth. Like the dominating man, the critic is also secretly imposing his domination. For ultimately only the resolute suppression of both external and internal nature can assure the rule of critical reason. The work of art's metaphysical truth-claim can only be sustained if "the surging life" within it appears "stilled, as if spellbound in a single moment."[16]

Comparable images of domination occur to Benjamin in the context of *Moscow Diary,* when he tries to become clear about his relationship with Asja Lacis. What Benjamin experienced existentially, in the constellation of city and woman, as the futile attempt to approach the beloved, is inscribed in the origin of the *Arcades Project* as an emblematic image. Paris, the "goddess" before whom the world pours out the cornucopia of literature in homage, desires itself to be read like a book in all its historical manifestations. Paris, as infinite library assembled from many zones of time and space, remains, as text, unfathomable. Paris, "city of mirrors," resists study and merely reflects its own image back at the reader. Nevertheless Benjamin undertakes the heroic projects of reading. The arcade, that threshold structure in which inside and outside, dream and wakefulness, the underworld of antiquity and the modern world of commodities blend into one another, appears to him as the possible point of entry into this labyrinth.

If the conception of the *Arcades Project* failed, it is primarily because of its internal contradictions. The element excluded from the text, which, behind the allegorical mask of woman and goddess, conceals its true meaning, that of the female element, nature, or the mass of exploited and repressed humanity—all this can be recovered for Benjamin's text only on condition that the text maintain its freedom from inherent structures of domination. Benjamin's attempt to fulfill this condition is evident in his self-imposed renunciation of the dialectical structures he had proposed as an organizing principle, as also in his obstinate insistence on working out the text's destructive elements. The enigma "Paris as Goddess" finds its solution in the failure of the *Arcades Project*, in the disintegration of the text into the tiniest fragments of documentary material and reflection, on which the writing subject no longer attempts to impose a structure of meaning. Grouped under the heading of key words and with both large and small alphabetical ordering sequences, the notes, excerpts, and brief reflections that constitute the *Arcades Project* were thus preserved in substantial files and, in 1982, published in two volumes.

In the impossibility of producing a coherent work, there is thus inscribed a utopia of writing and reading, purified from the elements of violence and domination, under whose historical assault it has taken shape under intense suffering. The "pure" text thus outlined excludes no one, indeed demands the inclusion of all readers. Every one of them can and must become his or her own author. The infinite number of possible readings, which in its fragmentariness the *Arcades Project* both offers and demands, may constitute that collective subject, which, in the concrete historical situation confronting Benjamin in the thirties, could not become manifest in the process of awakening.

Under pressure from Horkheimer, Benjamin turned his attention in 1937 to the working out of a partial aspect of the project that, in the original plan, figured as the fifth chapter with the title "Baudelaire or the Streets of Paris," and which gave promise of yielding a text publishable in the *Journal for Social Research*. During his studies for this task, undertaken in Paris in the first half of 1938, the proposed essay swelled once more into a new book, the success of which, he promised himself, would provide "a very precise model of the *Arcades Project*."[17] By the end of June 1938, when he left for a summer visit with Brecht in his Danish place of exile, Benjamin had organized the necessary materials to the point where he could go into "seclusion" in the peace of the fishing village and begin drafting the Baudelaire text.

The book, *Charles Baudelaire: A Lyric Poet in the Era of High Capitalism*, was to have a tripartite structure, to be organized dialectically on the model of the essay on *The Elective Affinities*.[18] In fact only the text of the second part, "The Paris of the Second Empire in Baudelaire," was completed during the summer in Skovsbostrand and sent for publication to New York at the end of September 1938. A draft prepared in the early summer of 1938 reveals that the book's first part was to portray Baudelaire as the "mixed" object of study that he has become through the historical tradition. Baudelaire's work, with its ceaseless oscillations between symbolic—that is, based on "natural correspondences"—and allegorical descriptive modes, would be

182

A portrait of Louis-Auguste Blanqui by Charles Baudelaire.

Charles Baudelaire, self-portrait.

shown to be itself ambivalent and partially responsible for its own errone-
ous reception; for the critics, with their traditional aesthetic theory, had
paid exclusive attention to Baudelaire's symbolic aspects, "holding uncriti-
cally to his opinions concerning the Catholicity of his literary works."[19]

Against this traditional misreading, the second part of the book, with
its three existing chapters, "Bohemia," "The Flaneur," and "Modernity,"
locates Baudelaire's work within the sociocultural context of his time. Here
Benjamin follows up on "Baudelaire's machinations in the place where they
are unquestionably at home"–in the bourgeoisie.[20] In the book's overall
context the completed part fulfills the function of rereading Baudelaire's
work in opposition to its traditional reception, by viewing it from the objective basis of the social relations conditioning its production.

Thus the chapter "Bohemia" analyzes the secret communication between the outsiders of post-revolutionary French society: the political con-
spirators, who as losers in the struggle end up in the underground and in
prison; the workers sinking to the level of Lumpenproletariat–and the
poet; the bourgeoisie no longer entrusts its defense to the poet, having
handed over that function to the adventurer Louis Bonaparte, and so the

poet must enter the marketplace and become a writer for magazines. Thus, in the first chapter Benjamin embeds the poet's social role in the social context of his time.

In "The Flaneur," he does the same for the content of his poetry, locating precisely its dominant experiences of shock, such as the individual undergoes in a crowd, and of the deathliness permeating the Parisian atmosphere. Finally, under the title "Modernity," the social experiences thus far analyzed are portrayed in their decisive impact on the poems' formal tendencies. In the work of the modern poet, the experiences of shock and death are expressed as allegories that, as "centers of poetic strategy," transpose a "putschist" technique into the heart of the poem itself, by assaulting the unprepared reader with the sudden violence of deeper meaning.[21] The structural homologies between the forms assumed by political revolt, the everyday social experiences of the individual in an urban environment, and the literary techniques of the *poète maudit* prove that the allegorical mode of expression conveys the authentic meaning of *The Flowers of Evil*. The attempt by bourgeois interpreters to incorporate these allegories into the tradition of symbolic poetry, using Baudelaire's own doctrine of "correspondences," is unmasked as a maneuver designed to cover up the revolutionary aspects of these poems.

The antithesis of the second part was to be followed, in the third part entitled "The Commodity as Poetic Object," by its "Marxist" resolution.[22] Like the first part, this synthesis remained unwritten, but sufficient material exists, in the files of fragments assembled for the *Arcades Project*, to permit a sketch of it in general terms. Through linkage to the first book of *Capital* and to Benjamin's own insights in his book on tragic drama, the allegorical form of Baudelaire's poetry was to be interpreted as a response to the universal commodity character of things under capitalism. "The allegorical perspective is always based in a devalued world of appearances. The specific devaluation of the world of things, expressed in the commodity, is the foundation of Baudelaire's allegorical intention."[23] Just as, in the commodity, a thing's exchange value conceals its use value, so, in Benjamin's interpretation of allegory, a thing's function as a sign conceals its true nature. Allegory thus recapitulates the qualities of the commodity, the fetish character that it establishes by alienating things from their functional relations to other things; allegory makes this fetishism "objectively evident."[24]

The allegorical intention thus is seen to be itself ambivalent. On the one hand it produces phantasmagoria, images that deceive and promote illusion. On the other hand, as direct expression of a reified world, it becomes, for materialist criticism, the starting point for the quest for historical truth. The "deceptive transfiguration, which is the norm for commodities when being exhibited" is aesthetically duplicated by allegory, which, like the commodity, presents things divorced from their natural context. The allegorical intention thus brings into the open the commodity's ultimate inherent logic; by destroying the illusion of organic continuities, allegory reveals the reification of the world under capitalism. The example chosen for a full demonstration of this process was to be the image of the whore in Baudelaire's poetry, since, in Benjamin's formulation, in her the commodity "endeavors to gaze at its own face."[25] The dialectical historian needs only to render visible what is always already operative in the organization of a society based on exchange value. He confronts the materialist base with its allegorical double, thereby stripping both of their phantasmagorical appearance. He is thus able to lay bare the nature of things that capitalism has distorted and to secure the negative image of their potential rescue.

Nowhere did Benjamin's understanding of Marxism as a critical methodology "of a heuristic, experimental kind" leave clearer traces than in the planned book on Baudelaire.[26] The social-historical analyses of the completed central section refer, when they interpret the poems of *The Flowers of Evil* as expressing an age of counter-revolution, to Marx's classic analysis of the failure of the 1848 revolution, which led from the workers' uprising with its dream of a social republic, through the parliamentary constitution of 1851 with its language of peace and order sustaining and sustained by the bourgeoisie, finally to the "eighteenth Brumaire of Louis Bonaparte."

Against the background of this "imperialist restoration period" described by Marx, Benjamin puts the values of *The Flowers of Evil* on display. The ambiguity inseparable from the poems thus becomes intelligible as the expression of a counter-revolution necessarily establishing itself following the defeat of the proletariat. The putschist tactics of the workers' leaders and the sinking of the workers to the status of Lumpenproletariat, like the perversion of writers into lightweight journalists or the retreat of Baudelaire into allegory, are linked indissolubly to the conditions prevailing after Louis Bonaparte's coup d'état. In Marx's words: "The constitution, the national assembly, the dynastic parties, the blue and red republicans, the heroes of Africa, the thunder of the *Tribune,* and the lightning of the daily press, all the literature, the political names and intellectual reputations, civil law and civil rights, liberté, égalité, fraternité—all this has disappeared like a phantasmagoria before the exorcizing words of a man whom even his enemies do not claim to be a master magician."[27]

Benjamin adds to Marx's ironic analysis of this counter-revolutionary "magic": All that has not simply disappeared, but has taken refuge, precisely as a phantasmagoria, in Baudelaire's literary work. He thus renders visible the "traces of barbarism" clinging to that work and telling of its origins.[28] The word *barbarism* points toward the time in which the critic Ben-

185

jamin projects his unique image of the past. Louis Bonaparte's Caesarism and the poet Baudelaire retreating into satanism and ambiguity are constructed as precursors of the fascist terror and the writer forced by it into exile. The flaneur's sense of well being in the crowd is described as the intoxication of the human being feeling himself to be a commodity, hence also as a premonition of what the proletarianized masses actually will become in every part of their being. In this analysis an unmistakable allusion is made to the fascist mass rallies, wherein what in the nineteenth century could still be enjoyed as unconscious aesthetic display is consciously organized in order to divert attention from capitalism's persisting domination. These manifestations, after 1918 as after 1848, are a consequence of the proletariat's defeat. In the Baudelaire book, as in Brecht's *Caesar* novel, written in both temporal and spatial proximity, Marx's analysis of the counter-revolution emerges as the perspective from which the social and political development of the Weimar Republic is criticized. However, what had still, in the nineteenth century, appeared to be a mere caricature and bloody episode on the way to the anticipated ultimate victory of the proletariat, now assumed in the twentieth century, in view of Hitler's seizure of power and the forthcoming world war, the seriousness of history's last days.

Under these auspices the epistemological grounding of Benjamin's critique turns into an assessment of the actual political situation. The parallel between Louis Bonaparte and Hitler, between Baudelaire and Benjamin, appears legitimate because the social conditions between 1848 and 1851, and between 1918 and 1933, remained fundamentally the same. For if the forms of social organization are based, now as then, on commodity exchange, then the hope for a revolutionary reversal of the reactionary development, which had endowed Marx's analysis of the Eighteenth Brumaire with its militant optimism, has proved illusory. Benjamin's historico-philosophical construction is based on the experience that history, once it has entered the stage of the commodity-producing society, can no longer generate anything qualitatively new, but, in the sense of Blanqui and Nietzsche, perpetuates itself as a fashionable renewal of a corrupt and forever unchanging world condition.

Seen thus, Benjamin appears both more rigorous methodologically and more pessimistic politically than Brecht, who projects the fascist dictatorship onto the Caesarism of the slave-holding society of ancient Rome; or even than Horkheimer, who, in his essay "Egoism and the Movement of Freedom," first published in 1936, describes the "leaders and leadership cliques" of the Renaissance and the French Revolution in terms of their relationship to the petty bourgeoisie.[29] In both Brecht's historical novel and Horkheimer's social-historical analysis, analogies to the present are drawn

Benjamin in front of Brecht's house in Denmark, 1938.

from the past in order that the reader can learn, on the basis of these parallels, to see through, hence to resist the fascist Führer-figures. Benjamin, far more radically, insists on the fundamental equivalence between the age of Louis Bonaparte and that of Hitler. In this perspective the revolution itself means something very different to him than it did to Marx and his successors. For Benjamin it is no longer that point at which society metamorphoses into a new form appropriate to the state of economic productive conditions, but rather the apocalyptic rupture of history as such. Benjamin's dialectical materialism in the Baudelaire book is directed towards this messianic vanishing point, without expressly formulating it.

Benjamin had been able to begin drafting "The Paris of the Second Empire in Baudelaire" under idyllic working conditions in Denmark: "I'm sitting at a heavy, spacious desk in an attic room, on my left the shore of the quiet, narrow straits, bounded by the woods on the opposite bank. . . . Brecht's house is nearby; there are two children whom I like; the radio; supper; a very friendly atmosphere and after the meal an extended game or two of chess. The newspapers arrive here with such delays that one more readily has the courage to open them."[30] It was the last time that Benjamin was to be able to work in peace. Toward the end of his Danish summer political reality caught up with him. To finish the work in the final weeks of September 1938, with the Sudeten crisis and the Munich treaty alarming the world, proved literally to be "a race against the war; and, despite all the agonizing fear, I experienced a feeling of triumph on the day when I had finally rescued (in the precarious security of a manuscript!) the piece on the flaneur, planned for almost fifteen years, from the world catastrophe."[31]

These words, expressing both Benjamin's pride in his achievement and its precarious creative circumstances, accompanied the manuscript to New York. His disappointment was all the greater when, after his return to Paris, he had to wait for weeks for a response. Finally, in a detailed letter from Adorno on November 10, he learned of the text's rejection by the directors of the institute. Paying no heed to the structural principle of the planned book, Adorno reproached the existing text with lapsing into an undialectical "reproductive realism" by linking "Baudelaire's pragmatic contents without mediation to neighboring aspects of the social history of his time, indeed to economic aspects as much as possible." Against this tendency, which "gave to the text itself a phantasmagorical character," Adorno decreed "in a straightforward Hegelian manner": "The materialist determination of cultural characteristics is possible only through the mediation of the total historical process."[32]

This curt rejection by the youngest member of the New York institute, whom Benjamin had viewed as his student and close friend, must have hurt him profoundly, especially in the insensitivity with which it ignored his precarious living and working conditions. "The isolation of my life here, and particularly of my work, makes me abnormally dependent on the reception given to what I produce," he acknowledged to Scholem.[33] A "period of lasting depressions" at the onset of the winter was the consequence.[34]

In addition, Benjamin's circumstances became increasingly gloomy. On his return from Denmark he found that his sister, with whom he had periodically lived in Paris, was "hopelessly ill."[35] The situation of his brother Georg, a socially committed physician and communist member of the town council of Berlin, had grown worse too. He had already been placed in "protective custody" by the Nazis in 1933; Benjamin remained in indirect contact with him through his sister-in-law Hilde. In November 1938 he had to tell Gretel Adorno: "My brother has been transferred to the penitentiary at Wilsnak, where he has to work at building roads. Life there is supposed to be still bearable. The nightmare haunting people in his situation is, so I often hear from Germany, not so much the next day at the penitentiary as the concentration camp, which threatens long-term prisoners."[36] Four years later Georg Benjamin was murdered in Mauthausen. Only the fate of his son Stefan could bring Benjamin some reassurance. After managing to flee Nazi-occupied Vienna for Italy at the last moment in the spring of 1938, Stefan had reached safety with his mother in London.[37]

Although Benjamin clearly understood that Germany's increasingly evident plans for an aggressive war would place his life in mortal danger, he did not yet seriously contemplate moving to London (the step being urged on him by Dora) or to the United States;[38] he must not, he felt, put the continuation of the *Arcades Project* at risk. Instead he promoted his French naturalization, as he wrote, "circumspectly but without illusions. If previously the chances of success were dubious, now even the value of such success has become problematic. The decay of civil order in Europe renders any kind of legalization delusive."[39] At the end of February 1939, the Gestapo in Berlin cancelled his citizenship on the grounds that he had published in the Moscow journal *Das Wort*. After that Benjamin had to use, as travel papers, "the French document giving legitimacy to refugees originating in Germany."[40] At the same time his financial situation also threatened to become untenable, meaning that he would have had to give up the small studio in Paris, which he had occupied since January 1938 at no. 10 rue Dombasle, in the fifteenth arrondissement. On 23 February 1939, Horkheimer wrote to him from New York that the institute was in serious economic difficulties, hence that he might possibly have to tell him "in the not too distant future that even with the best will we are not in a position to continue your research stipend."[41]

189

Immediately after receiving this letter Benjamin virtually begged Scholem to make possible a livelihood for him in Palestine, at least for a time, perhaps through a book contract from Salman Schocken. "There is no time to lose. What kept me going in earlier years was the hope of obtaining at some point a minimally decent job with the institute. By minimally decent I understand the life-sustaining minimum, which is for me 2400 francs. To sink again below that would not be bearable to me for very long. For that, the attractions of the present-day world are too weak and the rewards of posterity too uncertain."[42] Scholem evaded this despairing cry for help. One may assume that his disappointment at Benjamin's attitude ten years earlier played a role, at least unconsciously.[43] He concluded his response with the recommendation, illusory in view of the circumstances: "I wonder whether you shouldn't try to gain entry to the United States while there's still time, and whether that wouldn't really be better for you than anything else. With all good wishes, Gerhard."[44]

From this moment Benjamin knew that his life was in danger in Paris. "I live in anticipation of the news of a catastrophe breaking in on me," he wrote in April 1939.[45] For the first time he tried seriously, but without success, to move to the United States, at least for a few months. To this end he even made arrangements to divest himself of his favorite and only remaining possession, Klee's picture "Angelus Novus," which he endeavored to sell in America, through the mediation of a young acquaintance, Stephan Lackner, in order to pay for his passage.[46] Despite these multiple existential worries, Benjamin summoned up, with an extreme effort, the concentration to undertake the "reformulation of the flaneur chapter," which the institute had requested from him. In April he told Scholem that he was thinking of giving the new piece "a very wide range and an extreme philosophical tension."[47] In the revision of the central chapter of "The Paris of the Second Empire in Baudelaire," he sought accordingly to provide the metaphysical and epistemological apparatus that Horkheimer and Adorno had missed in the original; he thus concentrated the key motifs of the *Arcades Project* in a single text, which, in the dialectical structuring of the overall project, had been conceived as its antithetical nucleus.

The essay "On Some Motifs in Baudelaire" starts from the "loss of continuous experience" that characterizes life in the metropolis.[48] Its place has been taken by the "shock experience," which determines the interaction between the individual and the urban crowd, as well as mechanized industrial work and modern techniques of reproduction. Benjamin sees the common structural feature of all these phenomena, occurring simultaneously in the Paris of the nineteenth century, as the uprooting of both human beings and things from their natural context: in isolated alienation they are made

190

Walter Benjamin, 1939. (Photo Gisèle Freund.)

available for the installation of new structures of meaning. At the same time the displacement of experience by shock prevents the fulfillment of their "natural" life story, as Benjamin demonstrates in his analyses of industrial work, photography, film, and gambling. The accumulated meaning that surrounds things and people as a result of history, their "aura," is thus annihilated by the forms of social and economic organization in the modern world. Clearly Benjamin has introduced here the categories of his materialist aesthetic theory from 1935–36 into the analysis of the nineteenth century. Nevertheless the factual base that would underpin the structural relations between the various manifestations of shock, namely the commodity character of things and people in the capitalist economic and social order, is omitted from the late text.

Out of tactical considerations vis-à-vis his sponsors in New York, Benjamin passes over the materialist basis of his literary criticism, returning instead to the epistemology of the book on tragic drama, when he grounds the dominance of the shock experience in Baudelaire's poetry in the latter's melancholy consciousness of the world, in "spleen." In the condition of spleen, time appears as devoid of history, and experience as "collapsed into itself" because the contemplated object, under the melancholic's brooding gaze, loses the meaning that has accumulated within it through tradition. "The spleen . . . exposes the passing moment in all its nakedness. To his horror, the melancholy man sees the earth revert to a mere state of nature. No breath of prehistory surrounds it: There is no aura."[49] These and similar sentences in the essay, which was printed immediately after its completion in the last German-language volume of the *Journal for Social Research* and brought Benjamin "very considerable success in New York,"[50] suggest that this text is not the definitive synthesis of his metaphysical aspirations, as which it was praised by the author himself as well as by his New York correspondents.[51] Rather, the destructive events conditioning its production have left a deep imprint on it. The brooding genius, for which all experience has been stripped of its "prehistory," which means stripped also of its utopian dimension, is revealed to be Benjamin himself; as he confesses in March 1938 in his reaction to Hitler's entry into Austria and to the Republican defeat in the Spanish Civil War, he hardly knows where, in his own political experience, "to look for a concept of suffering and dying that is still meaningful."[52]

When Benjamin speaks in this context of "the Machiavellianism of the Russian leadership and the Mammonism of the French politicians," he is naming the deeper reason for his increasing historico-philosophical pessimism. Disillusionment with the politics of the left, particularly of the communists in the face of the dominance of fascism, had been growing in him since the beginning of his exile. He had always understood dialectical materialism less as a tool for political action than as a method of critical cognition. As he wrote to Werner Kraft in July 1934, it was essential to "dismantle the unfruitful pretentions to universal solutions for mankind, indeed to give up altogether the immodest perspective directed at 'total systems.'"[53] For this very reason he condemned the political errors of the left with unrelenting harshness, taking as his point of departure his own experiences in the last years of the Weimar Republic.

Thus, in a critical comment on Bloch's *Legacy of This Age,* he makes the objection that one cannot complain about the cultural politics of the Communist Party "without taking into consideration the corpus delicti of the castrated German intelligentsia."[54] The silence that greeted his own attempts at a materialist aesthetic in the years 1935–36 strengthened him in his view of the disastrous effect of popular front politics. Restating this view in terms of the internal French situation, he wrote to Fritz Lieb in July 1937: "They all cling to the fetish of the 'left' majority and it doesn't bother them that this majority pursues the very policies that, pursued by the right, would provoke insurrections."[55] In the discussions with Brecht in Skovsbostrand, in which the situation in the Soviet Union repeatedly played a central role, both men saw clearly the necessity "to show the official theoretical line to be catastrophic in relation to everything for which we have struggled for twenty years."[56]

The decisive turning point in his relationship to communism was for Benjamin, as for many contemporary intellectuals, the Moscow trials, which led him to declare already in August 1936 that he was "at his wits' end."[57] In the letter to Lieb quoted above, he offered the prognosis that "the destructive effect of the Russian events . . . will necessarily have an ever wider impact" and declared their most damaging effect to be "the silencing of the intellectuals."[58] These words allude to his own despairing helplessness at the betrayal of the revolutionary ideals on which he had based his hopes and his epistemology.

In his last years of exile, Benjamin became close to the political views of a group of French intellectuals around Georges Bataille, which called itself "Acephale." Disillusioned by communist politics, these people wanted to recover a place in life for the *sacré,* a concept of the sacred divorced from theology. Benjamin belonged to their outer circle, organized in the College of Sociology, for which he was scheduled to give a lecture on fashion; for unexplained reasons this did not happen.[59] The memoirs of Pierre Klossowski, a member of the group, convey the extent to which Benjamin's disintegrating political hopes impelled him back to the utopian conceptions of Fourier, then very much in vogue within the group:

193

Georges Bataille.   Pierre Klossowski.

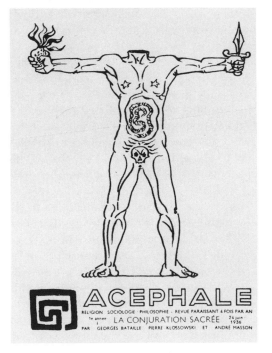

The cover of the journal *Acephale*.

194

In return we questioned him all the more insistently about what we guessed was his most authentic viewpoint, namely his personal version of a renewal of (Fourier's) phalansterie. Sometimes he spoke of it as an esoteric theory, at once erotic and craftsmanlike, auxiliary to his explicit Marxist conceptions. Common ownership of the means of production would permit the replacement of the abolished social classes by a society redistributed into affective classes. A liberated industrial production, instead of repressing the affective life, would multiply its expressive forms and organize its transformations; in this sense work would become the accomplice of desire and would cease to be its punitive counterpoint.[60]

To be sure, one must wonder whether this Fourierist social ideal, like communism before it, was not for Benjamin only an esoteric expression for his fundamentally Messianic hopes.

Benjamin's political despair becomes most apparent when one compares the 1935 outline essay for the Arcades Project with the second one, written in French in March 1939 at Horkheimer's behest, for an American patron who was to finance the project. Although in it the six main material divisions are retained from the original draft, indeed the dialectical antitheses between them are elaborated even more sharply, the historical optimism of the first draft has yielded to a profound resignation. In the place of his concluding methodological considerations Benjamin has now, with a lengthy quotation from Blanqui's text *Eternity by the Stars,* situated the "final, cosmic" phantasmagoria of the nineteenth century as the vanishing point in which its motifs converge. In Blanqui's doctrine of the return of the same the hope for "apocatastasis," which so energized the initial draft, is abnegated all the more cynically because Blanqui's doctrine is advanced by the pioneer of revolutionary change in this era himself. This disillusioned conclusion is not due exclusively to the fact that Benjamin rediscovered, in February 1938, Blanqui's forgotten cosmological speculation. The tremendous excitement he felt upon reading this text has to do, rather, with the way in which it confirms his own historical experiences. In a Europe acutely threatened by fascism and a France marked by the defeat of the popular front, it has become clear to Benjamin that there no longer exists a revolutionary class, toward whose potential action the historical materialist analysis of the nineteenth century could be directed.

The absence of a structure to the *Arcades Project* gains a precise significance in this context. The ordering of the materials according to both capital and lower-case alphabetical sequencing is not accidental. Such ordering produces an encyclopedia in which the key words of the universe are organized according to the rigorous but meaningless structure of the alphabet.

195

Like the contradiction between the materialist section of the 1939 outline essay and the despairing conclusion, the nonexistent structure of the work points to the absence of a collective subject that alone, in the act of awakening from the historical dream in the author's presence, could put the author in a position to structure the material, according to the meaning it would have for the awakening consciousness.

"Should awakening be the synthesis between the thesis of dream consciousness and the antithesis of waking consciousness? Then the moment of awakening would be identical with the 'now ($Jetzt$) of intelligibility,' in which things assume their true, that is surreal, countenance."[61] Such a "now of intelligibility" may still have been conceivable in 1935–36, in expectation of a popular front government; in 1939 such actualization of historical meaning had ceased to be possible. Indeed the collective subject destined to awaken had fallen more deeply than ever under the spell of the fascist nightmare.

The materialist historian Benjamin is thus confined to the role of collector, uprooting things from their material context without being able to supply them with any new one other than pure contingency. In the *Arcades Project,* Benjamin himself gathered materials delineating the collector's profile. The collector's drive for completeness, which condemns all collecting to remain fragmentary, is clearly annotated, as is his affinity with the student and with the allegorist, whose "profundity" is capable of justifying the attribution of any kind of meaning to any kind of object.[62] Not even the innermost source of the collector's passion, his fear of death, eluded Benjamin's scrutiny. Indeed he cites Paul Morand's telltale sentence: "The need to accumulate is one of the signs of impending death, in individuals as in societies."[63] Yet he was far from ascribing such motivations to his own activity.

The blindness of the normally so clear-sighted interpreter is evident in his commentary on an anecdote about the origin of Maxime Du Camp's *Paris: Its Organs, Its Functions and Its Life,* which he calls "one of the great factual source books on Paris." Bourget tells that Du Camp had had to visit the optician on account of an eye problem and, while waiting for his glasses to be ready, had gone for a walk on the Pont Neuf. At this moment the idea for his major work had come to him. "The quite small physiological decline, of which his visit to the optician had just convinced him, reminded him of what is so quickly forgotten, that law of inexorable destruction which governs everything human."[64] Benjamin disregards the evident connection between the personal glimpse of death and the resolve to write the encyclopedic work; in his commentary on the anecdote he limits himself to the surface structure of Bourget's text, stressing the "antique inspiration" of Du Camp's work. This slip is significant. Fear of death, as the core ele-

196

Walter Benjamin. (Photo Gisèle Freund.)

ment of the author Du Camp's intensive collecting and writing activity, had to remain concealed from Benjamin, since it would have opened his eyes to the real inspiration for his own obsessive piling up of material on Paris as the capital of the nineteenth century.

The awakening from the collective dream of the previous century, which Benjamin wanted to bring about in his *Arcades Project,* is ultimately revealed as the wish-dream of an individual abandoned by the collective subject of history. The dialectical construction of the second outline essay remains arbitrary in its formalist schema, because it no longer coincides with the real movement of history. It thus becomes the final and most profound phantasmagoria, its messianic face countered, on the Janus head of history now become apocalyptic, by the infernal face of Blanqui's vision. Benjamin was aware of the failure of his historico-philosophical intentions. Through the ruins of the *Arcades Project* there blows the wind of mourning. It is the mourning of one who has recognized that he is the only waking consciousness among so many sleepers.

On 1 September 1939, the German army invaded Poland. Benjamin, who had just concluded and mailed to New York his essay "On Some Motifs in Baudelaire," was, like all other German refugees in France at the outbreak of war, taken to a collection point and then interned in the "camp of voluntary laborers, Clos St. Joseph Nevers." He was totally exhausted. During

197

the march to the place of internment he collapsed several times. Nevertheless, as fellow prisoners reported, he endured the uncertainty and oppressive conditions of the camp with great composure. He tried to hold himself above water with philosophy courses for his fellow inmates and the planning of a camp journal.[65] At the end of November 1939, on the intervention of influential French friends, above all Adrienne Monnier and Jules Romains, he was released by order of an interministerial commission and permitted to return to Paris.[66]

During the three months in the camp he wrote nothing except for a dream protocol, which he drew up in French because of censorship restrictions and sent to Gretel Adorno in New York. With his doctor, Dr. Dausse, so he writes, he had descended into the underworld of a vast mine, where many people were resting on beds.

> I noticed among the women one, very beautiful, who was lying in a bed. Upon hearing my explication she made a brief movement, like a flash. She moved aside a tiny edge of the covering which sheltered her in her bed. Her gesture took less than a second. And its purpose was not to let me see her body, but the design of her bed covering, which evoked imagery analogous to that which I had written, several years earlier, to make a present of it to Dausse. I knew very well that the woman made the movement. Yet what had made me see it was a kind of supplementary vision. For as to my physical eyes, they were elsewhere, and I could not at all make out what the bed covering, which had fleetingly been opened for me, might offer.[67]

In the world of the dead, into which the author is led by his healer, nature and spirit are reconciled. The sight of the beautiful body and the reading of signs are intuitively experienced as identical. This unity is the guarantee of the "pure" text, in which everything that has been excluded lives again and through which the reader experiences perfect happiness. Benjamin concludes his dream protocol from the camp of Clos St. Joseph Nevers: "After experiencing this dream, I could not fall asleep again for hours. The reason was sheer happiness." Death had cast its redeeming shadow.

IX

The End of the Story

1 9 4 0

After his release Benjamin returned to a Paris living in darkness and readiness for air raids. He tried to reorganize his life as well as he could. The weakness of his heart, which had bothered him for a long time, had worsened to such an extent that he was forced "to stop every three or four minutes when walking in the street," in order to rest.[1] Nevertheless, as soon as it was possible, he resumed his interrupted work. On January 11, 1940, he had his reader's card for the Bibliothèque Nationale renewed for a year.[2] A few days later, in a letter to Gretel Adorno, he mentioned his indecision as to whether he should begin a new study—he had in mind a comparison between the autobiographies of Rousseau and Gide—or continue the work on Baudelaire, "which is decidedly closer to my heart than any other study, but which would not tolerate delay or interruption, not even to ensure the survival of its author."[3] When he told Adorno in May with no qualifications: "I have decided in favor of the Baudelaire book," he knew what the consequences of this decision could be.[4] At the same time he continued to look for an escape route. At the American consulate he took steps to obtain a quota-free visa, which would shorten the waiting period for passage to the United States; and he pressed Horkheimer to ensure that the institute would work energetically for his immigration to America.[5]

In the winter and spring months of 1940, before he returned to the Baudelaire book, he set down, in the "Theses on the Philosophy of History," thoughts of which he said that he had been "protecting them for

Benjamin's reader's card for the Bibliothèque Nationale,
dated 11 January 1940.

twenty years, even protecting them from myself."[6] Planned as a methodological clarification for the contemplated continuation of the Baudelaire study, but also as a fundamental consideration of the essence of historical time and the tasks of the materialist historian, the theses constitute, as Benjamin's last completed text, his intellectual legacy. Here, following the shock of the Hitler-Stalin pact, he delivers his harshest judgment on the "conception of progress as such," "at a moment when the politicians in whom the opponents of fascism had placed their hopes are prostrate and confirm their defeat by betraying their own cause."[7] To be sure, in this context he only actually names the naive optimism of the Social Democrats, but he is including the Communists when he criticizes the "vulgar-Marxist conception of the nature of labor": "It recognizes only the progress in the mastery of nature, not the retrogression of society; it already displays the technocratic features later encountered in fascism."[8]

With visionary relentlessness Benjamin criticizes the modern social and economic order that, in both capitalist and socialist variants, is based on the ruthless exploitation of nature. Benjamin's conclusion, which retains its actuality, is that a technologically driven domination of nature requires also a technology of social power, which bears within it the danger of imparting a totalitarian rigidity to society. Against this Benjamin endeavors, by recu-

200

perating Fourier's theory, to sketch a concept of liberated work, "which, far from exploiting nature, is capable of delivering her of the creations that lie dormant in her womb as potentials."[9] This kind of work, neither alienating the worker nor violating nature, would be possible to be sure only in a world transformed by a messianic revolution. Restating what he had written in *One Way Street*, Benjamin again defines the true concept of revolution as a rupture of the bad continuum of history. It is "the grasping of the emergency brake by the human race travelling in the train of world history," the dialectical "leap in the open air of history."[10]

At the same time that he condemns all revisionist politics, Benjamin subjects historicism to a devastating critique. Historicism's method is defined as empathy with the past, with the result that it never gets beyond the reproduction of the past power structures and, in the present, remains in thrall to the current rulers. Against it, Benjamin tries to formulate his conception of historical materialism in theoretical images and epigrammatic reflections, which are to assure its survival in better times. In a blend of Haggadah-like narrations and philosophical aphorisms, he bequeaths to posterity a text that, like its sacred analogue, requires commentary. In the endangered moment of the present, which threatens the individual with death, and European culture, together with its redemptive traditions, with final annihilation, Benjamin redirects the past towards the goal of "redeemed humanity."

In this final text Benjamin expresses his eschatological hope more clearly than he has done before; all despair has been set aside. Without regard for the necessities of the actual political moment, he formulates his goal: "To the concept of the classless society must be restored its genuine messianic face: this is in the interests of the proletariat's own revolutionary politics."[11] This restoration is viewed as the task of the materialist historian:

> Materialist historiography . . . is based on a constructive principle. Thinking involves not only the flow of thoughts, but their arrest as well. Where thinking suddenly stops in a configuration pregnant with tensions, it gives that configuration a shock, by which it crystallizes into a monad. A historical materialist approaches a historical subject only where he encounters it as a monad. In this structure he recognizes the sign of a messianic cessation of the progression of time, or put differently, a revolutionary chance in the fight for the oppressed past.[12]

In these sentences religious and political thinking have become one. In other words, politics has taken on an eschatological character; it can no longer be fulfilled in historical time but only in the final world judgment for which the historical materialist is preparing the verdict. At the center

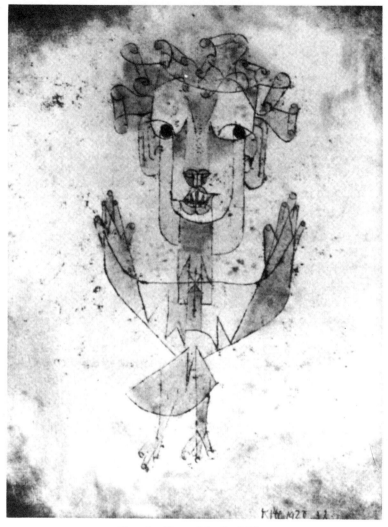

"Angelus Novus" by Paul Klee.

of his theses, Benjamin protrays the materialist once again in the figure of the Angelus Novus:

> A Klee painting named "Angelus Novus" shows an angel looking as though he is about to move away from something he is fixedly contemplating. His eyes are staring, his mouth is open, his wings are spread. This is how one pictures the angel of history. His face is turned toward the past. Where we perceive a chain of events, he sees one single catastrophe that keeps piling wreckage upon wreckage and hurls it in front of his feet. The angel would like to stay, awaken the dead, and make whole what has been smashed. But a storm is blowing from Paradise; it has got caught in his wings with such violence that the angel can no longer close them. This storm irresistibly propels him into the future to which his back is turned, while the pile of debris before him grows skyward. This storm is what we call progress.[13]

This picture presents the historian, turned toward the past, as one who experiences the failure of history and as one who himself fails. Nevertheless hope remains. Kafka's epigram, which Benjamin cites as commentary on Kafka's own failure, could also be applied to Benjamin himself: "Thus, as Kafka says, there is hope, infinite hope, but not for us."[14] In this negation of the human, the messianic force in Benjamin's thinking has both its origin and its goal. The dialectical materialist who lacks hope in and for human beings must put his faith in the eschatological catastrophe, which will restore the world in an instant and which gives a first inkling of itself in the saving "attentiveness" of the materialist historian.

From the outset this was the basis of Benjamin's composure amid his multifaceted failure. The most ancient figure in the Jewish tradition, the prophet, is reincarnated in a new form in Benjamin. On the basis of their double failure—the historical catastrophes experienced by their people and the utter inaccuracy of their political predictions—the prophets became all the more certain that these predictions would be vindicated in the realm of redemptive history. So Benjamin failed in his worldly politics, only to become all the more imbued with hope for the redemption of his world, which was the world of the European intellectual tradition.

In May 1940 the "phoney war" on the Western front came to an end; Hitler's troops marched into Holland, Belgium, and France. In mid-June, just before the German troops occupied Paris, Benjamin fled southward with his sister. He was able "to take nothing with him but his gas mask and his toothbrush."[15] His manuscripts and other possessions remained in Paris. He had entrusted the materials and preliminary drafts of the *Arcades Project* to Georges Bataille, who kept them in the Bibliothèque Nationale, thus assuring their survival. He left the manuscripts which seemed less im-

The cemetery at Port Bou overlooking the sea.

portant to him, as well as his correspondence, in his Paris apartment, where they were confiscated by the Gestapo. Today they are in the archives of the Academy of Sciences in Berlin.

From mid-June to mid-August he stayed in Lourdes, tormented by worries about saving his manuscripts and by "uncertainty" as to whether Horkheimer and Adorno would succeed in obtaining for him an entry visa to the United States.[16] The unbearable atmosphere of those summer months, in the little pilgrimage town overshadowed by the war, can be glimpsed in the description he gave at the beginning of August in a letter to his distant cousin Hannah Arendt: "Stifling weather reinforces my tendency to maintain the life of both body and spirit in a state of suspension. I wrap myself in reading: I've read the last volume of the *Thibaults* and *The Red and the Black*. My intense anguish at the thought of what is happening to my manuscripts is becoming doubly painful."[17]

In the second half of August Benjamin finally managed to reach Marseille, which was overflowing with refugees and where a few support committees were desperately trying to save the persecuted from the omnipresent Nazi agents. After he had obtained the American visa at the consulate in the last days of August—it had been issued as a result of Max Horkheimer's affidavit – Benjamin set out with an acquaintance, Henny Gurland, and her son, to leave France illegally, making his way by foot over the Pyrenees. In Banyuls-sur-Mer the little group was taken into the protection of Lisa Fittko, who with her husband and the support of the local mayor had organized a secret escape route over the mountains. On 25 September, they set out in the early morning to reach Spain by the "route Lister," unobserved by the "gardes mobiles" patrolling the border.

In her late recollections Lisa Fittko, who was herself making the journey for the first time on this day, emphasized Benjamin's self-discipline and remarkable staying power, in spite of the difficulties of the climb and his troubled health. She said that he was carrying a large black briefcase, which was "the most important thing" for him, since it contained his last manuscript. "The manuscript must be saved at all costs. It is more important than my own person."[18] Near the highest ridge Benjamin's strength was exhausted. "There was no path. We clambered between the vines, which were loaded with nearly ripe, dark, sweet Banyuls grapes. I think it was an almost vertical slope; but such memories sometimes distort the image of the landscape. It was here that Benjamin's strength gave out for the first and only time. More precisely, he made the attempt, failed and then made it clear to us that this climb was too much for him. José and I took him between us, he put his arms on our shoulders and we dragged him, with his briefcase, up the mountain."[19]

Toward evening the refugees, who had been joined en route by three other women, reached the Spanish border town, Port Bou. Since, as stateless people, they lacked French exit visas, they were turned back by the border guards. Next morning they were to be interned in a French camp. However they were allowed to spend the night in a small hotel in the town. There, on the evening of 25 September, Benjamin took an overdose of morphine tablets, from which he died at about ten o'clock the following morning. The briefcase with the manuscript, which Benjamin was concerned above all to save during his flight, has since disappeared. His companions, who after his death were permitted to travel on to freedom, arranged for his burial. His grave in the cemetery of the little town is no longer identifiable.

Notes

Translator's Note

The major publications by Walter Benjamin in book form in English are:

Illuminations, edited by Hannah Arendt, translated by Harry Zohn. New York: Harcourt, Brace and World, 1968; Schocken, 1969. Anthology.

Charles Baudelaire: A Lyric Poet in the Era of High Capitalism, translated by Harry Zohn. London: NLB, 1973; Verso, 1983.

Understanding Brecht, translated by Anna Bostock. London: NLB, 1973.

The Origin of German Tragic Drama translated by John Osborne. London: NLB, 1977.

Reflections, edited by Peter Demetz, translated by Edmund Jephcott. New York, London: Harcourt Brace Jovanovich, 1978. Anthology.

One Way Street and Other Writings, translated by Edmund Jephcott and Kingsley Shorter, introduction by Susan Sontag. London: NLB, 1979.

Moscow Diary, edited by Gary Smith, translated by Richard Sieburth. Cambridge, MA: Harvard University Press, 1986.

The Correspondence of Walter Benjamin and Gershom Scholem, 1932–40, edited by Gershom Scholem, translated by Gary Smith and Andre Lefevere. New York: Schocken Books, 1989.

Of these, only *Illuminations* has become very widely known. I have therefore cited the existing translations by Harry Zohn, in *Illuminations*, of: "The Storyteller," "Franz Kafka," "On Some Motifs in Baudelaire," "The Work of Art in the Age of Mechanical Reproduction," and "Theses on the Philosophy of History." All other translations are my own, and Dr. Witte's references to German originals

207

have been retained. Following are abbreviations used for editions of Benjamin's writings:

G S = *Gesammelte Schriften*, edited by Rolf Tiedemann and Herman Schweppenhäuser. Vols. I–VII. Frankfurt: Suhrkamp, 1972–1989.

B = *Briefe*, edited by Theodor W. Adorno and Gershom Scholem. Frankfurt: Suhrkamp, 1966.

S / B = *Walter Benjamin-Gershom Scholem, Briefwechsel 1933–1940*, edited by Gershom Scholem. Frankfurt: Suhrkamp, 1980.

Illum = *Illuminations*, Schocken paperback edition (details as above).

I. Childhood and Youth in Berlin (1892–1902)

1. G S VI, 465.
2. G S IV, 249.
3. Hilde Benjamin, *Georg Benjamin. Eine Biographie* (Leipzig: 1977), 13f. Gershom Scholem, "Ahnen und Verwandte Walter Benjamins," in *Bulletin des Leo-Baeck-Instituts 61* (1982), 30ff.
4. G S VI, 498.
5. G S IV, 264ff, 283ff.
6. Ibid., 261.
7. G S II, 375.
8. G S IV, 287.
9. Ibid., 253f.
10. G S VI, 475.
11. G S IV, 243.
12. Ibid., 270f.
13. *Berliner Kindheit um 1900* (Frankfurt: 1962), 79. This sentence is omitted in the version included in G S IV, 264.
14. G S IV, 266.
15. Ibid., 287.
16. Franz Hessel, *Spazieren in Berlin* (Munich: 1968), 141.
17. Hilde Benjamin, *Georg Benjamin*, 19.
18. G S VI, 474.
19. Ibid., 511.
20. G S II, 832.
21. Ibid., 9.
22. *Der Anfang* 2, Folge 1, Jg. Nr. 4. (Mai 1911), 80. (Not in G S).

II. Youth Movement, Judaism, Philosophy of Language (1912–1917)

1. B, 41.
2. Irmtraud and Albrecht Götz von Olenhusen, "Walter Benjamin, Gustav Wyneken

und die Freistudenten vor dem Ersten Weltkrieg," in *Jahrbuch des Archivs der Deutschen Jugendbewegung* 13 (1981), 98ff.

3. G S II, 836.
4. Ibid., 12–16.
5. G S VI, 476ff, and Martin Gumpert, *Hölle im Paradies* (Stockholm: 1939), 55.
6. B, 48.
7. G S II, 40f.
8. Ibid., 846.
9. B, 52.
10. Ibid., 70.
11. Gustav Wyneken, *Schule und Jugendkultur* (Jena: 1913), 92.
12. B, 44.
13. G S II, 838.
14. Ibid.
15. Ibid., 839.
16. Ibid., 838.
17. Ibid., 28f.
18. Ibid., 32.
19. B, 94ff.
20. Unpublished.
21. B, 93.
22. Ibid., 92.
23. G S II, 78f.
24. B, 110.
25. Ibid., 110f.
26. G S II, 82.
27. Ibid., 75.
28. Ibid.
29. B, 95.
30. G S VI, 481.
31. G S II, 240.
32. B, 157.
33. G S II, 123.
34. Ibid., 119.
35. G S VI, 478.
36. Gershom Scholem, *Walter Benjamin. Die Geschichte einer Freundschaft* (Frankfurt: 1975), 20f, 34.
37. B, 120f.
38. Gershom Scholem, "Walter Benjamin und Felix Noeggerath," in *Merkur* 35 (1981), 136.
39. Ibid., 141.
40. Ibid., 140.
41. B, 128.
42. G S II, 146.
43. Ibid., 150.

44. Ibid., 144.
45. Bernhild Boie, "Dichtung als Ritual der Erlösung. Zu den Sonetten von Walter Benjamin," in: *Akzente* 31 (1984), 23.
46. Walter Benjamin, *Sonette* (Frankfurt: 1986), 7, 56.
47. B, 127.
48. G S II, 147.

III. Art Criticism in the Spirit of Romanticism (1917–1923)

1. B, 140.
2. Scholem, *Freundschaft*, 50.
3. Ibid., 53.
4. B, 150.
5. G S II, 160f.
6. Ibid., 168.
7. Ibid., 163.
8. Ibid.
9. B, 252.
10. Georg Lukács, *Die Theorie des Romans* (Neuwied and Berlin: 1971), 6.
11. Ernst Bloch, *Geist der Utopie*, (Munich and Leipzig: 1918), 9.
12. Ibid., 272f.
13. B, 169.
14. B, 203.
15. G S IV, 441ff, 1016ff.
16. B, 208.
17. G S I, 78.
18. Ibid., 86.
19. Ibid., 119.
20. B, 219.
21. Ibid., 230.
22. Ibid., 239.
23. Ibid., 248.
24. Ibid., 303.
25. Ibid., 271.
26. G S II, 244.
27. Ibid., 241f.
28. B, 281.
29. G S II, 242.
30. B, 294.
31. Ibid., 281.
32. G S I, 126.
33. Hermann Cohen, *Ästhetik des reinen Gefühls*, 2d ed., 2 vols. (Berlin, n.d.), 123.
34. Wilhelm Dilthey, *Das Erlebnis und die Dichtung* (Göttingen 1970), 126.

35. G S I, 156.
36. Ibid.
37. Friedrich Gundolf, *Goethe* (Berlin: 1922), 566.
38. G S II, 175.
39. Ibid., 176.
40. Ibid., 199f.
41. Ibid., 194.
42. G S I, 134.
43. Ibid., 130.
44. Ibid., 176.
45. Ibid., 148.
46. Ibid., 196.
47. Ibid., 188.
48. Ibid., 169.
49. Ibid., 197.
50. Ibid., 196.
51. Ibid., 123.
52. G S VI, 493.
53. B, 172.
54. Siegfried Unseld, ed., *Zur Aktualität Walter Benjamins* (Frankfurt: 1972), 116.
55. B, 513.
56. Charlotte Wolff, *Innenwelt und Aussenwelt* (Munich: 1971), 206.
57. G S I, 173.
58. G S VI, 493.
59. Unseld, *Zur Aktualität*, 101.
60. Ibid., 116.
61. Ibid., 102.
62. G S I, 199f.
63. Ibid., 200.
64. Ibid., 192.
65. Ibid., 181.
66. Hugo von Hofmannsthal and Florens Christian Rang, "Briefwechsel," in: *Die Neue Rundschau* 70 (1959), 424ff.
67. Ibid., 440.
68. Hugo von Hofmannsthal, *Aufzeichnungen* (Frankfurt: 1959), 368.
69. Vorwort, in: *Neue Deutsche Beiträge* 1, Folge, 3, Heft (July 1923), 123.
70. B, 341.
71. Ibid., 327.
72. Ibid., 341.
73. Ibid., 400.

IV. History as Catastrophe: Anti-Classical Aesthetics (1923–1925)

1. B, 293f.
2. Chryssoula Kambas, "Walter Benjamin an Gottfried Salomon," in *DVJS* 56 (1982), 601–621.
3. B, 293.
4. Ibid., 298.
5. Ibid., 307.
6. Ibid., 306.
7. Ibid., 311.
8. Ibid., 299.
9. G S IV, 924.
10. Ibid., 929.
11. Ibid, 923.
12. Ibid., 926f.
13. Kambas, "Walter Benjamin," 613.
14. Adalbert Rang, "Florens Christian Rang," in *Die Neue Rundschau* 70 (1959), 456.
15. G S I, 897.
16. B, 310.
17. Ibid., 309.
18. Ibid., 374.
19. Ibid., 311.
20. G S I, 872.
21. B, 339, 326.
22. Ibid., 352.
23. Ibid., 354.
24. Ibid., 351.
25. Ibid., 358.
26. Ibid., 351.
27. Ibid., 355.
28. Kambas, "Walter Benjamin," 615.
29. B, 455.
30. Ibid., 372.
31. G S I, 227.
32. Ibid., 298.
33. Ibid., 392.
34. Ibid., 308.
35. Carl Schmitt, *Politische Theologie. Vier Kapitel zur Lehre von der Souveränität* (Munich and Leipzig: 1922), 9.
36. G S I, 887.
37. Schmitt, *Politische Theologie*, 37.
38. Georg Lukács, *Essays über Realismus*, in *Werke* vol. 4., (Berlin: 1971), 493ff. Printed with its later title, *Die Gegenwartsbedeutung des kritischen Realismus* (The Comtemporary Meaning of Critical Realism).
39. B, 366.

40. G S I, 408.
41. Ibid., 403.
42. Ibid., 407.
43. Ibid., 406.
44. B, 399.
45. G S I, 408.
46. Ibid., 343.
47. Ibid., 218.
48. Ibid, 217.
49. B, 392.
50. Ibid., 373.
51. Ibid., 381f.
52. Ibid., 403.
53. G S VI, 318.
54. Asja Lacis, *Revolutionär im Beruf* (Munich: 1971), 52f.
55. G S IV, 128.

V. Paris, Berlin, Moscow (1926–1929)

1. B, 368.
2. Louis Aragon, *Le Paysan de Paris* (Paris: Gallimard, 1961), p 87f.
3. G S IV, 135.
4. Ernst Bloch, "Revueform in der Philosophie" (1928), in *Erbschaft dieser Zeit*, Gesamtausgabe, vol. 4 (Frankfurt: 1962), 368ff.
5. G S IV, 89.
6. Ibid., 148.
7. Ibid., 122.
8. Ibid., 111.
9. Ibid., 119.
10. Ibid., 102, 109.
11. G S II, 622.
12. G S IV, 133.
13. Ibid., 113ff.
14. B, 433.
15. Ibid., 416.
16. Ibid., 414.
17. Ibid., 393.
18. Ibid.
19. G S III, 278.
20. Willy Haas, ed., *Zeitgemässes aus der 'Literarischen Welt' von 1925–1932* (Stuttgart: 1963), 477.
21. Kurt Koszyk, *Deutsche Presse 1914–1945, Geschichte der deutschen Presse, Teil III* (Berlin: 1972), 216.

22. B, 422f.
23. Benjamin to Thankmar von Münchhausen, September 14, 1926, unpublished.
24. G S VI, 316.
25. Ibid., 341.
26. Ibid., 393.
27. Ibid., 409.
28. Ibid., 358.
29. Ibid., 409.
30. B, 442f.
31. G S IV, 348.
32. G S VI, 358.
33. G S II, 743ff.
34. Ibid., 747.
35. Ibid., 757.
36. G S III, 174.
37. B, 523f.
38. G S II, 285.
39. Ibid., 289.
40. Ibid., 292.
41. G S III, 113.
42. G S II, 295.
43. B, 491.
44. Ibid., 431.
45. Ibid., 663.
46. Ibid., 455.
47. G S V, 1051.
48. B, 446.
49. Ibid., 455.
50. G S V, 1041.
51. Ibid., 1057.
52. B, 472.
53. Ibid., 483.
54. Scholem, *Freundschaft*, 172f.
55. Ibid., 174.
56. B, 463.
57. G S II, 705ff.
58. Scholem, *Freundschaft*, 196.
59. Ibid., 200.
60. Ibid., 207.
61. Ibid., 202.
62. G S II, 333.
63. Ibid.
64. Scholem, *Freundschaft*, 202.
65. B, 513.
66. Ibid., 493.

67. Ibid., 496f.
68. Ibid., 505f.

VI. Crisis and Critique: The End of an Era (1929–1933)

1. G S IV, 108.
2. G S III, 252.
3. Ibid., 172.
4. Ibid., 281.
5. G S II, 696.
6. Siegfried Kracauer, *Die Angestellten* (Frankfurt: 1971), 7f.
7. G S III, 224f.
8. Ibid., 219.
9. Ibid., 223.
10. Ibid., 225.
11. Johannes R. Becher, "Partei und Intellektuelle" (1928), in *Zur Tradition der sozialistischen Literatur in Deutschland* (Berlin, Weimar: 1967), 12ff.
12. G S III, 224.
13. B, 537.
14. Sabine Schiller-Lerg, *Walter Benjamin und der Rundfunk* (Munich, New York, London, Paris: 1984).
15. G S II, 1507.
16. Ibid., 1506, 638ff.
17. Scholem, *Freundschaft*, 198.
18. B, 534f.
19. G S II, 662.
20. Ibid., 523.
21. Ibid., 527f.
22. B, 518.
23. Bertolt Brecht, *Gesammelte Werke in 20 Bänden*, vol. 18 (Frankfurt: 1967), 85f.
24. Unpublished note, Bertolt Brecht Archive No. 332/49 (=Ramthun 16687).
25. Conversation between Brecht, Benjamin, and Ihering, unpublished typescript, Bertolt Brecht Archive No. 217/4–7 (=Rathun 18815).
26. Scholem, *Freundschaft*, 205.
27. B, 521.
28. Ibid., 509.
29. Ibid., 513.
30. Walther Kiaulehn, *Mein Freund der Verleger: Ernst Rowohlt und seine Zeit* (Hamburg: 1967), 150ff.
31. Scholem, *Freundschaft*, 206.
32. G S II, 339.
33. Ibid., 363.
34. Ibid., 353f.

35. Ibid., 353.
36. Ibid., 363f.
37. Ibid., 364f.
38. Ibid., 1125.
39. Ibid., 344.
40. Ibid., 367.
41. Karl Kraus, "Um Perichole," in: *Die Fackel* 852/56 (May 1931), 27.
42. B, 526.
43. Ibid., 531.
44. Ibid., 524.
45. Ibid., 544.
46. G S vi, 595.
47. Ibid., 586.
48. Ibid., 584.
49. B, 542.
50. G S vi, 602.
51. Scholem, *Freundschaft*, 223.
52. Schiller-Lerg, *Benjamin und der Rundfunk*, 106.
53. Scholem, *Freundschaft*, 225.
54. Ibid., 228.
55. S B, 22f.
56. Scholem, *Freundschaft*, 234f.
57. G S iv, 398.
58. S B, 28.
59. Ibid., 38.
60. B, 755. The typescript of this version is in the Bibliothèque Nationale (Paris), Walter Benjamin Collection. In the following discussion of the textual organization of *Berlin Childhood*, reference is made to this version, which for some time has been recognized as the only authentic one. It has been published under the title *Berliner Kindheit um neunzehnhundert. Fassung letzter Hand* (Frankfurt: 1987).
61. G S ii, 1064.
62. Marcel Proust, *A la Recherche du Temps Perdu*, part one (Paris: Ed. de la Pleiade, 1954), 5 f.
63. *Berliner Kindheit*, 9.
64. G S iv, 240.
65. Ibid., 242.
66. Ibid.
67. Ibid., 283.
68. Ibid., 273f.
69. Goethe, *Dichtung und Wahrheit. Werke*, vol. ix. (Hamburger Ausgabe), 523.
70. G S iv, 274.
71. Ibid., 296.
72. Ibid., 242f. The Paris version reveals some deviations from the printed text.
73. Ibid., 245.

74. Ibid.
75. Ibid., 239.
76. Ibid., 238.
77. Ibid.
78. Ibid., 250.
79. Ibid., 247.
80. Ibid., 275.
81. Ibid., 248.
82. Ibid.
83. Ibid., 254.
84. Ibid., 255.
85. Ibid., 253.
86. Illum, 130.
87. G S IV, 271.
88. Ibid., 272.
89. Ibid., 102.
90. Ibid., 109.
91. G S v, 785f.
92. Friedrich Weinreb, *Die Symbolik der Bibelsprache: Einfuhrüng in die Struktur des Hebräischen* (n.d.), 82.

VII. Emigration: The Theory of a Non-Auratic Art (1933–1937)

1. S B, 49f.
2. B, 586; S B, 101.
3. B, 595.
4. S B, 127.
5. Ibid., 58.
6. B, 602f.; S B, 126, 129.
7. B, 653.
8. Letter to Asja Lacis, undated (early 1935), in *Alternative* 59/60 (April/June 1968), 62.
9. B, 602.
10. Ibid., 704.
11. Ibid., 710.
12. S B, 171.
13. Ibid., 134.
14. G S I, 1012.
15. Ibid., 1013.
16. Rolf Tiedemann, ed., *Versuche über Brecht*. 5th edition. (Frankfurt: 1978), 133.
17. G S II, 1343.
18. Ibid., 1321.
19. Ibid,, 1346.

20. Ibid., 1352; Stephan Lackner, "Vor einer langen schwierigen Irrfahrt," from unpublished letters of Walter Benjamin, in *Neue Deutsche Hefte* 26, H. 1 (1979), 58.
21. S B, 122.
22. G S II, 1324.
23. Ibid., 783.
24. Ibid., 789.
25. Illum, 222.
26. Ibid., 234.
27. G S I, 462 (a passage omitted from the second version, the one translated in Illum).
28. Illum, 218.
29. G S II, 688.
30. Chryssoula Kambas, *Walter Benjamin im Exil* (Tübingen: 1983), 26ff.
31. Illum, 232.
32. B, 715.
33. G S I, 435; G S II, 800.
34. G S II, 696.
35. B, 722, 728.
36. G S I, 1023.
37. Bertolt Brecht, *Arbeitsjournal*, vol. 1 (Frankfurt, 1973), 16.
38. G S I, 997.
39. G S II, 795.
40. G S I, 1002.
41. Illum, 91.
42. G S II, 734.
43. Illum, 102.
44. Ibid., 88.
45. Ibid., 102.
46. Ibid., 95 (modified).
47. G S I, 1238.
48. B, 524.
49. S B, 172, 177.
50. Illum, 126.
51. Ibid., 122.
52. Ibid., 130, 114.
53. Ibid., 137.
54. Ibid., 126.
55. Ibid., 138–39.
56. B, 638.
57. S B, 155.
58. Ibid., 157f.
59. Tiedemann, *Versuche über Brecht*, 158.
60. Ibid., 160.
61. S B, 273.
62. Franz Kafka to Max Brod, July 5, 1922.
63. Illum, 134.

64. G S IV, 157.
65. Ibid., 228.
66. Ibid., 955.
67. Scholem, *Freundschaft*, 252.

VIII. Parisian Arcades (1937–1939)

1. B, 664.
2. G S V, 1162.
3. B, 659.
4. S B, 195.
5. G S V, 59.
6. Ibid., 1257.
7. Ibid., 47.
8. Ibid., 1058.
9. Ibid., 574.
10. Ibid., 578.
11. Ibid., 573.
12. G S III, 139f.
13. G S IV, 356.
14. Ibid., 358.
15. G S I, 181.
16. Ibid.
17. S B, 279.
18. G S I, 1079.
19. Ibid., 1150.
20. Ibid., 1167.
21. Ibid., 603.
22. Ibid., 1091.
23. Ibid., 1151.
24. Ibid., 1074.
25. Ibid., 671.
26. Scholem, *Freundschaft*, 258.
27. Karl Marx, Friedrich Engels, *Werke*, vol. 8 (Berlin: 1978), 119.
28. G S II, 477.
29. Max Horkheimer, "Egoismus und Freiheitsbewegung. Zur Anthropologie des bürgerlichen Zeitalters," in *Zeitschrift für Sozialforschung* 1936, Jg. 5. H. 2: 161–234.
30. B, 767.
31. Ibid., 778.
32. Ibid., 784f.
33. S B, 291
34. Ibid., 290.

35. B, 780.
36. Ibid., 781.
37. S B, 292, 317.
38. Ibid., 318.
39. B, 781.
40. S B, 304.
41. G S v, 1169.
42. S B, 300.
43. S B, Vorwort, 12.
44. S B, 303.
45. B, 814.
46. Lackner, "From unpublished Letters," 63: G S v, 1180.
47. S B, 305.
48. G S I, 607ff.
49. Illum, 185.
50. S B, 313.
51. B, 821.
52. Ibid., 747.
53. Ibid., 616.
54. To Siegfried Kracauer, January 15, 1935, in Walter Benjamin, *Briefe an Siegfried Kracauer* (Marbach, 1987), 80.
55. B, 732.
56. Ibid., 772.
57. Ibid., 722.
58. Ibid., 733.
59. Denis Hollier, ed., *Le Collège de Sociologie (1937–1939)* (Paris: 1979), 447.
60. Pierre Klossowski, "Entre Marx et Fourier," in *Le Monde*, 31 May 1969, 4.
61. G S v, 579.
62. G S I, 404.
63. G S v, 275.
64. Ibid., 144.
65. Hans Sahl, "Walter Benjamin im Lager," in *Zur Aktualität*, 74ff.
66. B, 834.
67. Ibid., 830.

IX. The End of the Story (1940)

1. B, 841.
2. Pierre Missac, "Walter Benjamin à la Bibliothèque Nationale," in *Revue de la Bibliothèque Nationale* 3, no. 10 (1983), 30f.
3. B, 842.
4. Ibid., 850.
5. Ibid, 843, 856.

6. G S I, 1226.
7. Illum, 258.
8. Ibid., 259.
9. Ibid.
10. G S I, 1232; Illum, 261.
11. G S I, 1232.
12. Illum, 262–63 (modified).
13. Ibid., 257–58.
14. S B, 273.
15. G S v, 1182.
16. B, 861.
17. G S v, 1182.
18. Lisa Fittko, "'Der alte Benjamin.' Flucht über die Pyrenäen," in *Merkur* 36, no. 403 (1982), 40.
19. Ibid., 44.

Index

223

Index

225

Scholem, Gershom (*continued*)
    120, 122, 125–27, 130, 133–34,
    154–55, 170–71, 189–90
"School Reform, a Cultural Movement,"
    23
Schultz, Franz, 68, 71–72, 86
Seligson, Carla, 28–29, 31
Seligson, Rika, 32, 37
Selz, Jean, 151–52
"Sleeping Beauty, The," 20–21, 86
"Society," 16–17
Sonnets, 37–38
Speyer, Wilhelm, 114, 132, 134
Spitteler, Carl, 25
Stalin, Joseph, 163, 200
Stone, Sacha, 91
"Storyteller, The," 16, 164–68
Strauss, Ludwig, 26–27, 114
Surrealism, 97, 106–8, 126

"Task of the Translator, The," 7, 51
Teaching and Valuing, 24
"Theses on the Philosophy of History,"
    55, 167, 199–203
Thieme, Karl, 172
"Thoughts on Aristocracy," 19

"Thoughts toward an Analysis of the
    Condition of Central Europe," 69–70
Toller, Ernst, 102
"Toward a Critique of Violence," 54–56,
    129
Tuchler, Kurt, 26
Tucholsky, Kurt, 117
"Two Poems of Friedrich Hölderlin,"
    32–33

Ullstein, Ilse, 18
Unger, Erich, 50

Valéry, Paul, 94, 97

Weltsch, Robert, 154–55
"What is Epic Theater?" 124, 126
Wilde, Oscar, 64
Wissing, Egon, 132, 134, 153
Wolff, Charlotte, 59
Wölfflin, Heinrich, 34–35
"Work of Art in the Age of Mechanical
    Reproduction, The," 21, 153–65
Wyneken, Gustav, 19–21, 23, 26–29, 34

Zucker, Wolf, 121